REWEAVING
THE WEB_

How together we can create a
human-centered Internet of trust

Richard Whitt

FIRST PUBLISHED IN 2024

© 2024 BY RICHARD WHITT, US, REWEAVING THE WEB

ISBN PAPERBACK [979-8-9910858-3-0]
ISBN HARDCOVER [979-8-9910858-1-6]
ISBN E-BOOK [979-8-9910858-2-3]

CREATED IN CONJUNCTION WITH THE BOOK SHELF LTD:

EDITOR - AMEESHA GREEN
TYPESETTER - KYLE ALBURQUERQUE
COVER DESIGNER - NIALL BURGESS
PROOFREADERS - GEMMA ROWLAND AND SHELBY JONES

CARLA ILLUSTRATIONS AND COMICS - MARTHA SPERRY

REWEAVING THE WEB [VERSION 1.0.22561.4563]

C:\USERS\RICHARD WHITT>

A BOOK ON REWEAVING THE WEB _

PRAISE FOR
REWEAVING THE WEB

"Whitt sets out an aspirational world in which digital technology becomes more helpful and less threatening. Definitely thought-provoking!"

— Vint Cerf, Chief Internet Evangelist, Google, and co-father of the Internet

"Richard Whitt brilliantly and meticulously constructs a complete overlay of the WWW (GliaNet) that is built on trust, where each of us enjoys autonomy and agency to control our data and safely use technology to benefit humanity."

— Susan Ness, former Commissioner, US Federal Communications Commission; Distinguished Fellow, Annenberg Public Policy Center, University of Pennsylvania

"Whitt's Reweaving the Web starts from a place that brought me, and many of us, to the internet—that it was an open space for human creation. Underneath our current experience, there are still opportunities for creativity, autonomy, and human values. We can still create a web that serves the many and not just the few. Richard's book calls us to that—to reexamine and reimagine what we accepted as normal on the web, and to join forces in doing so."

— Mark Surman, President of Mozilla Foundation

"We are increasingly living inside a computer - the internet which so seamlessly facilitates and mediates our lives, is moving deeper into our "offline" environments through the countless sensors and cameras of the "smart" city. What does that mean for our human freedoms of thought and action? Whitt helps us see the very real dangers, but more importantly, proposes ways to shift the balance towards the digital rights we all deserve."

– Jacqueline Lu, CEO and Co-founder, Helpful Places

"Reweaving the Web masterfully guides us towards a future where trust and human agency are at the core of our digital lives. A blueprint for reclaiming the internet for the people, by the people, Whitt's background enables him to provide readers with a clairvoyant vision for the future of the internet!"

– Joe Toscano, technology entrepreneur and former Googler

"Reweaving the Web perfectly contextualizes the challenges facing humanity and what the "coalition of the willing" can do to solve them. The book masterfully lays out the forces and choices that have led us here — for better or worse — and how we can use the "most transformative technology in all of history" to turn us back from the brink. It is Whitt's blending of economics, historical context, and solution sets that makes "Reweaving the Web" a must-read for policymakers on Capitol Hill and in state capitals alike. For that matter, the book is essential reading for anyone serious about the future of digital governance and personal agency."

– Tim Lordan, Executive Director, Internet Education Foundation

WWW.REWEAVINGTHEWEB.NET /CONTENTS

FOREWORD

BY DOC SEARLS

The Internet is us. It's people.

Terraforming Our Future

To the Internet, we are not "users," or "consumers," or "eyeballs," or "account holders." We are independent actors, operating as peers with every other person, organization, and thing—including the non-things called "clouds."

This is by design. TCP/IP, the base protocol of the Internet, is end to end. This means that every entity on it is an end, and there is no middle. In *The Rise of the Stupid Network*, David Isenberg explained that "The Internet breaks the telephone company model by passing control to the end user. It does this by taking the underlying network details out of the picture." That was in 1997, when David worked for AT&T. They fired him for saying what turned out to be entirely true.[1]

Likewise, in a 2000 interview with *Linux Journal*, Craig Burton described the stupidity of the Internet:

I see the Net as a world we might see as a bubble. A sphere. It's growing larger and larger, and yet inside, every point in that sphere is visible to every other one. That's the architecture of a sphere. Nothing stands between any two points. That's its virtue: it's empty in the middle. The distance between any two points is functionally zero, and not just because they can see each other, but because nothing interferes with operation between any two points. There's a word I like for what's going on here: terraform. It's the verb for creating a world. That's what we're making here: a new world.[2]

This new world is not Web 1, 2, or 3. It's zero: just getting started.

Or maybe 0.1, because we have only had the Internet we know since 1995, when commercial activity began[3] to explode on it. And we have been living digital lives, dependent on connected mobile devices and computers, for only about a decade or so. The Internet and digital technologies are two of the biggest and most powerful genies ever to escape their bottles and start granting wishes. And they will continue to do that for many decades and generations to come.

But here, in the early years of our webbed digital existence, problems already abound, or we wouldn't need Richard to write this book. Topping the list of these problems is a lack of personal privacy. Fortunately, we have had technologies to protect privacy in the natural world for almost as long as we have been human. One is clothing, and the other is shelter. One has zippers and buttons, and the other has locks on doors and shades and shutters over windows. These technologies serve two purposes. One is to stop unwanted advances into private spaces. The other is to signal what is okay and what is not.

In his book, Richard refers to these technologies as indicia of "personal contours," the psychologically safe zones of influence we establish, maintain, and evolve over the course of our lifetime. Unfortunately, the Web does not respect these personal contours. Instead, due to a lack of equivalent technologies on the Web, we can only go around naked. And as a lack of privacy protections allows easy money to be made at our expense, we are stuck in countless panopticons where we are constantly observed and manipulated. Richard calls this system "SEAMs," as in surveillance, extractions, analysis, and manipulations. This has become the dominant paradigm of the current version of the Web, as practiced by large online platform companies.

But that is not the end of the story. The Internet's open, stupid, and sturdy original infrastructure is still there. On it, we can have far more agency, freedom, and privacy protection than our deeply flawed early systems allow. This is what Richard proposes with his GliaNet initiative—a way to civilize our digital world so that it respects our personal contours and puts us back in charge. Here are some examples of what we will have when GliaNet becomes real:

- Networks of people who are truly social, comprised of human beings connected independently rather than trapped on commercial platforms.

- Being able to "intentcast" your purchase plans (think advertising in reverse), privately and across all possible sellers, and not just on separate e-commerce platforms such as Amazon, eBay, and Walmart.

- Having your own private shopping cart that you can take from site to site (an idea my wife had in 1995 when e-commerce first appeared).

- Having your own private AI working just for you, eliminating drudgework such as managing subscriptions, finances, health care, property, and other important stuff without relying on big uncaring companies that just want your money and your data.

- Assuring privacy through legally accountable contracts with the world's sellers, website operators, and service providers rather than mere promises to which you "consent."

The crucial point is that all these things and more are possible. *Reweaving the Web* presents a wealth of knowledge about how all of us can get involved and take concrete steps to move us into that far better digital world. Read on to see how we can do it.

Or better yet—weigh in and help out.

As I am fond of saying, don't be the pinball. Be the machine.

INTRODUCTION

FOUNDING A NEW ONLINE PARADIGM OF TRUST

"Certainty hardens our minds against possibility."

– Ellen Langer

This is a book about technology, about the online networks and systems of influence that in just the last thirty years have rapidly taken over our lives. It is a book about how we have become increasingly entangled in the aptly named "World Wide Web," and its many dubious denizens.

And yet, this is not just a book about technology. Rather, it is a narrative of the human values held by those people who built these networks. Their genius and hard work spawned digital tools of incredible potential to enhance our autonomy in the world. As it turns out, over time, those same tools have been adopted and applied by large companies in ways that constrain our very humanity. The book is also a counter-narrative of sorts, highlighting the technical creations of those dreamers and doers who are challenging the status quo that increasingly serves only a handful of people at the expense of the rest of us. Ultimately, though, it is a book about and for all of us, demonstrating how we can join forces with those same dreamers and doers to build a better Web that serves the many and not just the few.

The moment for such a counter-narrative has arrived. In the long shadows cast by a global pandemic, environmental crisis, economic disparities, political upheavals, and regional warfare, we have each earned the opportunity to pause and consider where exactly we are standing. By all accounts, the many intertwined social systems designed to protect and promote our interests—governmental, market, and social institutions—are not serving most of us very well. Some of these systems are failing spectacularly before our eyes, falling prey to black swans,[4] grey rhinos,[5] or simply the ordinary challenges of everyday life. Without lasting change, the likely pathways on our horizon are not promising either. The Web has not created these systemic challenges, but it has done little to solve them and, increasingly, has actually exacerbated them. However, as you will see in this book, there are other humanity-affirming technology pathways available to us—we just have to adopt them to our own ends.

Entangling Webs of Distrust

The Internet is arguably the most transformative technology in all of human history. In the 1970s and '80s, the Net was initially designed to place intelligence and control with ordinary people at the edges of the network. Such an empowering approach was considered dramatically, even radically, democratic. And yet, as the 21st century dawned, the World Wide Web—an overlay that sits uneasily on top of the original Internet's architecture—has become the actual medium for our day-to-day online interactions. Unfortunately, that medium has seemingly become dominated by questionable forces. Huge data-gathering companies have adopted business models premised on online surveillance, extraction of personal data, and biased algorithms. In turn, these technologies collectively prop up a growing flood of intrusive advertising, malicious bots, fake news, data breaches, identity theft, and more.

The common denominator seems to be that our fundamental freedoms as human beings—the thoughtful autonomy of our "inner" selves, and the impactful agency of our "outer" selves—are in real jeopardy. All too often, our predominant social systems negate personal context, ignore mutual relationships, and undermine more inclusive perspectives. In other words, they constrain more than they liberate. Even the "coolness" factor and convenience of our digital technologies mask subtle forms of (more or less) voluntary subjugation. In exchange for our personal data, and the willingness to have our behaviors and mindsets manipulated by others, we receive "free" service offerings.

Today, both corporations and governments are subjecting us to a one-sided onslaught of online platforms, computational systems, and interfaces. These all operate in the background of our devices, behind what could be thought of as our *screens, scenes, and unseens*. The purpose of this impressive yet fundamentally unbalanced "cloudtech" has become clearer over time: forms of control that engender money and power.

The Web's underlying economics have become the relentless financial imperatives of modern capitalism. In technical terms, these imperatives translate into the employment of information feedback loops of four interconnected user-related activities: surveillance, extractions, analysis, and manipulations (we will call these "SEAMs"). This ecosystem is fronted by multisided online platforms (MOPs), such as Google, Facebook, and Microsoft, who provide each of us with helpful tools, like email and social media feeds, in exchange for our personal data. In turn, that data is shared with many thousands of data brokers, whose sole purpose is to sell insights about us to advertisers and marketers who then pursue us relentlessly around the Web. It turns out that these often faceless and nameless data-based advertisers, marketers, and brokers (DAMB) firms are the actual subjects of these multisided transactions, while the rest of us are these companies' mere objects of scrutiny. In this uneasy (some might say "creepy") *Ads+Data* world, many of us are finding it challenging to continue supporting what was supposed to be a robustly free and open Web.

Among other drawbacks, this prevailing paradigm has helped fuel a monoculture of winners-take-most, from treating people as mere "users" in a landscape of "surveillance capitalism" to fostering a culture of amplified divisiveness and untruths. More dauntingly, these computational ecosystems of data, algorithms, and interfaces underly systemic failings, in some ways, entrench them even further.

Notably absent from this picture is a deep comprehension of the behind-the-scenes human infrastructure. Governance structures and processes are necessary to establish the duties of the online entities involved and the guardrails that will protect the autonomy, agency, and privacy of individuals and their chosen communities. In essence, what we call "governance" is designed to respond to all the pressing questions – the whys, whos, whats, whens, and hows—of a particular technology's use. And where tech companies and governments are failing to address this missing piece of the infrastructure recipe, they merely leave us with two words: "trust us."

Indeed, a crucial ingredient is missing today, and it is *basic human trust*, an assurance that our online interactions are founded on consent, accountability, and mutual benefit. With new technologies of data control now online—such as cloud computing, the Internet of Things (IoT), generative machine learning, augmented reality, and biometrics—the trust and accountability deficit is about to get appreciably worse.

Bearing all of this in mind, an obvious question to ask is: what are we to do about it?

The so-called realists would reply, "probably nothing." If anything, the largest corporate technology platforms seem to be capitalizing on the moment and getting larger and more powerful by the hour. Too many governments appear to be following suit. Perhaps at best we can muster some modest political or market reforms around the edges, compel the MOPs to be a bit more accountable and a bit less harmful, and call it a day. History proves that we honestly should not hope to achieve anything more.

Yet, the present moment invites us to refuse that outcome. We have in our hands an opportunity to reexamine the Web-centered governance assumptions that have accumulated over the past several decades. Holding these Web platforms and their ecosystems accountable for their practices is a necessary undertaking.

Nonetheless, greater transparency and accountability alone are not sufficient to alter our current trajectory. In the prevailing paradigm of the Web, an entirely new set of guiding principles is called for. This book proposes one set of solutions—focused on the complementary, more aspirational goal of building novel ecosystems that elevate, rather than constrict, the autonomy and agency of ordinary human beings vis-à-vis digital technologies. The argument is to build new webs that connect us, not bind us. Those that actively promote the best interests of "end users" as *actual*, real people.

Surfacing the Systems

As Ethan Zuckerman recently opined, "Information only works when it's harnessed to power."[6] Although they are crucial, courageous acts of witnessing by themselves are not enough to compel a corrupt system to change. Such transformations must start with two kinds of power: the ability to gain robust knowledge of the underlying system itself, and the ability to take advantage of various levers of opportunity to transform it.

Power is in the understanding and in the action. This book offers both kinds of power, and the encouragement to insist upon the availability of levers of real change.

In both regards, systems thinking can provide useful tools. On the understanding front, the iceberg metaphor is one example.[7] The tip easily seen just above the waterline is the event level—individual and seemingly isolated acts. Over time, and below the surface, these events can be linked as more meaningful patterns of behavior. Eventually, we can expose the deeper underlying system structures, which engender the underwater patterns and events.

Of course, our conceptual systems of things like "the Web" are frozen instantiations of people, behaviors past and present, both intentional and accidental, locked into path dependencies that today seem all but inevitable. These echoes from the past are still with us in varying ways. Initial biased beliefs, enacted into behaviors, molded into practices, embedded into institutions, promulgated in cultures, fed back into and bolstering the initial beliefs. Times a hundred, or a thousand, or a million. As with systemic economic or racial injustices, so with our technology paradigms and their human control cycles.

In this vein, what are the conceptual roots of something as pervasive as the existing Web paradigm? Shoshana Zuboff articulates the role of "surveillance capitalism" in the behavioral surplus of humans serving as a new means of production.[8] Tim O'Reilly blames a "Bizarro World" where companies seek to capture more value than they themselves produce.[9] Anand Giridharadas describes the makings of "MarketWorld" and those with concentrated power who engage in only partial and self-preserving good deeds in the place of real change.[10] Elizabeth Renieris posits that powerful technology companies actually weaponize a singular obsession with personal data.[11]

If we dig deeper, more expansive roots can be found. Yanis Varoufakis, for one, argues that capitalism has slowly given way to feudalism and that Web companies reap profits they derive from the rest of us even as they charge rents to app developers, marketers, advertisers—and ultimately, end users.[12] What I call "the SEAMs paradigm" may be another turn in that history, the digital era equivalent of the agricultural, industrial, and financial sector imperatives of market capitalism. For example, to systems theorists, "success to the successful" is a common dynamic of capitalism and other social systems, where wealth or power becomes concentrated in the hands of a few.[13] Similar forces appear to be at play in our political systems as well. To that end, counter-movements exist to challenge the unequal uses and abuses of power in society. Data feminism, for example, focuses on how data science intersects with social, racial, and gendered inequalities.[14]

To Jason Moore, a logic of extraction and exploitation sees the world and its inhabitants as resources to be "coded, quantified, and rationalized to serve economic growth..."[15] The imperative there "is to grasp the inner connections that conduct flows of power, capital, and energy through the grid of capital accumulation—and in doing so to shed new light on the limits of that very grid."[16]

Finding Our Leverage

A guiding light here is Donatella Meadows, the great teacher of complexity theory. Meadows argues that there are many ways to alter existing social systems so they "produce more of what we want and less of that which is undesirable."[17] She charts a dozen different kinds of leverage points to intervene in floundering systems. These include altering the commercial feedback loops, modifying information flows, and creating new forms of self-organization.[18] However, she notes that the single most effective approach is to directly challenge the existing paradigm—with its "great big unstated assumptions"—propping up a suboptimal system.[19]

We can do this in two ways: relentlessly pointing out the anomalies and failures of that prevailing paradigm, and simultaneously working with active change agents within the foundations of the new paradigm. As Meadows puts it, "we change paradigms by building a model of the system, which takes us outside the system and forces us to see it whole."[20] This book is firmly in the camp of describing the failings while building with the change agents.

The energy to drive change is found in the discrepancy between where people are currently and where they want to be. The creative tension between the two enables stakeholders to resolve in favor of their aspirations.[21] Bridging this gap can occur through high-leverage interventions, including engaging new stakeholders and learning from experience.

Even the obvious limits of leveraging our way to the possible can give us room to create. As Mark Taylor reminds us, a repeatedly misplaced promise of technology visionaries is that in the future, all will be possible without limits. To the contrary:

"Possibilities are inevitably limited by constraints that can never be overcome. The only viable freedom is not freedom *from* constraints but the freedom to operate effectively *within* them... [Nonetheless, constraints] are not merely negative but can be productive; indeed, there are no creative possibilities without significant constraints. Constraints provide the parameters within which thinking and acting must occur."[22]

Indeed, one person's constraint is another's way to leverage real change. And leverage points can and do become sources of power. As David Peter Stroh describes, the key is "to connect leverage points into a coherent path forward."[23] If computational systems (of data, AI, and interfaces) have become the fulcrum of the Web, then that is where the leverage resides. Some like Renieris argue that our human value should not be measured in bytes. If done correctly, however, those same digital technology tools can become implements that each of us wields in our own interest.

Creating a New Agential Paradigm

In light of our current shared crises, and with a deeper understanding of the current systems that envelop us, we can rethink and reshape how digital technologies are designed, in a way that promotes, and even enhances, our individual and collective humanity. The Web's prevailing paradigm need not become further entrenched as the de facto operating system. Instead, new paradigms are possible, ones more grounded in promoting the needs and aspirations of ordinary people. Such paradigms can become the animating ethos for a new generation of governance mechanisms to serve far more of us than are presently being served. They can actively promote the best interests of users as actual human beings by building virtual walls of protection where necessary, finding windows where possible, and opening doors where fruitful. All on our terms.

The initiative I will propose in this book is called "GliaNet," and it is an Internet overlay, one designed to create a more decentralized and empowering ecosystem of digital trust. The term was chosen for at least three reasons.

First, the ancient Greek word "glia" means glue, which here connotes the social bonds of trust that bind us together in fruitful social and economic relationships. These human connections are increasingly broken for most of us in the Web experience. Conversely, Web companies seek to entrap us within the sticky meshes of their own design.

Second, as in Spider-Man's credo, "With great power comes great responsibility." Too many companies operating online today lack the crucial elements of trust and accountability that should accompany—be bound to—their tremendous power and influence over our everyday lives.

Third, the cellular structures in the human brain—the glial networks—serve as important support functions to the neurons operating in parallel. Glial cells, in particular, provide vital protection of neural pathways, enhance their operation, and promote their health and well-being.

The GliaNet initiative then is premised on filling the Web's existing and widening gaps of *trust, accountability,* and *support*.

Ushering in a new ethos for digital technologies can also open up opportunities to drive societal shifts away from subpar systems. Perhaps, creating a human infrastructure of trust for our current challenges will pave the way for other forms of relational trust-building. Perhaps, treating data as a source of mutual relational benefits frees it up for as-yet-undreamed uses. Perhaps putting tech in the hands of ordinary citizens will give them power to exercise fruitfully in other domains of their lives.

Harnessing the Possible

Making real, lasting change is difficult. Altering governing paradigms is immensely hard work. However, the path we're on now is unattractive for a growing number of us. As our lagging systems struggle and strain to maintain viability, there is a window of opportunity to open up a bold new vision of human power and control in the computational era.

Ellen Langer's observation that the illusion of certainty prevents us from embracing what is possible still rings true. We have within us the wherewithal to do more—to challenge the supposed certainties of our time and seize the opportunity to create something better.

And Rebecca Solnit's words are especially salient here:

"Disaster sometimes knocks down institutions and structures and suspends private life, leaving a broader view of what lies beyond. The truth before us is to recognize the possibilities visible through that gateway and endeavor to bring them into the realm of the everyday."[24]

Our current predicament should instill within us a drive to discover or create places to put our trust and hope. To invent futures we all want to live in. Together, we can ensure the availability of online infrastructures that support, rather than thwart, robust autonomy and agency for all human beings. Then, humans, machines, and institutions can exist together on a far more level playing field. One where the bulk of humans are (more) firmly in charge.

My hope is that this book will spur people to peer more deeply into the one-sided interfaces placed in front of us. Online technologies should be spaces of human autonomy and agency, not extensions of society's already-pervasive asymmetries of power and control. The spaces of potential remain open before us. Let's see what awesome stuff we can build, together.

```c
int main(int argc, char *argv[]) {
   int sockfd, newsockfd, portno;
   socklen_t clilen;
   char buffer[256];
   struct sockaddr_in serv_addr, cli_addr;
   int n;

   sockfd = socket(AF_INET, SOCK_STREAM, 0);
   if (sockfd < 0)
      error("ERROR opening socket");

   bzero((char *) &serv_addr, sizeof(serv_addr));
   portno = atoi();
   serv_addr.sin_family = AF_INET;
   serv_addr.sin_addr.s_addr = INADDR_ANY;
   serv_addr.sin_port = htons(portno);

   if (bind(sockfd, (struct sockaddr *) &serv_addr, sizeof(serv_addr))
       < 0) error("ERROR on binding");

   listen(sockfd, 5);
   clilen = sizeof(cli_addr);

   newsockfd = accept(sockfd, (struct sockaddr *) &cli_addr, &clilen);
   if (newsockfd < 0)
      error("ERROR on accept");
```

```
}
int main(int argc, char *argv[]) {
    int sockfd, newsockfd, portno;
    socklen_t clilen;
    char buffer[256];
    struct sockaddr_in serv_addr, cli_addr;
    int n;

    sockfd = socket(AF_INET, SOCK_STREAM, 0);
    if (sockfd < 0)
        error("ERROR opening socket");
```

/PART ONE/WHAT'S AT STAKE (D < A)

```
    memset((char *) &serv_addr, 0, sizeof(serv_addr));
    portno = 8080;
    serv_addr.sin_family = AF_INET;
    serv_addr.sin_addr.s_addr = INADDR_ANY;
    serv_addr.sin_port = htons(portno);

    if (bind(sockfd, (struct sockaddr *) &serv_addr, sizeof(serv_addr))
        < 0) error("ERROR on binding");

    listen(sockfd, 5);
    clilen = sizeof(cli_addr);

    newsockfd = accept(sockfd, (struct sockaddr *) &cli_addr, &clilen);
    if (newsockfd < 0)
        error("ERROR on accept");
```

/C1/PROMOTING HUMAN AUTONOMY AND AGENCY

The World Wide Web is slowly but surely robbing us of our hard-fought individual and collective liberties—of thought, of decision, of action. Crucially, this subtle thievery is happening with our supposed consent—each keystroke, each voice command. Bit by bit, the Web is eroding what makes us truly human. This chapter will explore what is truly at stake in the current online environment: namely, the fragile yet necessary attributes of autonomy and agency for ordinary human beings.

Human Nature: Worth Promoting

Why should we begin here? Because any fruitful conversations about technology and economic and social systems are best grounded in the humans behind them all.

For thousands of years, philosophers and others have been debating the finer points of whether and how human beings are truly free, whether we have agency and autonomy. What has emerged from some quarters amounts to a rough consensus: we are neither totally free beings nor totally determined automatons. But between those two poles remains a vast area of contention.

With a nod to the experts, I am repurposing the two often-employed terms of autonomy and agency to give them a breath of new life. In general, autonomy can be seen as freedom of thought, while agency can be considered freedom of action— the inner realm and the outer environment, respectively. At the outset, the literature suggests that autonomy and agency can be viewed as two separable attributes of the human self.[25] Autonomy is self-direction, self-determination, self-governance.[26] It amounts to the freedom to decide who one wants to be, in one's thoughts and intentionalities. By way of contrast, agency is behavior, interaction, the capacity to take action.[27] It amounts to the freedom to intervene and act in the world. At the extremes, a child's simple robot can be said to have some agency without much autonomy, while a prisoner in a dungeon has some autonomy without much agency.

The two concepts of autonomy and agency amount to deciding to do something versus being able to do it. The freedom to create and determine your own motivations versus the freedom to act upon them.[28] They can be considered two flavors of human liberty and perhaps two fundamental ways to define the human self and its unique identity.[29]

At the same time, thought and action form part of a continuum of human beings existing in the world. The two concepts are closely intertwined and can be mutually reinforcing or degrading. They also are matters of degree across a blend of the inner and outer worlds. To capture this notion of continuity and blending, we will refer to a singular process of exercising "human autonomy/agency."

Let's say you are purchasing a new vehicle. What steps are involved in the decision-making process? Likely, at the outset, some vague (even unconscious) suppositions about the necessity of a car in modern society, emotional desires to own a certain "sexy" brand, and mental calculations of a cost/benefit analysis. At some point, the musings become an intention, marked by certain outward behaviors (checking online for specific offers) and actions (obtaining a bank loan), which led to the parking lot outside a local automotive dealer. Where autonomy ends and agency begins, a robust mix results in a brand-new hybrid vehicle parked in your driveway.

Human autonomy/agency can also be explored through the prism of two kinds of liberty: freedom *from* and freedom *for*. Freedom "from" something is considered the negative form, for example, in autonomy, it is the freedom from outside coercion and manipulation.[30] Freedom "for" something is deemed the positive form, for example, in autonomy, it is the freedom to develop our own thoughts and actions in creative ways.[31]

Both forms of freedom are not absolutes but are subject to a variety of internal constraints (urges, needs, genes, personality) and external constraints (environment, society, nature).[32] These constraints present differently in each culture and each individual. The key is whether and to what extent humans have some element of conscious sway over these "heteronomous" influences. Within the self-determination theory (SDT) school of human psychology, for example, autonomy is not defined by the absence of external influences but by our acquiescence to those influences.[33]

There are also important external bounds that communities can and do place on the exercise of human agency. Traffic lights, restaurant dress codes, not yelling "fire" in a crowded theater—examples abound. But more fundamentally, societies continually deal with the challenging tensions between freedom and justice. Human freedom is relativistic. As Camus put it, "[a]bsolute freedom is the right of the strongest to dominate," while "[a]bsolute justice is achieved by the suppression of all contradiction: therefore it destroys freedom."[34] To modern sensibilities, these tensions are best worked out in inclusive, democratic processes.[35]

While to some people, constraints on freedom present as significant limitations, they do not foreclose all degrees of independence. Indeed, our constraints are actually vital to our ability to experience our freedoms. If our options for groceries at the supermarket were unlimited, for example, we would be paralyzed by such an abundance of choices. As Taylor states, "The only viable freedom is not freedom *from* constraints but the freedom to operate effectively *within* them...." Constraints provide the parameters within which human autonomy and agency can occur.[36]

Further, even within those constraints, we are ceaselessly evolving as human beings. As Unger has argued, "The complex processual nature of the self—always changing and developing, always reflecting on and transforming itself, [is] never complete."[37]

It is worth noting that human autonomy/agency is not limited to certain cultures or certain times. While these attributes of self can be expressed in innumerable ways and are subject to different outside influences, there is abundant evidence that they still constitute universal and core capabilities for thinking, being, and acting in one's own world.[38]

Our Mediating Selves

Of course, human autonomy/agency does not exist in a vacuum. As embodied beings, we live within webs of mediation shaped by our social interactions.[39] By nature, we are mediating creatures, constantly interacting with and filtering the world through our sensory and conceptual systems. Mediation processes are part of our organic constitution, as our bodies and brains and minds constantly filter in the meaning and filter out the meaningless.[40] In this way, feedback is what allows information to become action, providing "the bones of our relationship with the world around us."[41]

As social beings, we have a long history of delegating our mediations to third parties[42]—news sources, government bodies, religious institutions, trusted friends, and the like. However, this mediation process takes on even greater importance with the advance of digital technologies, where technical interfaces and other tools are taking over more of the filtering work of our biology-based mediation systems.

Some might wish to shy away from the digital world to prevent this outcome, but the point is not to avoid all forms of mediation. On the contrary, it is difficult to imagine living in the world without some sort of filters in place. Rather, we should strive to understand how these mediations operate and take a hand in controlling the flows and interfaces that comprise them. We could invoke the noise/signal duality from information theory,[43] where the objective is to achieve human meaning by elevating the signal while depressing the noise.[44] Or better yet, we could find trustworthy outside mediators that compensate for our cognitive biases and shortcomings, rather than those that prey on our exploitable weaknesses. Much more on the latter point later.

To data scientists, the digital ones and zeroes stored at the data level are bountiful and complex. Usable information comes only from the abstract connection of these data points. Knowledge is the human understanding of the information derived from this data, while wisdom is found in the application of this knowledge. As we go up each level of the "data, information, knowledge, wisdom" (DIKW) hierarchy, the noise decreases and a usable signal appears.

A useful image for human mediation could be that of an enclosing bubble with semi-permeable barriers. By affirmatively pushing to expand the bubble outward, we can accept and bring into ourselves certain aspects of "the world." A new friend, a challenging book, an educational documentary. In contrast, by deliberately pulling back to contract the bubble inward, we can reject and move away from unwanted aspects of experience. When we are in charge of this boundary-making process, we can control (to some degree) our autonomy of thought and agency of action. When others are more in control of these continual expansion and contraction processes, the actual human at the center is less in charge.

My notion of *personal contours* stems from the territorial behaviors of people seeking "personal space" in physical places. Human beings naturally occupy land and property as their "own," typically with dwellings we consider to be our homes. This same instinct appears to drive our psychological need to establish boundaries between ourselves. Irwin Altman was the first to explore how these behaviors constitute "interpersonal-boundary mechanisms" (one of several) that we each use to define ourselves.[45] In Altman's analysis, these mechanisms are a means to the end of a desired level of privacy. In my own conception the end goal is broader than privacy—it encompasses optimizing an individual's autonomy of thought and agency of action.

Scholar Sandra Petronio furthered the general notion of human boundary-making in the context of privacy. In *Boundaries of Privacy*, she discusses her "Communication Privacy Management" (CPM) framework, where individuals regulate their personal boundaries in dialectical processes between privacy (closure) and disclosure (openness).[46] By its own admission, the CPM model only focuses on the one-way transmission of information from the person to the world.

As much as we seek to control access to the boundaries that let information out, however, we also should want to control access to the influencers that try to get their own information *in*. The CPM concept can be expanded to include the influence of others in our lives as forces that we either allow or refuse access to penetrate our personal boundaries. In this extended version of CPM, the conceptual boundaries of the self demarcate where our internal and external influences conjoin, intermingle, and often clash. Privacy certainly can be an important consideration here, but it is not the only or even the predominant one. My concept of "personal contours" is intended to capture this notion that each of us possesses individual influence boundaries that shift and evolve over time, affected in turn by the boundary layers of the people and institutions that surround us.

We can also put this well-grounded concept to work more strongly in the vernacular of human rights. We can imagine asserting the right to define and utilize outside mediation processes, and the resulting personal boundaries that help shape our lives. We could also assert the right to assign certain contour definitional and access rights only to those third parties who provide us with actual assistance and support. This may sound minor, but it is an important point. When trust is embedded in a mediating relationship, we can engage in opening up to a broader range of outside influences.[47] For example, if a close and trusted friend counsels you to seek professional help in dealing with a personal challenge, you will be more likely to lower your virtual barriers and truly listen. This type of intention-driven openness contrasts with forms of "faux" openness, such as advertising-based websites that offer us information or advice but in fact are doing so for financial motivations that can end up acting against our better interests.

As noted earlier, living life inevitably involves forms of mediation. Philosopher Roberto Unger has written cogently about this lifelong dialectic process, as "being in the world, without being of it."[48] He urges us to overcome the duality between exposure and sterility, or as he puts it, "engagement without surrender."[49] To the point, "It is only by connection with others that we enhance the sentiment of being and developing a self. That all such connections also threaten us with loss of individual distinction and freedom is the contradiction inscribed in our being."[50] In brief, we are "[c]ontext-shaped but also context-transcending beings..."[51]

Our Meaningful Selves

Mediation tools do not exist in a vacuum. As filtering agents, our personal identities are constantly changing and evolving blends of the autonomous and agential.[52] This means that our lives constantly flow with meaning. Fred Cummins observes that the human experience is characterized by our "embedding in webs of meaning" that arise from our participation in many types of overlapping systems.[53] It is arguable that much of this "meaning" may arise not only from our conceptual thought but from the raw feelings derived from our ancestral brains, based on genetic inheritance, sensory inputs, internal bodily inputs, and action dynamics.[54]

Our lived reality is a unique bundle of experiences, interactions, and relationships—a fluid mix of the past (memories), the present (moments), and the future (intentionalities). Hopes, fears, and aspirations are woven together with the experiences of others—family, friends, strangers, communities of interest. This feeling of autonomy and self-determination, as represented in the action of agency, "is what makes us most fully human and thus most able to lead deeply satisfying lives—lives that are meaningful and constructive—perhaps the only lives that are worth living."[55] My proffered term for this human experience, of the (potentially) meaningful flow of space and time, is the individual's *lifestreams*.

The mental image of a stream of thoughts and events is intended to convey a sense of flow, of forward movement, of blurred lines between thought and memory and action. In phenomenology and the 4e school of cognition, concepts like the self and the world, the inner and the outer, inhabit a continuum more than a duality.[56] Couldry and Mejias call these relational boundaries "the space of the self ... the open-ended space in which we continually monitor and transform ourselves over time."[57] This circle of inner and outer spaces never-endingly turns in on itself, in what they call "a materially grounded domain of possibility that the self has as its horizon of action and imagination."[58] Or, as Brincker says:

> "As perspectivally situated agents, we are able to fluidly shift our framework of action judgment and act with constantly changing outlooks depending on the needs and opportunities we perceive in ourselves and our near surroundings in the broader world.... [W]e continuously co-construct and shape our environments and ourselves as agents...." [59]

If we follow the 4e school of cognition on this, the function of natural and technological mediation processes is even more important. This model portrays a human in her environment as fully embodied, embedded, enactive, and extended (hence the four 'e's). And this means that the scope of human cognition is extracranial, constituted by bodily processes (embodied) and dependent on environmental affordances (embedded and extended).[60] For our purposes, if the self and the environment essentially create each other, whether and how other people and entities seek to control those processes is paramount.

Importantly, the twinned human autonomy/agency concept should not suggest a form of isolation or solipsism. The "cast-iron" and completely independent individual is simply an unsupported philosophical relic of the past.[61] On the contrary, experts have found that humans possess both individual and collective forms of autonomy and agency. In SDT psychology, people experience collective autonomy when they endorse and identify with other people and things.[62] Our relationships in the world make us social creatures; our connections to the world make us cultural creatures. Our mode of meaning is more than individualistic; it is collective. Ultimately, human autonomy/ agency embraces the liberty to define and enact our own semi-permeable boundaries between the self and the rest of the world.

As we have seen, the concepts of human autonomy and agency, mediation and meaning, are broad and deep. Hopefully, my construct of our personal contours, the boundaries guarding and promoting our lifestreams, give these concepts flesh and blood. Yet even this cursory treatment demonstrates how our technology systems can be engineered to extend—or constrict—the essence of our individual and shared humanity. Next, we will consider the societal angle in the tangled topics of power and accountability, consent and trust and ethics.

/C2/MOVING FROM POWER TO TRUST

As the Mark Twain saying goes, history doesn't repeat itself, but often it rhymes. Take the siege of Melos, during the Peloponnesian War between Athens and Sparta, which continues to resonate down through the centuries.

The story goes that the mighty Athenian empire invaded the small nation-state of Melos in the summer of 416 BCE and demanded that its citizens either surrender and pay tribute to Athena—or face annihilation. Such a minor event in the midst of a decades-long war would likely be long forgotten to most. For historian Thucydides, however, that particular moment merited his readers' attention. He produced a dramatic reenactment of a short dialogue between the threatening Athenians and the defenseless Melians. There, the Athenians coolly rejected every Melian argument for mercy, using the primary rationale of *realpolitik:* the nature of things.[63]

As Thucydides conveyed in the original Greek, "δυνατὰ δὲ οἱ προύχοντες πράσσουσι καὶ οἱ ἀσθενεῖς ξυγχωροῦσιν," a straightforward translation of which would be, "It is the nature of power that he who has it takes it; he who does not must submit." In that hugely asymmetric contest, the Melians nonetheless refused to surrender. And in turn they were slaughtered.

Thucydides possessed an uncanny ability to capture the timeless lessons of history in often painful manifestations, like the now-infamous siege of Melos. His teachings on human power, and the seeming inevitability of people amassing and using it against others, still resonates today. An appreciation for how and why humans employ power, and the supposed constraints such as governance, consent, and trust, will inform our discussion of the very real power dimensions at play in today's Web—and what we can do about it.

Power: Timeless Issues of Asymmetries

Power in human relationships and societies has long been recognized and studied in various forms and contexts. In order to understand the ways in which Web-based technologies can empower people—or be used against their best interests—we need a deeper appreciation for the very concept of power first.

Obviously, the use of direct physical force or the threat of it is its own form of power. In modern society, far too many regimes continue to resort to these visceral displays of violent power. In this book however, we are focused on the more subtle forms of power held by individuals or collectives over others.

In general terms, I would define human power as the ability to define, create, and enforce physical and/or conceptual boundaries of enclosure and inclusion between systems. This definition ties the use of power to shape and promote our personal contours, as discussed in Chapter One. Our ability to modify our surrounding environment, and what physicist Stuart Kauffman calls the "adjacent possible" of elements that can be explored just outside ourselves,[64] is a subtle yet important form of power. In this way, power is not a quality possessed by "someone else" to be used against us but something that we all have the ability to wield to protect, enhance, and promote our personal contours of autonomy and agency.

Steven Lukes has pioneered studies into the roots of power in modern society. In his seminal book *Power: A Radical View*, he posits that power is exercised by the most powerful actors in political systems under three "faces" or dimensions: decision-making power, non-decision-making power, and ideological power.[65]

- *Decision-making power* is the most familiar to us, where someone or something uses its authority to drive certain outcomes, whether in legislatures or on battlefields.

- *Non-decision-making power* lets a policymaker set the agenda in debates, thereby making certain issues unacceptable for discussion in "legitimate" public forums. Adding this face gives a two-dimensional view of power, allowing us to understand both current *and* potential issues, and expanding the focus on observable conflict to more overt or covert types.

- *Ideological power* allows a policymaker to influence people's wishes and thoughts. At its most effective, this dimension would lead individuals to want or do things that are opposed to their own self-interest.

These can be thought of as the three power dimensions of the "overt" of decision-making, the "covert" of non-decision-making, and the "latent" of ideology. Another way to conceive this is forming a continuum, from the physical to the political to the conceptual.

THREE DIMENSIONS OF POWER

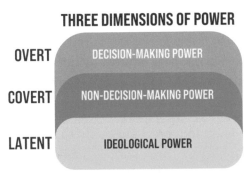

OVERT	DECISION-MAKING POWER
COVERT	NON-DECISION-MAKING POWER
LATENT	IDEOLOGICAL POWER

Importantly, these forms of power need not be limited to the political sphere but can be exerted in other institutional settings, such as markets, to control or influence outcomes. So, political actors, such as elected officials or unelected bureaucrats, can employ these types of power over each other or fellow citizens, and corporations can use these powers over consumers and would-be regulators.

At Melos, the overwhelming military strength of the Athenians was enough to win the day. But Thucydides wanted us to understand something more. He presented us with a tug of war over ways of thinking, which happens to align to Lukes' three modes. In keeping with the first dimension of overt power, the group with vastly superior military might set the terms. The debate between the invaders and defenders of the besieged city was held openly, between a representative group of the two parties. At the outset, in keeping with the second dimension, the agenda was dictated explicitly by the Athenian commander: surrender or die. Yet, much of the dramatic impact of this dialogue comes in Lukes' third "face" of the ideological, where the Melians raised a series of questions and offered arguments that sought to overcome the first two power predicates. Of course military superiority won out in the end, but not before the Melians compelled the Athenians to lay bare their rationale for the coming slaughter.

Lukes offers his third face as a critique of the behavioral focus of the first two dimensions. He believes that this third face allows one to study both latent and observable conflicts. As seen in the Melian Dialogue, tools such as social myths, language, and symbols are typically employed by those seeking an advantage in power relations via this third dimension. Lukes claims that a full critique of power should include both subjective interests and the actual or "true interests" of those excluded by the political process. Not just individuals in positions of authority, but entire systems of government and corporations can prevent the appearance of claims and frustrate their transformation into actionable issues.

One obvious question is: *why do so many of us fail to resist the rule of social elites?* In the 1970s, John Gaventa researched the phenomenon of *quiescence*: silent agreement by individuals and groups in the face of obvious inequalities.[66] He focused on how elites use power primarily to prevent the rise of conflicts via social quiescence, instilling powerlessness in others. To him, a lack of conflict is both an indicator and a consequence of the deliberate use of power mechanisms. Thus, the chief aim of power is to prevent groups of people from participating in decision-making processes, as well as gaining their passive agreement to a situation. In fact, as John Gaventa observes, one can participate effectively in the first overt dimension— by presenting well-defined claims and grievances—only after successfully overcoming the agenda-setting and ideological obstacles presented by the second and third dimensions. To those in power, these same sets of challenges present viable ways to thwart debate and maintain the status quo.

Gaventa's subsequent "power cube theory" builds on Lukes' notion, while presenting a more dynamic account of how power actually operates in the world.[67] His proposed three dimensions are: *Places* (from global to local), *Spaces* (closed, invited, and created), and *Forms* (visible, hidden, and invisible). That last category, Forms, essentially adopts Lukes' three faces, and could be labelled "action/agenda/influence." This continuum allows us to appreciate the various ways that power is acquired and employed in modern society, particularly via political and economic institutions. In particular, as we will see, the less direct-seeming forms of power (agenda and influence) are key to the persistence of the current Web paradigm and online companies' policies and practices.

More recently, John Allen laid out his three spatial vocabularies of power as: *territorial*, *networked*, and *topological*.[68] He invites us to rethink specific clear-cut categories such as here/there, inside/outside, and borders/border crossings, in the context of global power. As he explains, power is a relational effect of social interaction that can bridge the gaps between *here* and *there*, *absence* and *presence*, through a "succession of mediated relations or through the establishment of simultaneous presence." Indeed, Allen observes that power topologies come into play when actors can make their presence felt in ways that cut across proximity and distance. When an order issued on one side of the continent results in instantaneous military action on the other side, the ordinary human boundaries of time and place are blurred. In this way, powerful entities—using forms of connectivity—can draw distant others within close reach, while also constructing the close at hand from a distance.

As we will see, Allen's insight is eerily mirrored in the ways that Web companies use websites and apps and devices to impart to end users a sense of local control, while simultaneously exerting typically unseen forms of authority from afar.

Constraints on Power?

Of course, human power is not an absolute. It can and will always be limited by a variety of internal and external forces. Where those in charge seek to legitimate their use of power, they turn to several conceptual implements.

Governance: The Roles of Rules and Players

Governance is the system of distributed decision-making where certain people or entities possess the authority to make decisions that impact others. Governance channels power in ways that ostensibly provide transparency, accountability, and recourse to those who are governed. We can envision governance as a mix of *rules* (institutions) and *players* (organizations), where the rules are the governing human concepts that become instantiated by and for the players.

Much of human interaction and activity is structured in terms of overt or implicit rules. Institutions such as laws and contracts, norms and behavior codes, are the rules of the game, and they create the incentive structure of political, market, and social relationships. Markets in particular require conscious political effort to foster the trust-generating institutions necessary for them to function.

For decades, the school of New Institutional Economics (NIE) has been wrestling with questions about the appropriate institutions for a market economy. The fundamental tenets of NIE are that institutions matter and can be analyzed by tools of economic theory. In particular, institutions reduce information uncertainty and transaction costs.

Different institutional arrangements also lead to different trajectories and combinations of static and dynamic performance characteristics. A gamut of institutional choices differs by degree of coercion, flexibility, accountability, and formality. For example, social control can often be achieved through more informal, decentralized systems of consensus and cooperation, such as norms, rather than through laws.

There are roughly two ways that institutions can be established to engender social trust:

1. *"Macro"* governance means the public instruments, such as laws, regulations, policies, and standards, that are adopted by governmental bodies. These are intended to bind certain actors in society.

2. *"Micro"* governance means the governing instruments adopted by private actors, most notably corporations, to shape their interactions with others. These can entail codes of conduct, best practices, terms of service, policies, and other unilateral instruments.

Notably, in recent times, these public/private approaches have blurred, so that governments expressly leave certain governance areas to be occupied by corporate actors, who in turn use their power to influence the outcomes of multilateral governance processes.

In addition to the institutions-as-rules, we also have the various entities that actually play the game—organizations. These are groups of individuals bound together by a common purpose to achieve certain agendas. Their attributes include criteria to establish their boundaries, principles of sovereignty, and chains of command.

Organizations include political (governments and others parties), market-oriented (corporations, law firms, and trade unions), social (membership clubs), and educational bodies (such as universities). Much like institutions, organizations run the gamut from formal to informal, accountable to non-accountable, fixed to flexible.

In the United States, typical political bodies at the Federal level include the executive branch, the legislative branch, the judicial branch, and the "fourth branch" of independent agencies. Corporations also participate as advocates in this political ecosystem, along with many other types of entities, such as non-governmental organizations (NGOs).

Each organization is its own complex adaptive system, which among other things means that we should look beneath the surface to understand the actions of the disparate individuals within. For example, the consideration of an organization as a single outward-facing actor should not ignore potential human-to-human conflicts taking place within the organization. Moreover, organizational perspectives dictate how any individual views a policy issue. Whether you are a corporate chief executive officer (CEO), a public interest advocate, a political appointee chosen to run a government agency, or a career bureaucrat in that same agency, what you see typically depends on where you stand.

Players can also serve as external intermediaries between us and aspects of the world, whether invited or not. Their legitimacy can be linked to the presence of power asymmetries. As they gain scale and scope, our relationships/transactions/interactions with them can become more tenuous—less physically proximate, less transparent, and with less recourse and accountability. An example is the global holding company comprised of multiple online businesses. This distancing can be compensated for by certain social benefits, such as greater efficiency or reduced cost. But within my personal contours theory, this dynamic affects the opportunities and content of mediation processes, and the definition and availability of viable interfaces.

Challenges of Consent

The theories of power also consider its legitimate uses, that is, in cases where there is adequate consent by those who are governed. But what exactly constitutes consent? This is a trickier concept than one might first assume.

Consent theory describes whether one has freely bought into and agreed to be governed by another. In a recent paper,[69] Elizabeth Edenberg and Meg Leta Jones helpfully laid out the five key features of consent from a moral perspective:

- **Context**: A clear delineation of the background conditions

- **Scope**: A defined scope of action

- **Knowledge**: Relevant information

- **Voluntarism**: Freedom to choose from among viable options

- **Fairness**: Equitable treatment, including respecting other important rights

Importantly, even consent that is legally binding can fail to capture the morally legitimate transfer of an individual's rights and obligations.[70] A law can create certain privacy obligations on a company, for example, but still permit inadequate consent processes.

What then does it mean for a person to be free to provide legitimate consent to another? Where one human being is said to be acting on behalf of another, consent theory offers a useful but incomplete justification. As Don Herzog puts it:

"The claim that someone has consented or acted voluntarily may be rebutted with a surprising variety of counterevidence. One can say she has no alternative or no reasonable alternative, or didn't and couldn't have known about the alternatives that did in fact exist, or one can see the action in another context than the given one."[71]

Herzog points out that the political philosophies of libertarianism and paternalism are two extreme poles, seeing humans as either existential gods or helpless victims. In reality, most of human life is somewhere in the middle. This suggests hazy boundaries where consent theory applies easily on one hand and not at all on the other. In those hazy areas, consent theory can have some force but still competes with other views.

Of course, the claimed legitimate exercise of power is not limited to the political context of governments and citizens. To some economists, individuals in modern markets are said to consent voluntarily to the institutional structures of corporations (acting themselves as "natural persons") by taking on the economic role of the "consumer." Nonetheless, conditions such as the presence of monopoly power can constrain autonomy/agency opportunities and thwart legitimate consent.

In my personal contours theory, I presented the metaphor of virtual boundaries that surround us, allowing information and influences to flow between ourselves and others. A crucial question then is: *Have I granted consent to someone other than myself to mediate those flows and thereby gain levels of power over me?*

In the early 21st century, another power asymmetry has emerged—fueled by the technologies of communications and information networks. The Internet, with its human-facing overlay of the World Wide Web, introduced the concept of the consenting end "user." In many ways, the three worlds of the political, the economic, and the technological intersect at the Web. In this book, we will unpack these different yet hugely interdependent systems and the persistent power asymmetries that drive them.

Forms of Trust: Introducing Carla

It's December 2019, somewhere in a small town in America. Carla, a single mother, is busy with her day. From getting ready in the morning, to taking her young daughter Ada to daycare, putting in long hours at the office, and greeting her bed at night, Carla is enmeshed in a social world bound together by trust. Food and drink are provided by grocers, chefs, waiters, bartenders, baristas, farm workers, and butchers. Transportation is provided by taxi drivers, airplane pilots, flight attendants, school bus driver, and the crossing guard. Other needs are provided by the hairdresser, the clothing store clerk, the optometrist, the drugstore, the gardener, the postal worker, the election clerk, and her daughter's daycare providers. Plus countless supply chains of goods and services operating quietly behind the scenes. Not to mention Carla's fellow neighbors, patrons, citizens, and consumers.

The next day, Carla takes care of errands...

In a world where power is spread unevenly and freedom of thought and action is available at the whims of those who hold that power, a currency very much in demand is human trust. It is a truism that trust is the social glue, the foundational principle, that holds all relationships and binds us together.[72] From waking up in the morning to our daily routines, we rely on countless other humans to do the right thing, and at minimum not to harm us. Our lives are inhabited by those we trust (and of course many that we do not). These trusted intermediaries can be denoted by the term "trustmediaries."

According to noted expert Rachel Botsman, three basic kinds of trust have developed over human history:[73]

- *Local trust* is the original form between individuals, typically between members of small, local communities.[74] This interpersonal trust is in someone specific and familiar.

- *Institutional trust*[75] flows upwards to leaders, experts, and brands, traditionally including large entities such as churches, governments, the media, and corporations. To some, institutional trust has been declining due to an increasing number of (or more revelations about) scandals and breaches of faith involving these entities.[76]

- *Distributed trust*[77] flows laterally between individuals, enabled by systems, platforms, and networks.[78] Botsman believes this version to be in its infancy, and a source of potential upsides and downsides for users.[79] Distributed trust is based on reputation (what someone thinks about you), which Botsman considers to be "trust's closest sibling."[80]

We can think of these forms of trust as the *interpersonal*, the *social*, and the *distributed*. For most of human existence, we have held interpersonal trust with our closest family members and friends, and gradually added social trust as our institutions evolved and proliferated. We can see these forms of trust demonstrated in Carla's life. Only with the introduction of the Internet and the Web did we begin seeing early signs of distributed trust.

Regardless of the particular flavor, lack of trust in entities outside our inner circle should not be surprising. But in the past decade, a decided lack of trust by ordinary citizens and consumers has become increasingly noticeable across major societal institutions.[81]

One way that social trust can be created is for powerful actors to acknowledge and accept constraints on their behavior.

Certain fields, such as medicine and law and some in finance, formed professions, premised on adopting fiduciary duties such as care, loyalty, and confidentiality. Because these professions carry considerable entrusted power over their constituents (due to the asymmetry in expertise and shared confidences), such duties are intended to build trust with their constituents and are often embedded in ethical codes of conduct to bind each individual or entity. They can also be found in statutes or regulations adopted by governmental bodies.

In the online context, a leading cause of distrust is the mismatch in motivations.[82] Too many online entities typically treat those using their services as mere "users," rather than *bona fide* customers, clients, or patrons. This objectification of people carries over to their commercial practices, which as we will see rely heavily on overt command-and-control feedback cycles— all of which inevitably leads to a more trust-deficient Web.

A Matter of Ethics

Finally, there is a tool that many believe can effectively constrain the undue exercise of government and corporate power over the rest of us: ethics. Under this theory, powerful entities can be directed to abide by ethical practices and standards to address any power asymmetries that may exist.

Ethics is a challenging enough subject when limited to interactions between two human beings. When one side of the equation is an organization, such as a modern-day corporation or large government body, the role of ethics becomes more fraught. When technology is utilized as a form of mediation between the one and the many, a truly ethical outcome seems difficult to imagine.

We might ask: *can a company even have ethics?* Minka Woermann addressed this point in *On the (Im)Possibility of Business Ethics*, where she observes that standard ethical theories focus on the agent committing the actions, not the subject/object receiving them. She argues that these theories are flawed because they are unduly anthropocentric, logocentric, and egocentric.[83] Organizations are not human beings, but assigning them ethical expectations assumes that they are. Woermann also notes the fallacy of the free, intentional, fully informed individual as a moral and economic agent, which still dominates much of today's public policy thinking.[84]

Instead, she delineates "the ethics of complexity," which entails that every business decision has an ethical *dimension*. And she points out that true ethics cannot be determined in advance; rather, it results from the complex relations between corporate stakeholders and the larger environment. To Woermann, then, ethics should be viewed as an emergent property, which can only inform a corporate social responsibility (CSR) model but not be captured within it.[85] It is a concentric circle, starting from the organization, leading out to its economic, legal, social, and environmental responsibilities.

Another useful perspective is the nature of the connection between a human being and an entity of some type. When bonds are limited to one-off transactions based on fleeting interactions, the very notion of a relationship—let alone one premised on ethical behaviors—seems difficult to justify. But if based on a continuing series of interrelated actions, sustained by an expressly acknowledged series of consents, there appears to be a more legitimate basis for a relationship. In such a scenario, trust is *earned*, which invites the introduction of ethical practices. As we move forward, it is suitable to ask whether and how true relationships can be discerned and sustained.

In these first two chapters, we have sketched out the twin elements of human autonomy and agency, which are enhanced or reduced by constrained forms of societal power. Now the stage is set for the rise of the Internet and the World Wide Web, and the unique challenges and opportunities they present to all of us.

/C3/FROM OPEN NET TO STICKY WEB

From fire to the printing press to the digital computer, humans have employed technologies to modify and control their external environment, as well as augment their capabilities. Technology is embedded in, and can open up and enhance, our sensory and other bodily/conceptual/social systems. If the human mind truly is an extended and embodied locus of processes,[86] then technologies reside within that mediated zone.

While there are many forms of technology in the world, enabling sectors such as transportation, energy, healthcare, and bioengineering, this book focuses on *network* technologies of communications and information. A network is a type of system that has been designed, engineered, implemented, and operated by people. Networks can be found in many flavors along various continua: physical or virtual, formal or informal, centralized or decentralized, open or closed.

Various types of physical and virtual networks have been constructed over many decades to convey people, objects, and information between various places. In most cases throughout history, network industries—from stagecoaches and canals to the postal service, electricity, telegraphs, railroads, and airlines—have been subject to some form of government regulation and oversight.[87]

This chapter explores the nature of networks and the two great innovations in communications and information networks over the last 50 years: first the Internet, and then the World Wide Web. While these terms are often used interchangeably, they are in fact two distinct technology platforms. Understanding their respective histories, governing philosophies, and real-world instantiations helps us see the paradigm shifts that have brought us to today's online world.

Open Edges and Enclosing Cores

Networks are deemed by engineers to be "open" or "closed" based on their relationship to their respective environments. In the online world, "openness" is a concept with a lengthy history, but its precise aspects can be difficult to pin down.[88] The basic notion is that a more open network is designed to allow end users to have more control over their interactions, with the ability to introduce their own software, interfaces, and streams of data. By contrast, a more closed network excludes opportunities for individuals to control and define our own experiences.

Of course, this begs the question: *Where in the network do the controls actually exist?* This question translates into the physical placement of controlling mechanisms, either at the "edges" of the network—where the end user resides—or at the "core"—where the network operator resides. So, the question of how centralized a particular network is ties directly to the concept of openness.[89] Indeed, to Andrew Russell, the perceived tensions and tradeoffs over control that is (in his words) "decentralized" (at the edges) and "centralized" (at the core) "has been the perpetual preoccupation of the builders of information and communications networks."[90]

Over many decades, telephone networks were built consisting of "smart" switches at the core and "dumb" devices at the edges. The standard Bell telephone sitting at the edge is all but useless without being connected to the intelligence residing in the phone network infrastructure, and it exemplifies this design philosophy. These telephone networks became known as closed, especially as the more open Internet was introduced.

Similarly, in the enterprise and government worlds, the 1950s and 1960s were dominated by mainframe computers. These large computational machines were linked to their end users with comparatively simplistic terminals at the endpoints. As with the telephony networks, most of the intelligence was built into the core computing functions. Only when personal computers came onto the scene in the 1970s did some of the computing power begin to shift to the "edges," with the end user.

Over the last 50 years, we have seen several paradigm shifts as our information and communications technologies have continued to evolve. In one conception, this is the history of power, control, and freedom moving between entities operating at the core (the "providers") and the edge (the "users").

Another key question is: *Who decides where to place the boundaries between the edge and the core of the network?* What entities have power over the mediation points and interfaces that create the inward spaces we can control, as opposed to the outer spaces controlled by others? Picture a simple spider web. First, there is just the environment. Then, a spider spins a web, creating an inside/outside demarcation. To the spider that web becomes a staked claim, a psychic investment, in a particular inner territory carved out of its environment. This becomes a space to be protected and defended, and ultimately a way to capture, control, and benefit from parts of the outer—to bring the outer inward.

In my personal contours theory, humans construct their own webs, from physical structures (buildings, vehicles, clothing) to social networks (family, friends, acquaintances) to conceptual territory (me, me and us, versus them/others). These are the webs we weave ourselves, as *human conceptual systems*. To be open is to have a more permeable boundary to allow our own signals into the world and allow in others' signals. To be closed is to have a less permeable boundary.

As we will see, the Internet and the World Wide Web have become emblematic of this constant tugging between openness at the edges, and enclosure at the core.

The Fundamental Layer: The Internet

The Internet was born and raised not from the market, but from an unlikely confluence of government and academic forces. Many hundreds of people contributed to what eventually became the "Internet project" over several decades of development, from designers and implementers to writers and critics. The participants came from universities, research laboratories, government agencies, and corporations.[91] Many of them worked on the technical standards that would provide the essential building blocks for various online technologies to follow.[92]

A brief overview of the Net's roots, processes, and people will shed some light on how it actually operates.

From Top-Down Government Management to Bottom-Up Guidance

The Net was actually born from several different projects in the late 1960s and 1970s, all funded and controlled in some manner by national government agencies. However, the early homogeneity of design and top-down control slowly gave way to a heterogeneity of design and bottom-up governance. In some sense, the nature of process followed the nature of function.

In 1968, the U.S. Department of Defense's Advanced Research Projects Agency (DARPA) awarded contractor BBN the first government grant to construct and develop ARPANET.[93] This single network was intended to allow dissimilar computers operating at different sites to share online resources.[94] DARPA eventually selected ARPANET as its primary host-to-host communications system to facilitate the sharing of mission-critical data between disparate systems. One key feature was its Interface Message Processors (IMPs)—packet-switching nodes and network protocols that connected different networks together.[95]

Beginning in 1968, Vint Cerf and Bob Kahn did much of their work on the Transmission Control Protocol-Internet Protocol (better known as "TCP/IP") software suite under DARPA's auspices and funding. Rather than addressing how to communicate within the same network, Cerf and Kahn tackled a far more challenging problem: linking disparate packet-switching networks with a common set of protocols. The landmark Cerf-Kahn paper of 1974 developed TCP as a means of sharing resources that exist in different data networks. Subsequently, the Internet Protocol (IP) was separated out to logically distinguish the packet addressing and packet sending functions.[96] Seeing the immense usefulness of this approach, the U.S. Defense Department adopted TCP/IP as an official standard in 1980, and then incorporated it within ARPANET in 1983.[97] This work served as a crucial bridge to the next development phase of what now is known as the Internet.

Moving beyond ARPANET, the top-level goal for the new Internet project was to develop "an effective technique for multiplexed utilization of existing interconnected networks."[98] Initially these non-military networks were limited to academic research facilities. The National Science Foundation (NSF) and others recognized TCP/IP as the primary means of solving that difficult task of connecting disparate networks, and the protocol suite was incorporated into its NSFNET research network in 1985. Starting in the late 1970s, other bodies began to appear with the objective of helping steer the course of this growing new "network of networks," including the Internet Configuration Control Board (ICCB) founded by Vint Cerf in 1979, the International Control Board, and the Internet Activities Board.[99]

Commercial services were authorized to use the Internet beginning in 1989, and with that authorization came a plethora of new technical bodies involved in some element of Internet governance or standards. In particular, the Internet Engineering Task Force (IETF), founded in 1986, is the institution that developed the core networking protocols for the Internet (including IPv4, IPv6, TCP, UDP, and countless others).[100] Its stated goal is "to make the Internet work better."[101] The Internet Society (ISOC) arrived in 1992, along with the Internet Architecture Board (IAB). The Internet Corporation for Assigned Names and Numbers (ICANN) appeared in 1998.

As government control and funding declined, commercial and non-commercial entities alike stepped into the breach to guide the Internet's continuing evolution. The resulting broader global vision of both process and rules "overshadowed the orientation that initially had been pursued by the government agencies focused on building specific military applications."[102] The Internet was becoming a platform available for *anyone* with a virtual connection.

Rough Consensus and Running Code

Given its unique heritage, the Internet's early shaping principles and operating rules were premised on freedom of interaction:

- *The lack of a central command unit:* with consensus-driven, democratic processes to define operations

- *The principle of network neutrality:* a simple network with intelligence residing at the end points

- *An open access principle:* local networks joining the emerging global Internet structure[103]

By contrast, the legacy telephone networks that served their customers were highly centralized operations, which included restrictions on people adding their own software or hardware implements.

One key part of how a network actually operates is its *technical standards*—the language that computers, phones, software, and network equipment use to talk to each other.[104] In turn, *protocols* are the widely recognized technical agreements among computers and other devices that determine how data moves between physical networks.[105] Internet pioneer Steve Crocker states that a "culture of open processes" led to the development of these standards and protocols that became building blocks for "the Net."[106] Informal rules became the pillars of Internet culture, including a loose set of values and norms shared by group members.[107] An early adopted document states that IETF should act as a trustee for the public good, with a requirement that all groups be treated equitably, and with an express recognition of the role of stakeholders.[108]

Unconventional technical bodies accompany these informal rules. Today, for example, there is no single governing body or process that directs the development of the Internet's protocols.[109] Instead, there are multiple bodies and processes of consensus. Much of the "governance" of the Internet is carried out by multistakeholder organizations (MSOs) such as ISOC and ICANN. Over the last two decades, these entities have largely established the relevant norms and standards for the global Internet, but despite this, "they are little known to the general public and even to most regulators and legislators."[110]

The IETF is a good example of this. This body develops many of the standards and protocols that are adopted to run the Internet. It is open to any interested individual, meets formally three times a year, and conducts activities through working groups in various technical areas. Its primary way of collecting and organizing viewpoints on proposed standards is the Request for Comment (RFC).

RFC 1958: The Internet's Four Design Principles

How the Internet runs is completely dependent on the software code implemented, of which its fundamental nature is created and shaped by engineers.[111] Indeed, "the Internet's value is founded in its technical architecture,"[112] and DeNardis points out the key role played by protocol standards in creating the Internet's "logical" layers:

"The Internet 'works' because it is universally based upon a common protocological language. Protocols are sometimes considered difficult to grasp because they are intangible and often invisible to Internet users. They are not software and they are not material hardware. They are closer to text. Protocols are literally the blueprints, or standards, that technology developers use to manufacture products that will inherently be compatible with other products based on the same standards. Routine Internet use involves the direct engagement of hundreds of standards... ."[113]

The IETF has clearly enunciated how its technical standards are imbued with certain values. The organization proclaims that "the Internet isn't value-neutral, and neither is the IETF.... We embrace technical concepts such as decentralized control, edge-user empowerment, and sharing of resources, because those concepts resonate with the core values of the IETF community."[114] So, how are these values reflected in the Net's actual design principles?

Understanding the what, where, why, and how of the Internet's architecture makes a big difference in understanding its immense role in modern society. Back in 1996, IETF's RFC 1958 probably best summed it up in saying, "in very general terms, the community believes that the goal is connectivity, the tool is the Internet Protocol, and the intelligence is end to end rather than hidden in the network."[115] Modularity or layering is the logical scaffolding that makes all of this work together.

So, consistent with RFC 1958 and other sources, we can discern a list of four major design attributes:

1. the structure of layering (the what)
2. the goal of connectivity (the why)
3. the tool of the Internet Protocol (the how)
4. the ends-based location of function (the where)[116]

But what does this actually mean?

The Law of Code: Modularity

The modular nature of the Internet describes the "what," or its overall structural architecture. "The use of layering means that functional tasks are divided up and assigned to different software-based protocol layers."[117] For example, the "physical" layers of the network govern how electrical signals are carried over physical wiring. Independently, the "transport" layers deal with how data packets are routed to their correct destinations, and what they look like. Finally, the "application" layers control how those packets are used by an email program, web browser, or other user application or service.

RFC 1958 reports that "[m]odularity is good. If you can keep things separate, do so."[118] This simple and flexible system creates a network of modular "building blocks," where applications or protocols at higher layers can be developed or modified with no impact on lower layers, while lower layers can adopt new transmission and switching technologies without requiring changes to the upper layers. Reliance on a modular system of layers greatly facilitates the unimpeded delivery of packets from one point to another. Importantly, the creation of interdependent layers also creates interfaces between them, which allow each layer to be implemented in different ways.

Smart Edges: End-to-End

The end-to-end ("e2e") design principle describes the "where," or the place for network functions to reside in the layered protocol stack. The general proposition is that the core of the Internet (the network itself) tends to support the edge of the Internet (the end user applications, content, and other activities).[119] RFC 1958 states that "the intelligence is end to end rather than hidden in the network," with most work "done at the fringes."[120] Some have rendered this broadly to mean that dumb networks support smart applications.[121] A more precise technical translation is that a class of functions can generally be more completely and correctly implemented by the applications at each end of a network communication. By removing interpretation of applications from the network, it vastly simplifies the network's job: just deliver IP packets and the rest will be handled at a higher layer. In other words, the network should support generality, as well as functional simplicity.[122]

The e2e principle suggests that specific application-level functions "ideally operate[] on the edges, at the level of client applications that individuals set up and manipulate."[123] By contrast, from the network's perspective, "shared ignorance is built into the infrastructure through widespread compliance with the end-to-end design principle."[124]

To have a fully functioning network, the edge and the core need each other. And they need to be connected together.

A Network of Networks: Interoperability

To become part of the Internet, owners and operators of individual networks voluntarily connect to preexisting networks. As a result, RFC 1958 puts it plainly: the goal of the Internet, its "why," is connectivity. This amounts to moving traffic—data packets—transparently and seamlessly from point A to point B.[125]

The Internet's goal of open and voluntary connectivity requires technical cooperation between different network service providers.[126] Networks of all types, shapes, and sizes voluntarily choose to interoperate and interconnect with other networks. They do so by agreeing to adopt the Internet's protocols as a way of passing data traffic to and from other entities on the Internet. So, "[i]f you want to put a computer—or a cell phone or a refrigerator—on the network, you have to agree to the agreement that is the Internet."[127]

In their book *Interop*, Palfrey and Gasser observe that "[t]he benefits and costs of interoperability are most apparent when technologies work together so that the data they exchange prove useful at the other end of the transaction."[128] Without interoperability at the lower layers of the Internet, interoperability at the higher layers—the human and institutional layers—is often impossible.[129] Their concept of *interop* is to "embrace certain kinds of diversity not by making systems, applications, and components the same but by enabling them to work together."[130] If the underlying platforms are open and designed with interoperability in mind, then all players—including end users and intermediaries—can contribute to the development of new products and services.[131]

Agnostic Protocols: IP

RFC 1958 calls the Internet Protocol (IP) "the tool" that made the Internet what it is.[132] The design of the IP, or the "how," allows separation of the networks from the services that ride on top of them. The IP was designed to be an open standard that anyone could use to create new applications and networks. Because the IP is standardized and non-proprietary, the things users can do on top of it are incredibly diverse. As Palfrey and Gasser say, "The system has standards at one layer (homogeneity) and diversity in the ways that ordinary people care about (heterogeneity)."[133]

By nature, the IP is completely indifferent to both the underlying physical networks and the countless applications and devices that use those networks. In particular, the IP does not care what underlying transport is used (such as fiber, copper, cable, or radio waves), what application it is carrying (such as browsers, e-mail, instant messaging, or MP3), or what content it is carrying (text, speech, music, pictures, or video). Thus, it enables any and all user applications and content. As Doria says, "By strictly separating these functions across a relatively simply protocol interface the two parts of the network were allowed to evolve independently but yet remain connected."[134]

Not only does IP separate the communication peers at either end of the network, but it also maintains a firm separation between the entities above and below it.[135] This is another example of how two discrete elements (in this case, modular design and agnostic protocols) work closely together to create a distinctive set of network functions.

The End Result: A Simple, Open, and Generative Feedback Network

So, to the countless software engineers who developed the Internet over several decades, its key attributes amount to the goal of connectivity (the why), the structure of layering (the what), the tool of the agnostic Internet Protocol (the how), and the end-based location of function (the where).[136] In each case, its design was founded on specific engineering principles grounded in human values: openness, connection, diversity, and user control.

The design features also reinforce one another. For example, the layering attribute is related to the end-to-end principle as it provides a framework to place functionality at the relative edge within the network's protocol stack.[137] RFC 1958 states that to keep the complexity of the Net at its edges means keeping the IP layer as simple as possible.[138] In turn, giving the IP a central role in the Internet is also "related loosely to layering."[139] The combination of these four design attributes has certainly allowed end users to utilize the Net as a universal platform for their activities.[140]

The end result is that the IP has helped to fashion what some call a "virtuous hourglass" from disparate activities at different layers of the network. In other words, the Net drives convergence at the IP (middle) layer, while facilitating divergence at the physical networks (lower) and applications/content (upper) layers. The interconnected nature of the network allows innovations to build upon each other in self-feeding loops.

Through its revolutionary design attributes, the Internet became a true *network of networks* over several decades. Its unique decentralized, peer-to-peer configuration enabled participants to interact from "the edge"—symmetrically, with little need for intermediaries. As Doc Searls and David Weinberger, both longstanding fellows at the Berkman Klein Center at Harvard summarized back in 2003, "the Net is a world of ends. You're at one end, and everybody and everything else are at the other ends."[141] As a result, the Internet has become the ultimate complex adaptive system, an enabling platform, and a common resource—supporting commerce, information exchange, entertainment, and free expression.[142]

And Now, the Web Overlay...

Understanding the advent of the World Wide Web is key in discerning how we got to the murky situation we find ourselves in, where our human autonomy and agency is more or less up for grabs. Such knowledge also demonstrates what is required to raise an effective challenge.

The software protocol that powers the World Wide Web was invented by Tim Berners-Lee in the late 1980s. His objective was straightforward: while the Internet was an incredibly open means for end users to interact, it was often difficult for non-experts to set up and operate their own portals in the Net. For the ordinary person, a more simplified set of interfaces was necessary to truly democratize the underlying resource. Berners-Lee sought to fill that gap.

The Web was first initiated in 1989 by CERN (the European Organization for Nuclear Research), and it was introduced as an "overlay" to the Internet in the early 1990s. This essentially means that the Web operates as another layer *on top of* the TCP/IP protocols, while also bringing its own separate interfaces to the network edges. In 1994, the World Wide Web Consortium (W3C) was formed to evolve the various protocols and standards associated with the Web. The W3C produces widely available specifications, called Recommendations, which describe the Web's building blocks.[143]

The Web can be defined as a collection of different websites around the world, containing different information shared with clients (edge devices) via servers (computers). This client-server relationship lies at the heart of the Web. The software that resides on the user's device—initially the desktop computer but now mobiles and other devices—is called the "client." The "server" is a second computer physically situated elsewhere, typically in a large data center.

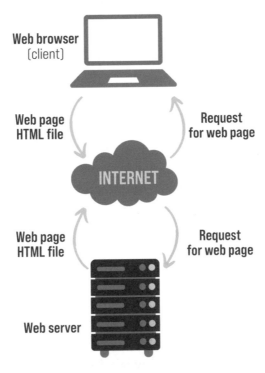

Client-server relationship

By the client-server nomenclature alone, we might expect that the "client" controls the relationship, while the "server" subserviently obeys the client. But as the Web has evolved, the reality has become very different.

Web 1.0: client-servers and browsers

The Web is based on several different software-based technologies: Web browsers, Hypertext Markup Language (HTML), and the Hypertext Transfer Protocol (HTTP).[144] Collectively, these innovations introduced a number of important improvements to the average person's experience of the Internet.[145] In particular, the combination of the browser, the client-server arrangement, and cookies revolutionized how end users could interact with each other, and with online content.

The browser is a species of client software which the end user utilizes to access different pages on the Web and displays content, such as text, data, pictures, animation, and video. Initially, web browsers were used only to "surf" the Web, but they developed the ability to conduct searches, send emails, and transfer files.

Importantly, from the end user's point of view, the Web is a portal leading to a vast, global assortment of content. The ability to browse websites opened up the network of networks as a democratic platform for literally billions of people around the planet.

Doc Searls, one of the most insightful observers of the Web, has noted that with the advent of the browser:

"The Web became a World Wide Free-for-all. Literally. Anyone could publish, change and remove whatever they pleased, whenever they pleased. The same went for organizations of every kind, all over the world. And everyone with a browser could find their way to and through all of those spaces and places, and enjoy whatever "content" publishers chose to put there. Thus the Web grew into billions of sites, pages, images, databases, videos, and other stuff, with most of it changing constantly."[146]

Sounds pretty cool in theory, right? Unfortunately, it turned out that at the root of the client-server relationship lies a fundamental tradeoff. In creating new opportunities for the "end user" to interact with a vast array of online resources, the client-server configuration opens the door to more asymmetrical arrangements between users than the underlying Internet with its end-to-end design principle. Those individuals or entities on the server side could begin dictating the user interfaces, accruing user data, and analyzing user behaviors. Ironically, the two sides over time began shifting roles, so the "server" became the actual controlling principal (the subject), while the "client" became relegated to a mere "user" (or object).

In retrospect, this initial centralizing overlay to the Internet was termed Web 1.0, and then came...

Web 2.0: cookies

In the early 2000s, companies such as Google and Facebook discovered the benefits of using multisided platforms on the Web. This configuration was based on a longstanding economic model, where companies (for a price) bring together buyers and sellers at a convenient location.[147] In the Web context, software applications such as email, search, and social media feeds are provided to users, typically for free on one side of the platform. Advertising and marketing providers that operate on the other side of the platform gain access to the user's personal data and serve the user ads. This advertising revenue accrues to the Web platform in the middle, acting as an intermediary between the two sides. This dynamic will be explored in more detail in the next chapter.

In this phase of the Web's evolution, perhaps the best representative is something that sounds innocuous, even playful: the cookie. Lou Montulli invented that piece of code as a simple way for websites to remember their visitors and handle user logins. These same HTTP cookies (so called because they are powered by the Web's foundational protocol) also gave online visitors a way to remember where they were when they last visited. These tiny crumbs of code made browsing the Web smoother and more convenient.

Essentially, cookies are just a token, a string of text that one computer leaves with another computer that acts as a virtual bookmark. Over time, companies realized that HTTP cookies enable the computer servers to track the activities of the client browser. As a result, corporate servers began depositing cookies onto every browser that visited their website.

Colloquially, there are two types of tracking cookies. The "first party" cookie is created by the website the user is actually browsing. The "third party" cookie is generated by other websites than the one being browsed, usually because they are linked to advertisements that appear on the page. Every ad on a page can generate a separate cookie, even if the user never clicks on the ad. Advertisers, analytics firms, and others can then track the individual's browsing history across any websites that contain their ads. Over time, these entities can build detailed user profiles, based on browsing history and other online behaviors. Doc Searls described this move to third-party cookies as crossing an important privacy threshold; "a personal boundary that should have been clear from the start but was not."[148]

Web 2.0 extended: mobility and the cloud

As Web platforms like Google, Facebook, Microsoft, and Apple grew in size, their architecture evolved into a more efficient way of serving up information. Once residing in a few centralized data centers, their servers were now residing in interwoven sets of data centers spread across the globe. As these data centers grew in size and scale, this became known as the "cloud era."

On the other end, for the users, the launch of Apple's first iPhone became a watershed event. For the first time, humanity had the sheer computing power, content, and applications of mainframe computers, but all in the palm of their hands. Google's introduction of the Android operating system to power a less expensive array of smartphones and other devices accelerated this shift. This combination of the ubiquitous cloud and the near ubiquity of smartphones greatly extended the reach of the Web.

The Web's simple interfaces and ease of use also meant that ordinary people quickly adopted it as the preferred means of accessing the Internet. More proprietary online portals provided by CompuServe, Prodigy, Yahoo, and others gradually declined in popularity. With a global array of servers, a browser on every computer and handheld device, and cookies proliferating on those browsers, web platforms became the near-ubiquitous manner for end users to procure and pay for services and mobile apps—via the data they reveal and the content they produce.[149] Because the platforms provide useful services, often at no upfront cost to users, over time they seemed to most people impossible to replace.

One natural result of this overlay to the original Internet is the facilitation of functional asymmetries between Web participants. Platform-based companies used their control over operating systems and devices and media platforms to quickly become the new uninvited intermediaries between people and the sites and apps they sought to reach.

At the same time, this arrangement continued a crucial trend: the illusion of end user control. The seeming ability to connect with anything and anyone through a few clicks on a smartphone or laptop conveys the sense that the user of this software and hardware is in charge. The reality is far more dubious. In each instance, the Web platforms control the localized interfaces and how they are used from afar.

These shifts away from the open, edge-based freedoms built into the underlying Internet have not gone unnoticed in Silicon Valley. In fact, many Web-based companies openly welcomed them—for their own reasons. In the next chapter, we will see why.

/C4/HERE COME THE MOPS

As you have no doubt noticed, our society is beset by significant power asymmetries. These asymmetries are no accident—in part, they are the product of centuries of efforts by entrenched entities to gain control over finite resources: finance, land, and labor. At the same time, humans have used governance instruments like laws and regulations, and social norms like consent and ethics, to engender the trust necessary for our social institutions to succeed and even flourish.

The web platform companies that have arisen in the early 21st century appear to be replicating this historic pattern of power through extraction. In this case, the resource is not other people's labor, or the remains of dead dinosaurs, but the digitally encased actions of those who utilize such platforms: data. With personal and environmental data gathered and mediated through interfaces, and analyzed via highly sophisticated algorithms, platform companies have tilted the proverbial playing field towards their own interests over ours.

As we are seeing, as online users we now have fewer actionable rights than when we are offline customers, clients, patrons, or citizens. In a short formula, our collection of digital rights amounts to less than our analog rights: $D<A$. This chapter takes a closer look at exactly how this erosion of human autonomy and agency was accomplished. The rest of the book then offers specific ways that these influences can be countered.

From here forward we will be referring to the web platforms as multisided online platforms, or "MOPs." As well as being a handy acronym, and more descriptive of the many-sided economic aspect of the Web version of the platform, this wording highlights the extractive nature of their business model. In brief, these entities use their online machinery to "soak up" our personal data, and "wring it out" into their computational systems for analysis and response. With ready access to financial resources, technical expertise, and our eyeballs and wallets, these MOPs are busy deploying advanced technologies that together comprise vast *computational systems*. All this tech occupies increasingly significant mediation roles in the lives of ordinary people.

The Unbalanced Economics of Online Platforms

As we saw briefly in the last chapter, many web companies discovered the benefits of operating a multisided platform. This approach has deep economic roots. For thousands of years, markets were primarily physical and local.[150] At certain times and in certain places, buyers and sellers connected through farmers' markets and trade exchanges.[151] These organized gathering spots connected participants to engage in market transactions and other social interactions.

This connectivity function of the ancient Athenian agora over time became its own standalone business model. These exchanges do not necessarily (or solely) produce goods or distribute services of their own; instead, their primary value is their ability to directly connect different customer groups and enable transactions. In short, they are useful platforms for carrying out commerce. In more modern terms, we can think of the shopping mall as occupying a similar connectivity role.

While prevalent throughout history, these market exchanges have only recently received serious attention in economic literature. Back in 2002, noted French economist and Nobel-winner Jean Tirole first used the phrase "multi-sided markets" in his analysis of modern-day platforms such as the credit card business. Since then, the term "multi-sided platform" or MSPs has gained general uptake. In more recent years, business analysts have deemed these platforms superior to traditional linear pipeline markets.[152]

Technical Fabric of MOPs

Computational systems are comprised of three nested physical and virtual basic components: information (data), devices (interfaces), and analysis (algorithms).[153] These systems combine various overlays (web portals, social media offerings, mobile apps) and underlays (network infrastructure, cloud resources, personal devices, and environmental sensors).[154] Considerable quantities of data derived from users' online activities supplies the virtual fuel.[155] Indeed, those same forces now are operating in the "offline" space, whenever we approach a store's sales counter, or use an appliance, or pump gas, or pay our bills. In each instance, an entity seeks to learn more about us, in order to sell us a product, or a service, or even (in the political context) an idea. For these transactions, what a computational system does is a combination of digital flows, physical interfaces, virtual computation, and human decision-making.

The largest MOPs—Google, Meta/Facebook, Apple, Microsoft, Amazon—have woven highly lucrative ecosystems around their computational systems.[156] This assortment of data-based advertisers, marketers, and brokers can be thought of as the "DAMBs." At the intelligent core of their computational systems is the algorithmic element itself—what we will call *Institutional AIs* (artificial intelligence). As we will see, these computational systems pose a singular challenge: they not just collect and analyze data; they are used to shape our perceptions and increasingly, our decisions.

Importantly, these immensely powerful "cloudtech" constructs belong to, and answer to, only a relative few in society. The situation is becoming even more challenging, as new generations of "intelligent" devices and applications are introduced into our physical environment. These include the Internet of Things (IoT), augmented reality (AR), biometric sensors, distributed ledgers/ blockchain, and quantum computing, culminating for some in the enticing vision of the "smart world."[157] Collectively, all this smart technology threatens to overwhelm us with its pervasive, intrusive, and relentless operations.

Many of us prefer that others mediate for us in facets of our life. Among other benefits, this allows us to offload the cognitive and decisional loads to someone else. This is an understandable tradeoff for living a modern life. With the rise of computational systems, however, Institutional AIs are poised to become increasingly influential and decisional agents in our lives.

Data: Extractive Assets

By now, data has become a well-worn concept utilized in every conceivable commercial context. Once, data was merely a set of passive measurements fed into static models, yielding limited insights. Then, it became more active—as part of the voluntary online interactions between "users" and "service providers" via various websites and apps. Now, data is "the new oil." As Srnicek puts it, "Just like oil, data are a material to be extracted, refined, and used in a variety of ways. The more data one has, the more uses one can make of them."[158]

Data has become a means of quantifying tracings of the world, and us. It is fast becoming an active agent in its own right, representing literally every aspect of existence. Freed from the shackles of the personal computer, data is free to roam throughout the world, in mobile form (smartphones and wearables) and environmental form (IoT and AR). Viewed in this way, data can be literally everything.

Human beings express themselves in a variety of contexts:

- the personal: in one's own thoughts and feelings
- the social: in communities of interest, including families, friends, and colleagues
- the economic: creating, buying, selling, and sharing
- the political: influencing government actions

Each of these human modalities of expression leaves its own "data trail" for others to follow, collect, and utilize.

Indeed, the global research firm IDC estimates that the amount of digital information i.e., data, in the world doubles every 18 months.[159] And according to IBM, 90 percent of the data in the world has been "created" (their term) in the last few years. So, what some have labeled "Big Data" is actually the three Vs of volume, velocity, and variety.[160] That enormous flood of data should not be a surprise, given the fact that "the collection of data today is dependent on a vast infrastructure to sense, record, and analyze," as Nick Srnicek explains.[161]

The economic agreement or compact that the MOPs have fashioned with users has entailed "giving away" our data from online interactions, based on vague online terms of service, in exchange for useful services and goods. Now, even third parties that we have no prior relationship with can gain access to and utilize our data. In this alarming way, data commodifies all of us into mere users and consumers, in all aspects of our personal, social, economic, and political lives. This same model now is being imported, without much forethought, into the brave new world of personal and environmental devices, machine learning systems, and AR.

Today, personal data can be seen as operating removed from the individual, both geographically and conceptually. This distance creates an unhealthy dynamic, where data is decontextualized and disembodied. The simple fact is that the human being can become lost in a numeric haze.

Unfortunately, the genie cannot be put back into the bottle. These technologies exist and are being employed to harvest personal data. Data will be collected and will be used in some fashion. So now, the question should be: by whom, and under what circumstances?

Algorithms: Institutional AIs

Companies have a singular focus in their collection of all this data: analyze it. The optimal method that humans have created to conduct such analysis is the algorithm, a set of software-based rules for solving a problem by sifting through data inputs and rendering decisions.[162] Problem-solving machines have been known since early Egyptian times. But today, the algorithms of machine learning, fed by massive amounts of data, dwarf any such machinery of the past.[163] When the algorithms achieve a certain level of sophistication and autonomy, the shorthand phrase for most of us is "AI."

As noted earlier, AI networks that are created, trained, and deployed by corporations and governments can best be thought of as "Institutional AIs." These algorithmic elements of computational systems churn through data to discern insights that in turn help develop tactics to get people to make one set of decisions over another.[164] As such, Institutional AIs pose a fourfold societal challenge as they are pervasive, consequential, inscrutable, and (in)fallible:[165]

- *Pervasive*: They lurk behind every online screen, environmental scene, and bureaucratic unseen (defined in the next section) in our lives.[166]

- *Consequential*: They make decisions that affect every one of us, from online recommendation engines to speech bots in our living rooms to decision engines in every corporate and government office.[167]

- *Inscrutable*: They often utilize deep neural networks and machine-learning-based systems, virtual "black boxes" where ordinary humans (and even expert software engineers) often cannot perceive or understand their operations, and the basis for their outputs.[168]

- *(In)fallible*: They raise major societal issues—regardless of their accuracy. Where their insights and inferences are correct, it means they have amassed highly sensitive correct profiles, which could be used to our detriment.[169] When their insights and inferences are flawed, it means they have amassed highly sensitive incorrect profiles, which also could be used to our detriment.[170] The choice seems stark enough: either the all-knowing panopticon of Orwell's *1984*, or the bureaucratic fog and confusion of Kafka's *The Trial*. Or the worst aspects of both.

In particular, with the rise of virtual assistants such as Alexa, Google Assistant, Siri, and Cortana, consumers are not only purchasing mobile devices but also home devices that include AI-based agents.

Beginning in 2024, the buzzword has been "chatbot." Built on generative AI platforms, such as ChatGPT, chatbots are poised to revolutionize many aspects of modern life, from education to employment to healthcare and beyond. While the sheer power and reach of these cutting-edge virtual technologies is impressive, the very real human beings behind the scenes are often overlooked. It is a fair statement that these innovations would not exist were it not for the financial benefits that their creators and implementers seek.

In reality, these AI agents waiting in the background "scenes" are an integral part of the feedback loops that these companies deploy. This means there usually is a single entity truly calling the shots: the corporation with financial motivations. Again, as with the online "screens" of our mobile phones, the human being residing in the home environment of their own living room is the object of the technology.

Many futurists tout existential concerns about AI taking over the world—"AI vs. Humans." This is the classic fear of AI general intelligence (AGI). Think *Terminator*, *The Matrix*, or any one of dozens of other dystopian fictional treatments. To be clear, this book does not wrestle with AI as a long-term existential threat. Many already have articulated these concerns, valid or otherwise. Instead, this book explores AI as an "essentialist" threat, with the increasingly plausible scenario that only a handful of people with the know-how and resources for creating Institutional AIs will be able to control the rest of us. Rather than machines becoming more like humans, their hoped-for outcome is humans who behave more like machines—whether serving the interests of governments (political power) or corporations (financial gain).[171] After all, as we utilize digital technologies in our everyday lives, we are being trained to think and react in increasingly crabbed and predictable ways.[172]

But perhaps our best recourse is to fight back with similar algorithmic technologies, just on our own terms. Indeed, perhaps we should be forging a third trendline to break out of this dynamic: "Intelligence Augmented," meaning humans enabled and enhanced by machines, or "Human Algorithms." Humans should be empowered to become *more* human— enabled, enhanced, and augmented by our machines and other technology tools.

Eventually, there may well be an Orwellian-style scenario: perfect information at the core and no privacy at the edge, with little to no recourse for affected individuals. This vision is an extreme one. Nonetheless, elements of less absolute scenarios are still at odds with the human values of individual autonomy, institutional accountability, and innovative advancements.

Interfaces: Control Points

Interfaces are an often-overlooked part of the story. They are the means by which we humans interact with the technology in question, and vice versa.

As we have seen, mediation is a key function of many types of modern technology, and the computer is its own locus of mediation, a process or active threshold situated between two states. An interface can be understood as a particular physical or virtual place or moment where one party transforms a fluid mediation zone into a pre-defined, fixed form of interaction. If mediation is a potentiality, the interface is the actual point of control.

In the physical world, interfaces can be specialized sensors, codes, switches, or chemical structures. They also can be icons, symbols, indexes, and diagrams. They can be levers, steering wheels, doorways, mobile apps, fences, office layout schemes, international borders, or telecommunications infrastructure. Indeed, our hands are prehensile general-purpose interfaces with which we embody cognition and manipulation.

Interfaces exist throughout digital networks. Three examples of this are graphical user interfaces (GUIs), which are designated interfaces for end users, APIs, which are designated developer interfaces, and the web browser.

For network designers, inherent decision points include who decides to have a mediation point, who creates it, where it is placed, and how rigid/porous it is. Furthermore, each decision point involves inherent tradeoffs between polarities such as openness and enclosure, freedom and control.

Alexander Galloway argues that the interface is perched on the mediating thresholds of self and world.[173] It is an area of choice—not a thing, but an effect, a process, or a translation; a "fertile nexus."[174] He muses about the interface as "a middle – a compromise, a translation, a corruption, a revelation, a certainty, an infuriation, a touch, a flux..."[175]

Benjamin H. Bratton similarly speaks of interfaces as mysterious zones of interaction that mediate between different realities.[176] For him, interfaces fix and limit possibilities. Each interface is open for some and closed for others. Or more philosophically put:

"Interfaces are thresholds. They connect and disconnect in equal measure, structuring flows by combining and segmenting it, enabling it or frustrating it, bridging unlike forms over vast distances and subdividing that which would otherwise congeal on its own."[177]

One notable trick is that interfaces, like an app or mobile screen, feel very much like they are "ours." In XR (extended reality), the interface becomes even more encompassing and problematic. At the same time, the MOP itself is becoming more like its own virtual entity, complete with new sensing systems (personal, wearable, and IoT devices), neural systems (AI/machine learning (ML)), and perception systems (AR). Seen in this way, the platform's reach and ability can exceed any single human being, or even large groups of humans.

Asymmetries of Our "Screens, Scenes, and Unseens"

Every day, we interact with computational systems via three kinds of digital interfaces: *screens, scenes, and unseens*.[178] Online *screens* lead us to search engines, social media platforms, and countless other web portals.[179] The Institutional AIs in the computational systems behind them render recommendation engines that guide us to places to shop, videos to watch, or content to read.[180] More ominously, these systems (with their user engagement imperative) tend to prioritize the delivery of "fake news," extremist videos, and dubious advertising.[181]

Environmental *scenes* are the "smart" devices—cameras, speakers, microphones, sensors, beacons, actuators—scattered throughout our homes, offices, streets, and neighborhoods. These computational systems gather a mix of personal (human) and environmental (rest of world) data from these interfaces.[182] Your neighbor's Ring doorbell is just one example.

Bureaucratic *unseens* are hidden behind the walls of governments and companies. These computational systems render judgments about our basic necessities and personal interests.[183] These decisions, which also often utilize Institutional AIs, can include life-altering situations, such as who gets a job or who gets fired, who is granted or denied a loan, who receives what form of healthcare, and who warrants a prison sentence.[184] And here, we don't even get the benefit of a screen or a speaker as a potential mediation point.

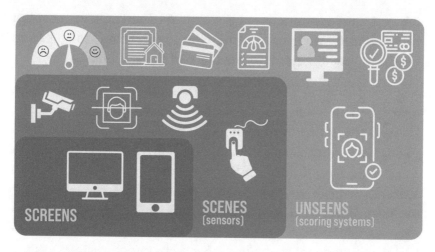

Interestingly, the progression of interface technologies tends to evolve from more to less visible (or even hidden) forms. What was once an obvious part of the user's interactions with a system has gradually become embedded in local environments and sometimes even vanishes altogether. As computer scientist Mark Weiser put it over 30 years ago, "the most profound technologies are those that disappear. They weave themselves into the fabric of everyday life until they are indistinguishable from it."[185]

Human engagement with these receding interfaces also becomes less substantive as part of a "deep tension between convenience and autonomy."[186] From typing on keyboards to swiping on screens to voicing word commands to the implied acceptance of walking through an IoT-embedded space, the interface context shapes the mode and manner of the interaction. In the parlance of systems theory, the feedback loops between the user and the network become more attenuated, or disappear altogether.[187] In these settings, traditional concepts like notice and choice can become far less meaningful. The tradeoff for us is exchanging control for simplicity and ease.

To some, this change is all but inevitable. The rise of generative AI has brought about a radical rethinking of how humans should interact with computational systems. As The Economist touted for example, accommodating the "all-seeing, all-hearing chatbots" could herald the "twilight of the screen age."[188]

Not surprisingly, the MOPs' computational systems work best for them when they operate in the unseen, less so in the scenes, and worst in the screens. This is because attenuation of interfaces means less human attention, and less opportunity to engage thoughtfully and deliberately with the technology systems. Interfaces can remove friction, but they can also exclude thoughtful engagement. In this way, technology moves from being a tool for the many sitting at the edges to becoming an agent of the underlying cloudtech systems. While this progression may bring some benefits, it also muddles the motivations of the MOPs and their DAMB ecosystem, and all the computational systems operating quietly behind the screens, scenes, and unseens within which we live our daily lives.

Three Challenges of Algorithmic Decision-making

The following brief examples highlight the as-yet unsolved societal challenges we face with the data-AI-interfaces capabilities that create our screens, scenes, and unseens.

Fake news (screens)

The United States presidential campaigns of 2016, 2020, and 2024 have spotlighted a troubling trend: many individuals and groups have the ability to harness computational systems technology to propagate disinformation, deep fakes, and slanted perspectives in ways that can influence political elections.

Those propaganda campaigns benefit from the ways that the MOPs use their computational systems to drive up emotionally charged traffic. Heightened emotions means greater user engagement, which means more money from advertisers. The truth loses relevance in such a scheme of pernicious feedback loops. These disinformation campaigns highlight how the current MOPs approach allows them to benefit financially from the social ills they feed.

Autonomous vehicles (scenes)

Today, human beings in control of vehicles make split-second decisions about what actions to take (or not take) in a potential impending accident. What would an algorithmic system decide to prioritize in the event of a potential accident?

- The driver's safety

- The passenger's safety

- The other driver's safety

- Damage to the driver's vehicle

- Damage to the other driver's vehicle

- Damage to other property

- Harm to pedestrians, and which ones

- Harm to animals

And more to the point, who will these fine-tuned choices be decided by? The car manufacturer? The software system? The federal regulator? The insurance company? The individual driver?

Biased algorithmic systems (unseens)

Currently, humans employ rough rules of thumb to identify and rectify forms of discrimination in everyday life. Now, and increasingly, market and political institutions are employing algorithmic systems to help make decisions about a variety of life-affecting situations, like:

- Who gets a job
- Who gets fired
- Who receives a loan
- Who receives what form of healthcare
- Who receives government assistance
- Who receives a prison sentence

One huge challenge is that the datasets can be skewed, and/or the algorithms themselves include inappropriate parameters. But again, how is bias to be defined in a host of contexts? And who makes these types of decisions for the rest of us?

Sir Tim's Misgivings

As it turns out, even the Web's original creator now wants to see its undoing. In recent years, Sir Tim Berners-Lee has openly critiqued how the Web's uses and misuses have evolved over time. In a 2019 interview,[189] he discussed how the Web has become a reflection of humanity's behaviors:

"Did we imagine that people would do bad things on the web? Absolutely. From very early on, we knew that if it's a powerful technology, then it's going to be used for good and bad, just like all other powerful technologies. But initially our feeling philosophically was that the Web should be a neutral medium. It's not for the Web to try to correct humanity. The Web would hopefully lead to humanity becoming more connected, and therefore, maybe more sympathetic to itself—and therefore, perhaps less conflict-ridden. That was our hope. But in general, we expected day-to-day life on the Web to be like day-to-day life on the street, to have its rough edges and its smooth edges."

What Berners-Lee realized, however, is that the Web's very architecture was driving the bad stuff. Indeed, the Web's structure can facilitate human freedom and choice and diversity, but also invites what could be thought of as abuses by design. Low-entry barriers invited spammers. The client-server architecture introduced hackers and breachers. Anonymity/pseudonymity served up trolls and bots.

And the Web's ubiquity led MOPs and their DAMB ecosystem to develop novel ways to deliver ad-based content (pernicious or otherwise). This cycle only became more pervasive, from surveilling online individuals to extracting and analyzing their personal data to using persuasive techniques to convince them to do something or buy something.

But rather than just criticizing what his invention has been transformed into, Berners-Lee also pointed a way forward:

"I've got a vision for an alternative world, in which that data does exist, but it's at the beck and call of the user themselves. Where the apps are actually separated from the data source. So when you use an app, it asks, where do you want me to store the data? And you have complete control over who gets access to it. It would be a new world. We're talking about a future in which these programs work for you. They don't work for Amazon, they don't work for Apple."

His revelation and proposed alternative Web is a yardstick for much of what follows here.

/C5/CEDING OURSELVES TO SEAMS OF CONTROL

Together, algorithms, devices, interfaces, and applications are being deployed as cutting-edge methods to extract the newest prized economic resource: our data. While web users tend to be drawn to platforms by siren songs of convenience and functionality, the MOPs and their DAMB ecosystems have their own pecuniary motivations. As such, this chapter focuses on the prevailing ways that Web-based companies develop user profiles which, in one expert's phrasing, "datafy" each of us.

While the human story of financial motivations is a timeless one, these Web-based economic and technological implements are unique in history. Collectively, these institutions now have the means and the incentives, on an unprecedented scope and scale, to substitute their own motivations for our hard-won human intentionalities.[190] As Adam Greenfield puts it, "the deeper propositions presented to us" by contemporary digital technologies are that "everything in life is something to be mediated by networked processes of measurement, analysis, and control."[191] For those who find this vision and the practices that support it problematic, the overarching "why not something different" of this book promotes one form of a concerted pushback. The call to arms: we can let someone else's financial imperatives define the whole of our digital identities—or we can realize and act upon the immense potential to create something far better for ourselves.

One-sided Platforms

All MOPs create value by matching different groups of people to transact. As Shoshana Zuboff and others have detailed,[192] the web platform ecosystem that dominates today is premised on several sets of players. The end user occupies one end, the platform/provider of the content/transactions/services occupies the middle, and the DAMBs occupy the other end.[193] The configuration is simple enough: the platform/provider supplies offerings at little to no upfront cost to the user, while data and information gathered about the user is shared with the brokers, who use the information to target their money-seeking messages to the user.[194] The platform/provider in turn takes a financial cut of these transactions.[195]

In this DAMB ecosystem model, it is increasingly common for the end user to be the "object" of the transactions, while the

DAMBs are the MOPs' true customers and clients.[196] As such, it is an unbalanced platform model, where one side obtains decided advantages of power and control over the other.[197] While Web users do receive benefits in the form of "free" goods or services, they are paying through the extraction and analysis of their personal information—and the subsequent influencing of their aspirations and behaviors by the MOPs and DAMBs.[198] Nonetheless, users of their services often do not fully realize their secondary status in the modern-day online platform.

Most people believe that their digital self is represented by the content they share online, be it posting on social media or sending an email or digital message. They may have a presence on multiple social platforms, contribute to a blog, or even own a website. However, online we are not just the content that we voluntarily contribute. We are also the data traces that are left in our wake as we search and surf and purchase and connect. We are also the human connections we seek out via social media. If we consider the whole of our gathered data, there is far more, and in much greater detail, than many of us might imagine. In other words, our personal contours in the online world are more porous and "leaky" than we may have thought.

A significant amount of information gleaned about us exists in marketing, advertising, and sales databases, scattered far and wide throughout countless networks. In general, the complexity of the DAMB landscape makes it all but impossible for any individual to successfully and completely map out the locations of all their acquired data. What we do know is that data is gathered in many places—then collected, pooled, shared, sold, and resold. Data scraped from the Web can be aggregated to form a detailed data profile about any individual to target advertisements and other pitches to them, and otherwise influence their behaviors and actions. Information contained in these data profiles may also be used for credit scoring, employment checks, insurance assessments, and more. Developing a clear-eyed view of the way our personal data is handled in marketing databases is a good first step in better understanding the potential for a deeper, richer digital identity. As we will see, however, more than transparency will be necessary to overturn this extractive paradigm.

While network effects and other economic factors make the current MOPS and DAMBs ecosystem model seem inevitable, and even irreplaceable,[199] nothing about this configuration of players is determined. Only two decades have passed since the model first gained traction in the commercial Web.[200] Countless more balanced options are available to be explored, where the end user is a true subject of the relationship. It is only today's Web that is premised on this unbalanced approach.

Digital Neoliberalism

Of course, the financial incentives here matter enormously. The money trails that MOPs find relevant should be equally relevant to the rest of us.

Evgeny Morozov, a longstanding critic of the technology sector, has observed how the real risks from technologies such as AI come not from the tech itself but the underlying political system.[201] He notes that what he calls the "neoliberal creed" has been adopted unabashedly by the major U.S. technology companies as they roll out their AI-based computational systems. Morozov observes that neoliberalism includes three abiding principles:

- The market bias: Private markets are superior to public institutions.

- The adaptation bias: Markets treat symptoms, not diseases.

- The efficiency bias: Efficiency supersedes social concerns.

Or as Milton Friedman put it succinctly, "There is one and only one social responsibility of business—to use its resources and engage in activities designed to increase its profits." To some, this market "fundamentalism" seems too extreme, and the recent debates over "shareholder" versus "stakeholder" capitalism is one reflection of this uneasiness. While web companies publicly embrace their commitment to values such as social good, how they actually design and deploy their technologies speaks volumes about their actual motivations.

Indeed, neoliberal thinking has helped shape our perceptions of the world around us. One example of this is the economic concept of the endogenous versus the exogenous. The endogenous is deemed to be the economic activities that take place within a particular economic system, while the exogenous (often called the externality) are the activities that occur outside the system. These externalities are deemed simply not to matter. With the assistance of aligned economists, this dichotomy involves drawing imaginary lines across the world that best suit the profit motive. Pollution is a good example, a deliberate drawing of endogenous/exogenous lines so that the negative externalities of a spoiled environment are not paid for by the economic activities that actually caused them. This artificial equation leads to personal profit over the public good. Efficiency, another neoliberal value, is also limited to the extraction of resources for private gain, rather than to maintaining a positive relationship with the larger environment.

Eric Schmidt, former CEO of Google, has succinctly made both the neoliberal and technology solutionism points. When asked about the US government regulating the practices of companies that are developing and deploying advanced AI capabilities, Schmidt insisted, "There's no way a non-industry person can understand what is possible. It's just too new, too hard. There's not the expertise. There's no one in the government who can get it right. But the industry can roughly get it right."[202] In his view, public institutions like Congress, and social concerns about bad outcomes, are secondary to the superior wisdom and efficiencies of large tech companies.

When however these questionable philosophies are put into practice by modern-day corporations, ordinary humans are at a decided disadvantage. In the US at least, the corporation is treated as a natural person, with a full panoply of human rights. These include freedom of speech (which essentially means spending their money to influence political and social systems), freedom to invent (which means enduring intellectual property rights designed for solo human inventors), and equal protection under the laws vis-à-vis actual human beings. But unlike the rest of us, corporations never need eat, or rest, or expire. They encapsulate the twinned realities of human rights and inhuman capabilities.

The larger point is that we have adopted a specific form of market-based economy, one that depends on the corporation as its prevailing organizational form, and the neoliberal creed as its governing philosophy. When married to the powerful technologies of the Web, and its proponents' technological solutionism, the combination is difficult to resist. The end result is what I call the "SEAMs paradigm."

SEAMs Feedback Cycles

As we have seen, computational systems require fuel—steady streams of data that render compensation to the MOPs, DAMBs, and other stakeholders in the web platforms ecosystem. The resulting feedback cycle consists of surveillances, extractions, analyses, and manipulations—what we can call "SEAMs." As Stafford Beer states, "the purpose of a system is what it does (POSIWID)."[203] And so we can consider the SEAMs cycle to be the purposive *action verb* of many computational systems.

SEAMs cycles harness four interlocking control points of the computational action verb.

- S is for surveilling, via devices in the end user's physical environment.[204]

- E is for extracting personal and environmental data encased as digital flows.[205]

- A is for analyzing, using advanced algorithmic systems to turn bits of data into inference and information.[206]

- M is for manipulating, influencing the users' outward behavior by altering how they think and feel.[207]

The point of this elaborate set of systems is not in the "SEA" control points, though they are troubling enough. It is the M of manipulations. By focusing primarily on the user data flowing in one direction, we easily can overlook the direction of influence back at the user. Yet, these cloudtech systems both import reams of data *and* export many forms of influence.

Extractions

SEAMs
cycles

Surveillance

Analysis

Manipulations

In today's world our data is increasingly used by many companies as part of SEAMs cycles...and this impacts everyone, every day...

Interestingly, the SEAMs cycle can be seen to correlate to John Boyd's concept of the Observe, Orient, Decide, and Act (OODA) feedback loops developed by the US military. Boyd's insight is that competitive advantage comes from shortening the lag time between the four steps of collecting data, analyzing it, making a decision, and carrying it out.

The "M" Word

Some may find the nomenclature of manipulations unduly harsh. But by definition, to manipulate means to manage or influence skillfully; it also means to control someone or something to your own advantage.[208] Both meanings match what the SEAMs cycles are actually doing.

The institutional imperative is straightforward: create as much influence over users as you can, so you can make as much money as possible. The predominant MOPs and their DAMB ecosystems would forego the considerable expense and effort of investing in and deploying the SEA elements, if they were not yielding hugely successful M outcomes.

To be clear, those with economic and political power have always wielded technological tools to exploit and even manipulate the consumer, the citizen, the human. The history of more benign examples of influence (advertising and marketing) and more pernicious ones (propaganda) is a long one.[209] In consumerist societies, advertising and marketing practices have long been used to persuade people to buy goods and services. These practices have morphed over time with technological advances: from newspapers to radio to TV—and now to the Web.[210]

What has changed is the sheer power of these new 21st century ecosystems. As Luciano Floridi puts it, "The digital revolution has radically transformed the power of marketing."[211] The combined reach of the SEA control points—the near-ubiquitous devices, the quality and quantity of data, and the advanced AI— all feeds directly into a greatly empowered "M" element. There is also profound human psychology operating in these design decisions. What Zuboff calls the "shadow text" gleaned from human experience helps MOPs in turn shape the "public text" of information and connection.[212] Algorithmic amplification of attention-grabbing content further adds to the creation of an online reality.[213] As the feedback cycle progresses, the entire construct constantly evolves to incorporate ever more subtle nudges, cues, "dark patterns,"[214] and other questionable innovations.

Floridi argues that the marketing imperative behind modern-day computational systems "sees and uses people as interfaces." These systems fail to respect human dignity for individuals and disregards "what is ethically good for them intrinsically and individually."[215]

Zuboff's Economies of Action

Shoshana Zuboff's in-depth empirical analysis has shed much-needed light on the people behind the algorithms and their desire to manipulate end users' behaviors. Senior software engineers and businesspeople at major MOPs confided in her that "the new power is action," which means "ubiquitous intervention, action, and control."[216] These Silicon Valley residents use the term "actuation" to describe this new capability to alter one's actions, while Zuboff labels it "engineered behavioral modification."[217] She details three different approaches aimed at modifying user behavior: tuning, herding, and conditioning.[218]

- "Tuning" is the subliminal cues and subtle nudges of "choice architecture."[219]

- "Herding" is remotely orchestrating the user's immediate environment.[220]

- "Conditioning" reinforces user behaviors, via rewards and recognition.[221]

In all three cases, the end goal is the same: to get a person to do something they otherwise would not do—or as Zuboff puts it, to "make them dance."[222] For example, in the case of content delivery to the user, the platform makes more money on content that drives higher engagement, which can entail dis– or misinformation, and extremist content.[223] By programming the system to promote—and amplify—certain kinds of content, the platform is also "programming" the user to accept and interact with that content.

On the selling side, MOPs and their DAMB ecosystem partners can also utilize detailed information about the user to extract the maximum amount of money they will willingly part with for a service or product.[224] In 2015, the Obama Administration released a white paper arguing that such "differential pricing could be conducive to fraud or scams that take advantage of unwary consumers." It is unclear whether we as end users fully appreciate this practice. When this first-order price discrimination technique is employed, it marks a clear case of using extensive knowledge about us *against us*.

Losing Our Autonomy

Importantly, much of this cloudtech activity happens outside our conscious view. As Zuboff says, "there is no autonomous judgment without awareness."[225] Frischmann and Selinger make a similar point as what they call "techno-social engineering" can shape our interactions via programming, conditioning, and control—engineered by others, and often without our awareness or consent.[226] To them, it is the technology that shapes the contours of our autonomy and agency, rather than the other way around.

Moreover, the sense of "faux" agency provided by robust-seeming interfaces leads many users to believe they are in charge of their online interactions. And when we are unaware of the manipulation, as Slavoj Žižek says, "our unfreedom is most dangerous when it is experienced as the very medium of our freedom."[227]

These insights about MOPs behaviors aligns well with Gaventa's earlier power cube:

- Places: Global corporations operating via web cloudtech appear to users as if local via interfaces and apps.

- Spaces: These same corporations use open-seeming interfaces such as application programmable interface (APIs) to control our experiences.

- Forms: These companies employ ideological power (hidden/ invisible setting of agendas) as a means of influencing/ manipulating users.

Mixed Motives in Advertising-Supported Search Engines

In 1998, two doctoral students at Stanford published a paper detailing the prototype of a large-scale hypertextual web search engine. In an appendix, they observed that the predominant business model at that time for commercial search engines was advertising. The students cautioned that "the goals of the advertising business model do not always correspond to providing quality search to users." Based on simple reasoning, and to historical experience with other media, "we expect that advertising-funded search engines will be inherently biased towards the advertisers and away from the needs of the consumers."

This "search engine bias is particularly insidious" because of the difficulty, even for experts, to accurately evaluate search engines. As a result, the authors concluded, "less blatant bias are likely to be tolerated by the market" because of the difficulty in detection coupled with the significant market effect.

The authors of this Stanford research paper? Larry Page and Sergey Brin.[228]

In 2000, their new company Google introduced text-based advertising above search results. In 2007, Google purchased DoubleClick, an online advertising company with deep ties to the nascent DAMB ecosystems of online publishers, advertisers, marketers, and brokers. In 2009, Google introduced product listing ads. Over time, "ad creep" has meant more space is allocated to advertising, with a growing number of ads, locations, and size. The "mixed motives" inherent in the MOPs business model, in this case of online ads supporting Web portals such as the search engine, were now up and fully running.

Interestingly, Google appears to perceive itself as the ultimate champion of the user, not the advertiser. In its 2004 Founders' Letter, as Google was being taken public, Larry and Sergey insisted that "serving our end users is at the heart of what we do and remains our number one priority."[229] Elsewhere, they claim that "we built Google search for consumers, not web sites."[230]

In their research paper, however, Brin and Page concluded that the inherent mixed incentives for search engine providers means "it is crucial to have a competitive search engine that is transparent and in the academic realm."[231] Presumably, such competition would help put useful pressure on the search engine in question to respond more to the end user side of the MOPs equation. The challenge, of course, is that the ads-based Web has become so lucrative to online companies, so seemingly indispensable to advertisers, and so convenient (meaning "free") to end users that few entities to date have mustered any minimally competing alternative.

Moving Beyond the SEAMs Cycles

In the new Computational Era, we are not just existing in the modes of "data extraction and analysis," as Hal Varian of Google puts it. It is the Manipulation mode of using data extraction and analysis to influence, even coerce, thought patterns and behaviors, which is emblematic of the new world order. The MOPs are not just "soaking up" (importing) user data—they are pushing out (exporting) ways of influence. In particular, we need a renaissance in more deliberate and relational forms of mediation if we are to avoid a future centered on AI-based systems controlled by others.

We are witnessing astounding technical advances, accompanied by reduced personal autonomy, and growing wealth disparity. Whether you want to call it a paradigm shift, an inflection point, or some other fancy term, the point is that dramatic changes in the tech world are causing huge societal change (yet again), in uneven and disproportionate ways. Nonetheless, the MOPs era has not yet run its course. There is much yet to be decided, created, and disseminated in the unexplored future. And there is time yet for a course correction.

What will constitute this as-yet undefined next phase in the ongoing datatech dynamic between cores and edges, layers and platforms, data brokers and "users"? As with the glial networks in neuroscience, dark energy in physics, and "junk DNA" in biology, the answer to the challenge is right before us. If only we can discern that next pathway, hidden behind the very concepts we employ to help us make sense of the world.

We can only see what our mental and physical apparatuses allow us to see. All of us wear conceptual shades, blinding us from recognizing a world beyond concepts such as "technology" and "markets" and "states." Yet, these concepts can be swapped out for new ones that better serve our needs.

On the surface, the SEAMs cycles paradigm remains firmly entrenched. Still, as we will see further in Chapter 19, cracks in the edifice *are* appearing. Policymakers have enacted laws and regulations that at least in theory constrain Web companies' activities. The online advertising business is not quite as successful as has been, well, advertised. End users are beginning to express unease about the length and breadth of data extraction. Companies like Apple find ever-growing market share as they shut down certain surveillance avenues (while still profiting from others).

Despite this, as the next chapter will explain, the laws and policies adopted so far to curtail those who employ the SEAMs cycles have not (yet) curtailed SEAMs-based incentives. As such, technology companies sprouting up everywhere continue down the familiar path of the Web's predominant business model. Our personal contours are under daily assault from the very technologies we employ to our presumed benefit. We cannot plausibly hope to retain much of our independence of thought and of action in the face of such relentless, pervasive, and super-intelligent SEAMs cycles.

However, the challenge is not to defeat the SEAMs cycles paradigm, but to move past it—with compelling value propositions for consumers, for Web companies, and yes, for advertisers. And as today's technology and economic and political systems are what we have to work with, they are the best tools available to push back with. In parts II, III, and IV, I will propose tangible ways to accomplish just that.

/C6/THE HAZARDS OF ACCOUNTABILITY

For those who find the picture painted so far troubling, there are two fundamental options. One is to take steps to make the MOPs and their DAMB ecosystem players more accountable for their actions. The other is to create entirely different ecosystems based on a very different ethos and overarching paradigm. While this book calls to press forward on both fronts, it focuses primarily on the latter. As this chapter will show, holding the MOPs accountable for their actions is necessary, yet insufficient. At best, it amounts to protecting us from some of the bad behavior of those with power, rather than granting us our own power to enhance and promote our best interests.

The Limits of Markets

In capitalist societies, many experts point to markets as the preferred way for disputes between producers and consumers to be rectified. But the brief history of end users seeking alternatives to the MOPs and their business models is not encouraging.

In 2009, researchers Christopher Soghoian, Sid Stamm, and Dan Kaminsky released a piece of software they called a "Do Not Track" (DNT) header. This became an official HTTP header field, adopted by the World Wide Web Consortium, suitable for embedding in web browsers. Its purpose? To allow end users to opt out of online tracking by websites. As noted earlier, the Web allows MOPs and other online companies to use third-party cookies to collect data from end users as they click on websites—including from sites that user browsers have never even visited. This practice quickly caught on and became a major feature of online advertising and marketing. With the DNT header, the researchers believed that allowing end users to opt out of such tracking would end these practices.

Mozilla first adopted the DNT header capability into its Firefox browser and soon, others followed. A decade went by. In 2019, the W3C Tracking Protection Working Group was disbanded. The rationale was straightforward: an "insufficient deployment of these extensions," and no "indications of planned support among user agents, third parties, and ecosystems at large."[232] In other words, not enough people had adopted the add-on, and not enough entities were supporting it.

The overarching reason for this was not difficult to understand. Whatever the merits of the DNT header for end users, nothing compelled the web companies to agree to honor it. For the vast majority of websites, the experience remained the same. Third-party cookies would attach to the browser, and the individual would be tracked as they surfed. And so the tracking continued, only more deeply ingrained than ever.

As this example demonstrates, MOPs and their DAMB ecosystems do not work for us. They work for themselves. And the financial incentive structures that the Web unleashed have become embedded in the very computational machinery these companies have built and deployed throughout the globe. The result is an environment dominated by MOPs and their DAMB ecosystems. In this context, how can we employ the rules and players of governance to restrain those unwanted behaviors?

The Limits of Governance

From the outset, we have to recognize the pronounced limitations of governance as practiced in the real world. As discussed previously, governance is essentially the prescribed set of Rules (institutions) and Players (organizations) that collectively manage power dynamics and interactions within a given human system. We can denote two kinds of governance: the macro (public rules and players) and the micro (private rules and players). In both cases, it turns out, others are deciding the MOPs and DAMBs governance practices for you.

Nicolas Suzor helpfully delineates how the legitimacy of a particular governance scheme depends on the consent of those being governed. He offers "digital constitutionalism" as the frame to examine legitimate consent in the digital world.[233] The most basic value of the rule of law is "that power is wielded in a way that is accountable, that those in positions of power abide by the rules, and that those rules should only be changed by appropriate procedures within appropriate limits."[234] Such accountability requires the presence of "restraints on the arbitrary or malicious exercise of power."[235] Unsurprisingly,

Suzor finds that the MOPs have largely evaded seeking true consent for their marketplace practices.

Public governance

In the first category of public governance, those in the United States and other democratic-leaning countries rely on our representative political systems. Here, we face neoliberalism again, dominated by large vested interests (such as MOPs and DAMBs) with deep pockets and business models to protect and extend. The average citizen appears to have little chance of creating meaningful change in such political and market systems.

Prevailing approaches to countering the negative impacts of MOPs and their DAMB ecosystems amounts to accountability measures that seek to minimize their harmful consequences. Theoretically, making these systems more accountable to the rest of us limits their unilateral reach and authority. Representative steps taken by various citizen advocacy groups in the public policy realm to improve MOPs accountability include:

- increasing government oversight of large platforms

- policing and punishing bad behavior

- creating greater transparency to benefit users

- improving corporate protection of personal data

- reducing algorithmic bias in corporate and government bodies

- introducing ethics training in computer science

To be clear, each of these actions is hugely important and necessary to make the MOPs and DAMBs more answerable to the rest of us. As one beacon of light, Europe's General Data

Protection Regulation (GDPR) passed in 2018 "is a notable achievement in furthering the cause of [protecting] European citizens' personal data."[236]

Nonetheless, such accountability measures likely are not enough, even together, to significantly alter power imbalances in the current digital landscape. Crucially, in most instances, these steps still leave the SEAMs cycles paradigm intact. The computational systems themselves remain largely under the direct control of the underlying MOPs and their DAMB ecosystem players, with their enormous financial and political advantages, and the winner-take-all "network effects" they enjoy.[237] The MOPs' ability to challenge and then, if necessary, absorb government accountability mandates may be unprecedented in modern political history.

The concern is that large players can often gain the advantage of "regulatory lock-in," that is, the ability to influence or evade government rules in ways that smaller players cannot duplicate.[238] This threat has been well-articulated in the MOPs' ability to comply (or approximate compliance) with GDPR.[239]

Moreover, regulatory solutions based on making incumbent players more accountable typically rely primarily on behavioral remedies—what could be considered "thou shall not" or "thou shall" injunctions.[240] Such regulations can be difficult to define, adopt, implement, and enforce.[241] Such behavioral remedies also tend to leave existing power asymmetries in place.[242] On the Web, one symptom of this is users' current struggles with "consent fatigue" when facing numerous cookie consent notifications with every click on a website or app.[243] These notification requirements, stemming from Europe's GDPR data protection regulations, ironically render consent a largely useless tool to garner legitimate user approval for the MOPs' actions.

A larger concern is that, as citizens, we tend to rely on public governance institutions to make important decisions on our behalf. An example of this is a one-size-fits-all privacy law that establishes limitations and allowances for the uses of personal data. However, as autonomous beings, each of us has personal contours of influence that we try to manage on a daily basis. Having the ability to fully exercise our control over those boundaries can be challenging. For most of us, consequential decisions about our lives are rendered by corporations, or the government. If governance creates a floor of accountability, I would argue that each of us still should retain the ability to assess and impose our own individualized ceilings. In philosophical terms, this could be seen as a basic protective foundation of "paternalism," combined with various openings for "libertarianism." Otherwise, denying the opportunity to exercise autonomy and agency is denying part of what makes us human.

Ultimately, an exclusive focus on accountability may end up conceding too much to the status quo. As Catherine D'Ignazio and Lauren F. Klein observe concerning the current data extraction environment, accountability measures by themselves can amount to "a tiny Band-Aid for a much larger problem."[244] They believe such measures have the unintended consequence of entrenching existing power. And so, core aspects of the prevailing SEAMs cycles paradigm, and its enacting business models, may well remain intact. Even promising proposals to grant users the ability to monetize their personal information can be seen as accepting the reductivist Silicon Valley credo that "personal data is the new oil."[245]

Private governance

This leaves us with private or micro governance. The most commonly used term to describe this approach is "self-governance," a practice that MOPs have become particularly adept at. For the most part, private governance is exemplified by policies adopted by corporations, such as terms of service (ToS), acceptable use policies (AUPs), and privacy policies. These documents tend to be drafted unilaterally and enforced by (again) the deep pocketed MOPs and DAMBs, eager to protect market power.

As Suzor reveals, the limits of micro-governance in the digital world are especially egregious. Any legal relationship between online providers and users is considered to be one of firm-to-consumer. Users are thought of as having voluntarily accepted the terms of participation in private networks such as Web platforms. Their options are essentially two: take it or leave it. As a matter of governing social media platforms, Suzor explains that:

"It is very seldom transparent, clear, or predictable, and providers often purport to have absolute discretion on the exercise of their power to eject under both contract and property law. Essentially, providers have control over the code that creates the platform, allowing them to exercise absolute power within the community itself. The exercise of this power is limited by the market and by emergent social norms, but it is barely limited by law."[246]

For most people, our interactions with MOPs are governed by their ToS. In all cases that Suzor examined, these documents provide broad, unfettered discretion to platform owners. In particular, "users are constrained in their power to negotiate with platforms or exit established networks."[247] In short, "these contracts are simply unlikely to ever reflect an optimal bargain," as for platform owners they "are almost universally designed to maximize their discretionary power and minimize their accountability."[248] In other words, the MOPs hold the pens to determining whether and how they agree to constrain themselves.

The Limits of Privacy

Privacy is a similarly cramped concept. Protecting our privacy can be an important tool for protecting the self. Still, the SEAMs cycles are one reason why privacy on its own is insufficient to protect ordinary humans from unwanted incursions.

To the average person on the street, the concept of privacy as an individual has been sold as an irrelevant luxury. Scott McNealy of Sun infamously remarked back in 2003 that "You have no privacy—get over it."[249] While at Google, Eric Schmidt posited that "if you have something that you don't want anyone to know, maybe you shouldn't be doing it in the first place."[250] These types of comments suggest that those within the MOPs and DAMBs ecosystem hope to instill us with a sense of resignation, of learned helplessness, if not outright shame, to counter our natural desire to protect our personal and private self from intrusive eyes.

Not surprisingly then, two common refrains we might hear from individuals regarding their online privacy are "they already have all my data anyway" and "I have nothing to hide." In both cases, the person likely presumes that the MOPs and DAMBs are utilizing a linear mechanism to acquire pieces of their daily life—their name, their credit card numbers, an unflattering photo, their favorite beer—to create a profile from which the platform will simply try to sell them goods and services.

As we have seen, this folk understanding minimizes the threat. The Communications Privacy Model mentioned earlier exclusively focuses on the one-way protection of the private nature of our information. By contrast, the shaping function of the dynamic "M" element in the SEAMs cycles is not as well understood. Players in the MOPs DAMB ecosystem not only want to discover something we might want in order to sell it to us. The ultimate goal is to export their influence, conscious or otherwise.[251] They want to make you *do* certain things—buy goods and services, provide content, take a stance on controversial issues, cast a vote for a certain political candidate—that *they* want you to do.[252] Their end game is to manipulate and alter our thoughts (autonomy) and behaviors (agency), simply because it makes for better business.[253] Using privacy policies as a shield to defend our sphere of intimacy and vulnerability, our personal contours, is a poor match for determined SEAMs cycles-based manipulation.

Furthermore, the concept of privacy typically extends only to what is thought of as "personal data." Other forms of data—from shared, to collective, to non-personal—seem ill-suited to individual privacy.[254] Still, other areas of human life (for now, at least) are lived outside the reach of the data realm. Yet, the SEAMs cycles churn through all types of data, with potentially pernicious impacts on human society. These impacts include those externalities that can harm society in general—such as the flood of disinformation—even if certain specific individuals are not directly harmed.[255]

Aligning our public policies to protect only our privacy views the human as a narrow enclave of "internal" things to be placed off limits from unwanted "external" forces. A more robust portrait sees the fully autonomous and agential human as the center point of complex social and institutional influences. Giving each of us the ability to enhance and promote ourselves in the world better reflects that human reality.

Scholar Sacha Molitorisz agrees with the notion of reframing privacy as a relational good.[256] He points out that other proposed models for privacy fail to adequately describe the human being in all her relevant personal, relational, and social contexts. "None of us is a being simpliciter; we are all beings-in-relation."[257] By contrast, what has been termed the "access model" theory of privacy best fits our embodied, embedded, social selves. As he notes, privacy always involves access, and the right to privacy that "others be deprived of unauthorized access to me and to information about me."[258] One may or may not always control that access, as in cases where the law or other external constraints circumscribe our choices, but nonetheless the ability to control access always in theory remains. Molitorisz gives us a more robust version of privacy than is typically presented to us in policy debates, one we can fold nicely into the personal contours theory.

In short, reducing the harmful actions of an already powerful status quo is vital, but by definition produces only partial societal gains. The point however is not to abandon these efforts, but to *supplement* them. These accountability-type policies offer a much-needed but ill-fitting shield. The times call as well for introducing sturdy swords to make up for the inherent gaps.

And thankfully, our democracies do offer some pathways for meaningful change. In Part Four, we will examine how devising a policy design space populated by a new "digital common law" offers some prospects for moving beyond the Web we have today.

The Limits of Consent

What then is left in terms of holding MOPs and DAMBs accountable for their actions? Above and beyond the limitations we can find in both public and private governance, we have the core principle of consent. As long as individuals (acting as consumers, citizens, or users) willingly accede to a power-based relationship, current laws would deem the requirement of consent to have been satisfied. This means we have agreed to surrender control to someone else over aspects of our personal contours, including privacy. At least that is the theory. The reality is far murkier, and more problematic.

Many tout Europe's GDPR as the gold standard for protecting an individual's privacy and personal data. As mentioned earlier, one of the ways that an entity can abide by GDPR's requirements is to obtain valid consent from its end users. But as consent is a highly flawed mechanism in the typical context of websites and users, many of GDPR's constraints on data uses have no real teeth.

With Don Herzog's treatment of consent in *Happy Slaves*, the notion of volunteering to be governed by another person or entity requires significant unpacking. In the Web context, the SEAMs cycles paradigm chugs away under the pretext that the end user has agreed to grant access to their personal data, to have detailed dossiers prepared and shared, and to be influenced by the best manipulation engines available. And in the case of private governance, ordinary end users have very limited options aside from departing the platform and giving up the benefits of being a connected human.

Edenberg and Jones earlier pointed out for us the five necessary elements that form the moral core of consent: context, scope, knowledge, voluntarism, and fairness. The "notice-and-consent" model set up by most web companies fails most, if not all, of these elements:

- In nearly all cases, the context of the background conditions, and the scope of the "clearly defined boundaries" of the permission granted, is rarely given in full or readily understood by the user.

- Knowledge as "epistemic competence" is difficult where key factors such as the context and scope are obscure.

- Voluntariness is also problematic where the consent is free from coercion or manipulation. "Your money or your life" does not provide a sufficiently free choice.

- Finally, fairness is at risk where society itself is conflicted over what social goods are provided in these situations.

Elizabeth Renieris finds similar sizable cracks in the Web's notice and consent regime.[259] The legal defects include the notices, agreements, and licenses presented by websites and apps to users. Ostensibly, they provide transparency and knowledge to form the basis of a valid consensual arrangement. But in reality, these amount to a one-sided mechanism, drafted by company lawyers and presented to users in a "take it or leave it" fashion. No negotiation is ever contemplated, as would be the case in a more typical marketplace transaction between willing buyers and sellers.

Likewise, Renieris finds a plethora of practical defects, such as the quantitative challenges of considering so many notice and consent announcements in daily digital interactions. These bring us the dreaded pop-ups, banners, and tick boxes that seek our approval for countless interactions on the Web. However, as technology evolves away from the GUIs found on our screens, to the "scenes and unseens" of voice, gesture, gait, and even brain interfaces, authentic consent seems all but impossible. As Renieris puts it, relying on real-time affirmations in these environments will become "wildly untenable."

The qualitative challenges center on many of the defects outlined by Edenberg and Jones, set against the cognitive limits of the human mind. Renieris also observes the "context collapse" that occurs when the digital realm squeezes down all of our weighty real-world actions and behaviors "into a series of one-dimensional clicks and scrolls." The notice and consent construct also underplays the complex, multidimensional nature of the Web, with its "toxic, extractive practices of parasites and surveillance capitalists in the parallel dataverse."[260]

Lisa LeVasser and Eve Maier also examine the basis for "consent overload" online.[261] They cite Nancy Kim's now-classic formulation of the three elements that must be included for valid lawful consent: "an intentional manifestation of consent, knowledge, and volition/voluntariness."[262] Digital consent experiences fail all three elements, including the lack of any actual negotiation or bargaining process.

Finally, Neil Richards and Woodrow Herzog recite many of these same drawbacks in what they term "the pathologies of digital consent."[263] They decry what they see as three such pathologies: the unwitting, the coerced, and the incapacitated. Interestingly, their proffered solution (to be discussed in the next part) is the trust-based approach of fiduciary relationships.

These are not mere academic quibbles about the validity of consent between one party and another. The implications are quite significant in whether or not an individual has given valid consent to other entities' uses of their personal data, and subsequent attempts at manipulation.

One salient example is the ongoing debate over cookies. In the parlance of data marketers, there are three categories of personal data: zero party, first party, and third party. Zero party data is information that an individual has "willingly" provided in exchange for an inducement, such as a product coupon. This information is especially valued by marketers because it offers direct insights about the person. First-party data is information that a website or app collects from an individual based on their activities or interactions from that domain. An example is someone who browses on a website looking to purchase something. Such activities have been deemed by the courts to create enough of a voluntary relationship to allow the site to collect certain data about those interactions. Again, that data is highly relevant to marketers.

By contrast, as we have seen, third-party data is the primary basis for the empires built by the largest MOPs: information gleaned from cookies and other tracking mechanisms that follow individuals around the Web. This non-consensual data is increasingly coming under pressure from regulators, and legal instruments such as GDPR, as not providing a basis for valid consent by the individual.

If we pause to take a closer look, however, it is clear that the voluntariness of consent is key to whether data can reasonably be deemed to be zero party, first party (and thus fair game to marketers), or third party—and thus warrants some limits being placed on its uses. But as we have seen, consent is a highly fraught mechanism for discerning the actual intentions of the human being behind it, and so these presumed distinctions can seem increasingly meaningless. True consent requires authentic relationship, as we will see in Part Two

CONCLUSION TO PART ONE

As we have seen, the SEAMs feedback cycles entrenched in the business models of the MOPs and their DAMB ecosystems are pervasive, pernicious, and very real. Their prevalence in the Web has resulted in the loss of human autonomy and agency. In short, our digital selves currently have fewer rights than our analog selves. Or, *D<A*.

What is there to be done about this? As we have seen, utilizing traditional accountability policy tools such as improving privacy and requiring consent are useful, but they get us only so far. We remain largely stuck in the transactional Web that others have woven for us. But what if there were another way, a pathway that led to enhancing human autonomy and agency via computational systems? Thankfully there is, as we will explore in the remainder of this book.

No more of this.

```
}
int main(int argc, char *argv[]) {
   int sockfd, newsockfd, portno;
   socklen_t clilen;
   char buffer[256];
   struct sockaddr_in serv_addr, cli_addr;
   int n;

   sockfd = socket(AF_INET, SOCK_STREAM, 0);
   if (sockfd < 0)
      error("ERROR opening socket");
```

/PART TWO/FIGHTING FOR OUR DIGITAL AGENCY (D > A)

```
   memset((char *) &serv_addr, 0, sizeof(serv_addr));
   portno = 8080;
   serv_addr.sin_family = AF_INET;
   serv_addr.sin_addr.s_addr = INADDR_ANY;
   serv_addr.sin_port = htons(portno);

   if (bind(sockfd, (struct sockaddr *) &serv_addr, sizeof(serv_addr))
      < 0) error("ERROR on binding");

   listen(sockfd, 5);
   clilen = sizeof(cli_addr);

   newsockfd = accept(sockfd, (struct sockaddr *) &cli_addr, &clilen);
   if (newsockfd < 0)
      error("ERROR on accept");
```

INTRODUCTION TO PARTS TWO AND THREE

In Part One, we saw how the MOPs and their DAMB ecosystems have successfully wielded SEAMs feedback cycles to exert control over the Web. These next two parts dive into GliaNet, a proposed new Web ecosystem, premised on the HAACS paradigm, of human autonomy and agency via computational systems. Part Four then provides a detailed theory of change and action plan—the "how" —for bringing each of these related elements of human governance and edgetech capabilities into reality. The overarching premise is that each and all of us should have available the entities, practices, and technologies that allow us to "hack back" at the SEAMs paradigm and its dubious benefactors.

As we shift towards a more relational and humanistic approach to stewarding our digital lifestreams, we enter a new world of trust-based legal mechanisms. The GliaNet initiative seeks to harness countless positive impacts on human autonomy/agency from computational systems. On the "CS" side of the HAACS ledger, this means creating ecosystems that include new kinds of information constructs, agential entities, AI applications, and network interfaces. Each of these modalities, in turn, pushes back emphatically against the four basic controlling elements of SEAMs cycles.

However, technology alone is not enough. We need new "rules of the road," in the form of governance principles that extend throughout the Web's layers. And the objective is more ambitious than merely restraining the pernicious acts of incumbent market and government players. Rather than solely minimizing the harms of the incumbent MOPs and their DAMB ecosystems (which is hugely necessary work in its own right), the goal is to maximize the positive impacts from newly-formed platforms that we control ourselves.[264] In that way, people online can move from a digital world founded on a limited form of negative rights ("freedom from" the more egregiously bad stuff), to one that rests firmly on positive rights ("freedom for" the good stuff).[265] Starting from protecting the person, through to enhancing and promoting their autonomy and agency.

As noted earlier, economic and technology systems are rooted in basic human behaviors. No MOPs or DAMB ecosystems, no computational systems or asymmetric interfaces, no SEAMs cycles have any meaning outside the purview of the human motivations sustaining them. And so, we cannot hope to push back successfully against the SEAMs paradigm and its supporters without a firm grasp on what exactly we are fighting for.

Part Two proposes that we start with the human in the middle, then work forward. So, we will be seeing more of Carla and her early 21st century life. In her daily thoughts and movements, in both analog and digital spaces, we will sketch a picture of what it will mean to bring real change to the Web. This involves moving from the transactional to the relational, from constraining certain market players to empowering the rest of us. In particular, recognizing our personal contours and digital lifestreams in the online realm and enhancing them with governance instruments and technological implements.

Importantly, the GliaNet initiative is one person's unfinished work, intended as a promising research agenda for some of us to explore. At this early stage, the proposed HAACS paradigm represents an adaptable stance, far better evolved and fleshed out organically by many people, both bottom-up and top-down. We will discuss these opportunities in Part Four, with the introduction of a provisional theory of change premised on numerous and continuing collaborations among stakeholders. What follows here should be taken as an open invitation to engage in the conversation.

/C7/GLIANET: A DIFFERENT WEB

"Your reaction to the datafication of life should not be to retreat to a log cabin in the woods, for they too are full of sensors; but to aggressively seek control of the data that matters to you. It's good to have recommenders that find what you want and bring it to you; you'd feel lost without them. But they should bring you what you want, not what someone else wants you to have."

— Pedro Domingos, *The Master Algorithm*

It seems that the Internet may have lost its way. Or, perhaps we have managed to lose the Internet somewhere along the way. As we have seen, the "network of networks" is running just fine, operating more or less as intended. Rather, those of us utilizing the Web, sitting precariously on top, have strayed away from the Net's foundational values of openness, its functional attributes of edge-based power, its inclusive decision-making processes.

The Internet's standards and protocols were intended to give preference to, and empower, the many people at the ends of the network connections, not the relative few entities operating at the center. To date, the reality has been otherwise. We could argue that the current ethos of the Web as an overlay has been co-opted in ways that have served to entrench certain asymmetries of power.

At the same time, much of the individual, social, and economic value inherent in the Net and the Web is locked away in separate silos and fiefdoms, subject to the MOPs' limited incentive structures. As individuals, and as collectives, the vast potential of our human autonomy and agency in the digital space remains largely untapped. Opportunities to enhance human well-being continue to be wasted each and every day.

This chapter presents the basics of the GliaNet initiative and its proposed humanistic foundations, which differ radically from the extractive Web that we have come to know and (largely) accept.

Designing a New Kind of Web

As we have seen, the Internet is premised on four foundational design principles: the "what" of modularity, the "why" of connectivity, the "how" of agnostic IP, and the "where" of the end-to-end principle. These principles remain highly operative as we map out the shape of a new overlay to coexist alongside— perhaps eventually replace—the current Web. So, what would that alternative overlay look like? The fundamental concept underlying GliaNet is to ground our technology systems in human priorities, then working our way out to the technologies. We start with the human being.

So What Is GliaNet?

The GliaNet initiative proposes a tight bond between two sets of activities: governing our institutions, and building our technologies. Typically, these two activities are seen as occupying separate spheres, of law/policy/ethics and software/ hardware engineering. When it comes however to ensuring that our digital technologies work on our behalf, and not someone else's, we must see human governance and tech design as all but inseparable. Part Two of this book will focus on the human governance component, with trustworthy intermediaries acting in our best interests, while Part Three will focus on the ethical design principles for edgetech. These governance and technology considerations notably blend together.

So how did this project come to be called GliaNet? Its roots may help convey its purpose. "Glia" is the Ancient Greek word for "glue." At least three metaphorical meanings for the original Greek term are relevant here:

- **Trust:** As the saying goes, "Trust is the social glue of relationships." Today, there appears to be a fundamental lack of trust in our institutions and by extension, the Web. In markets, politics, and ordinary human connections, trust is the key element in voluntary relationships based on openness and mutual benefit.

- **Accountability:** In the comic books and movies, Uncle Ben tells his nephew Peter Parker (aka Spiderman), "With great power comes great responsibility." To the extent that power and accountability have become unmoored on the Web, these two principles belong together again somehow. You could say, glued back in place, where they belong.

- **Support:** A third meaning is derived from the fantastic true story of the glial networks in our brains. In the late 19th century, while mapping the human brain, all that scientists could see were the fast-moving electrical impulses passing through the grey matter of the neural networks. By contrast, the white matter glial cells, operating only on chemicals, were too slow moving to be readily observed. And so was born the incorrect assumption that the glial networks' only task is to glue together neurons. In the past decade, we discovered that glial cells are the fundamental support networks of the brain—protecting, promoting, repairing, enhancing. (Apparently, Einstein had no more grey matter than normal, but he did have far more white matter).

Interestingly, the brain's glial networks can be broken down into three basic functions: protecting the brain's workings from harm, enhancing its fundamental capabilities, and promoting new network functions.

As you will see, these same "protect/enhance/promote" supportive aims find their way into the basic governance and technology elements of the GliaNet ecosystem. Today, each of us needs and deserves an online counterpart to the brain's glial networks—a comprehensive variety of services, applications, and offerings that together create a *digital life support system* for us. Trust, accountability, and support are three of the core human-empowering elements that are in short supply on the Web today. GliaNet seeks to bring them back in abundance.

Importantly, GliaNet is also a multi-layered ecosystem. This means that the technological implements are not separate pieces, but are actually married to the governance instruments. This holistic approach is essential. Technology without governance devolves into a fight for supremacy; governance without technology is empty words on a page, unable to take form and action. GliaNet proposes providing both, as reflected in its intertwined foundational principles: *D>A* (our digital rights should exceed our analog rights), and *e2a* (edge-to-any capabilities).

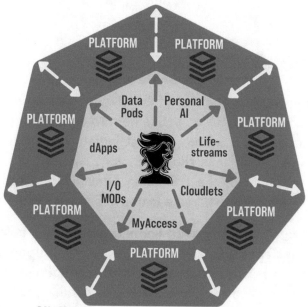

GliaNet = a digital life support system

Finally, in the GliaNet ecosystem the term "GLIA" is also an acronym that carries multiple intended impacts. The "GL" denotes the governance layers necessary for a more human-centered online environment. The "IA" in turn stands for a variety of preferred outcomes: individual autonomy, institutional accountability, intention augmentation, intelligent agency, and innovation enhancement.

One important point to emphasize here is that the GliaNet initiative depends for its success on healthy market dynamics. The premise (further laid out in the provisional theory of change in Part Four) is that a fully functioning marketplace of willing buyers and sellers can produce trustworthy intermediaries and empowering technologies that further our human autonomy and agency. It is conceivable that this premise is misplaced, that the Web's current reliance on extractive and manipulative processes is just too powerful to be dislodged by superior commercial alternatives. This book takes on that challenge.

Three Human Pillars

Before moving into the rest of Part Two and the crucial role of governance, it is useful to pause here to consider a few of the foundational pillars to the GliaNet initiative. By starting with the person, rather than the technology, we can recognize at the outset some of the animating humanistic attributes that otherwise tend not to surface in conversations about the Web.

We will touch on three such normative attributes below. First, the GliaNet approach suggested above relies upon an ethos premised on a form of stewardship of our digital ecosystems. Second, one objective of this ethos is to generate forms of data equity for as many people as possible. Third, this goal can be accomplished by creating relationships of Net privity through the use of trusted intermediaries operating under fiduciary based duties to protect, enhance, and promote our best interests.

An Ethos of Stewarding Digital Ecosystems

Today, the Web no longer provides an adequate foundation for empowering ordinary people. Increasingly, as we become digital beings, our technologies are shaping us as much as we shape them. We need to envision and hold much-needed societal conversations about issues such as control, trust, and accountability. We need new technology overlays to the Net and Web that embody core human values.

While the "Code" of computational systems and the "Players" of ecosystem stakeholders should be relatively straightforward, establishing the "Rules" for our proposed new human-centered paradigm is more challenging. Many varied governance regimes intersect and interact across different geographic and political zones. As such, the suggestion here is to take a broad governance approach that can welcome many of these regimes under one all-encompassing umbrella.

Selecting "stewardship" as that unifying concept likely requires some initial explanation. Why should we consider digital stewarding as a way to inform and pull together this proposed new paradigm? In brief, because stewardship can give us a compelling perspective, a strong sense of direction, and actionable paths forward.

Inspiration for digital ecosystem stewardship is drawn in some measure from modern-day environmentalism[266] (and also emanates from religious movements[267]). Respecting and caring for the integrity of the natural world is the cornerstone of being an environmental steward. This stance recognizes how humans have the power, and often the incentives, to harm or even destroy natural ecosystems. But with the right incentives, they also have the power to coexist and even encourage the flourishing of human beings along with other beings in the natural environment.

What makes for a healthy ecosystem? A general definition is the balanced flows of matter, energy, and information between and among the many players in the environment, in ways that provide mutual benefit. If we think of the world at large of computational systems (the Code, the Players, the Rules) as its own natural ecosystem in a similar holistic fashion, we can open up new perspectives.

If, for example, a digital ecosystem has intrinsic worth, then the goal is the health and well-being of the ecosystem itself. The ecosystem is the beneficiary, in whole as well as in its many constituent parts. In the environmental context, that is where stewards typically come into the picture.

It may be said that one mission of a digital steward is to foster the success of the human and virtual infrastructures of the evolving digital world. A digital steward's aim would be to respect and care for the integrity of the digital world, as an extension of core human values. In this way, stewardship can be seen as honoring, in principled fashion, the relational, contextual, and mediating aspects of digital life.

As noted, existing societal systems are rooted in human power. This suggests that being a good "steward" is not blindly following the existing power structures and incentives. Nor does stewardship entail engaging in "ethics washing," or viewing ethical conduct as merely a box to be checked in a product's journey to the market. Instead, one role is to test, and even challenge, those power asymmetries, those assumed constraints. To some, this means that stewardship is a vocation grounded in human ethics.[268]

One suggestion is to describe the practices and end goals of the digital steward as constituting an ethos. The word "ethos" is ancient Greek for "character." It connotes the fundamental ideals, beliefs, or values that characterize and guide a particular community of people.[269] In this instance, the notion resonates because it captures a variety of the technology and governance implements that could be explored, and ultimately utilized, to carry out the role of digital stewardship.

In brief, the ethos for a new stewardship of digital ecosystems could include three elements:

- A stance: Highlight the desirability of infusing humanistic values and beliefs throughout the ecosystem.

- The processes: Engage with an inclusive universe of stakeholders, with an emphasis on the typically underrepresented.

- Some guidance: Create and advocate for design principles to guide the creation, deployment, and use of digital technologies.

One hoped-for end result is garnering increased trustworthiness in the underlying technologies. As per Botsman, this can mean both enhancing the upward institutional trust flows (between individuals and entities) and the lateral distributed trust flows (between individuals and networks). The latter should be especially germane with new technology overlays that tap into what we will call "edgetech" capabilities, such as distributed computing, federated learning, differential privacy, and trusted execution environments. While much research and engagement needs to be done, such trustful technology enhancements can unlock mutually beneficial opportunities for all stakeholders.

Achieving Data Equities in Digital Economies

The term "equity" has two well-defined connotations: (1) fair and just treatment of an individual or group, and (2) economic value of a financial instrument. Equity also has a third meaning, when referencing the Middle Ages laws originating in the English chancery, which were designed to protect citizens' rights and enforce duties.[270] The equity courts offered a "gap-filling" forum, intended to redress injustices that were not adequately dealt with by existing laws.

Here we can take "data equity" to mean the creation of equitable "gap-filling" mechanisms that address existing justice and market shortcomings, enabling people to more fully exercise their freedom of action, or agency. In our modern data economy, the roles of the haves and the have-nots are played by "surveillance" capitalists and everyone else in the data economy, respectively.

As D'Ignazio and Klein see it, equity in the data economy is a concept that directly challenges power because it acknowledges and works towards dismantling sizable structural differentials.[271] As they explain, equity is "justice of a specific flavor," which takes into account the historic roots of differential power.[272] Equity is also "both an outcome and a process," requiring those in positions of relative power "to listen deeper and listen differently" to those marginalized by the status quo.[273] By contrast, concepts like greater transparency and accountability by themselves do not go far enough to dismantle structural power, and they can even have the unintended consequence of further entrenching dominant market players.[274]

When following the concepts of data equity as laid out by D'Ignazio and Klein, we should build new governance systems that contain the means of inclusive processes (justice), which in turn lead to the ends of optimal economic outcomes (value). These systems should grant individuals and communities greater agency to participate in key decisions around uses of their data. These stakeholders should also be empowered to engage more closely with MOPs where data is being utilized, and otherwise ensure that their multiple roles in data value chains are fully recognized.

Both flavors of data equity (processes rooted in structural justice and outcomes of optimal economic value) can be actualized through the equitable forum of data stewards and other trusted intermediaries that sit between data-sharers (principals) and data-requesters. These entities can utilize governance, technology, and structural measures to unlock the full potential value of user data while still safeguarding and elevating individual and collective agency. In doing so, these stewards can correct the power imbalances between people (as individuals and collectives) and platform-based ecosystems. Data stewardship, founded on a "laddering" of rights and duties, is an essential starting point to considering a new data paradigm.

Achieving Net Privity

As we have seen, the current Web rests largely on the transactional mode of individuals interacting with websites and apps in exchange for their personal data and opportunities to be influenced by others. Such fleeting connections seem a poor basis for establishing and growing a genuine relationship between the person and the entity.

The GliaNet initiative rests on a very different presumption about relationships. To ground this further, we will draw on not just the ethos of stewardship but also the legal doctrine of privity. In recent years, the term "privity" has been confined to contract law and defined as a relationship that exists between two contracting parties. This normally equates to a straightforward "meeting of the minds." However, in 1997, Nick Szabo offered a novel interpretation in an prescient online piece titled "Recovering Privity."[275] There Szabo reconstituted the legal concept of privity and applied it to the dawning information age. In his view, privity has far deeper roots than our "parched" modern-day version. In common law, he argues, the term was used to denote the creation of a boundary around two parties, defined by the scope of knowledge, consent, and control. Those within that boundary were said to be "in privity."

The linguistic and semantic relation to "privacy" is no surprise. When adding control to privacy, privity becomes in Szabo's term a generalized "meta-relationship," where those within the bounds of the relationship are protected from those outside it. The resulting "clarified boundaries of knowledge, control, and responsibility within and between relationships, is ideal for specifying a variety of cyberspace relationships, whether informal or formalized via legal code or software."[276]

Obviously Szabo's conception of privity as boundaries in a meta-relationship has much in common with my notion of protecting and promoting our personal contours. The GliaNet initiative seeks to implement this resuscitated concept of privity in stewarded ecosystems of trust. Moving beyond the transactional mode of passive users and barely accessible web entities, we can explore the "Net privity" of relationships founded on boundary layers of earned trust, mutual consent, and enhanced human agency.

/C8/DIGITAL LIFESTREAMS

"Before there are data, there are people...."

– D'Ignazio and Klein

Earlier, the notion of *lifestreams* was introduced as a way of capturing the essence of living in a world that provides opportunities to express our autonomy of thought and emotion, and agency of action. This chapter combines the lifestreams concept with the digital environment presented by advanced computational systems. As we will see, what we have come to call "data" is an ill-fitting shorthand that fails to capture the varied, social, contextual, and situational aspects of our *digital lifestreams*. Proposed alternative data narratives should prove superior to the prevailing extractive metaphors.

Discovering Quality in the Quantitative: Digital Lifestreams

Perhaps few words in the 21st century have been so widely employed, debated, misunderstood, and abused than "data."[277] While its provenance extends back several hundred years— well before the annals of modern computer science—data has been a rhetorical concept from the beginning, deriving much of its meaning from the times.[278] Indeed, for some 200 years, the notional West and global North have been building a world based on the collection and analysis of data.[279]

Today, the thing we call data is increasingly being defined for society by corporations and governments with their own stakes in the outcome.[280] Their conception of data as a resource derived from human beings for power and money reflects the extractive perspective foisted by MOPs and their DAMB ecosystems. Such definitional exercises tend to obscure the very human motivations that drive the Web's SEAMs feedback cycles. But there are other ways of perceiving the 1s and 0s that are meant to reflect the full range of our inner and outer aspects as human beings.

The concept of *digital lifestreams* presented here seeks to take back some of that definitional authority. That alternative conceptualization begins with a grounding in the more humanistic term described above as lifestreams, which embraces experiential flows about an individual, and their relationships and interests in the world. The "digital" represents the technology-based encasement of those flows.

Moving from Data Extractions to Digital Lifestreams

Technically speaking, data is a string of binary digits (ones and zeroes) intended to connote a piece of reality.[281] Data is a well-known term from computer science, often conceived as something for entities to manage in an information lifecycle.[282] Over time, concepts of data have been imported into the real world of human beings. Each of our lives is now represented in digital code by MOPs, DAMBs, government agencies, and others.[283] Three foundational points warrant emphasis.

We are more than just data

It may sound obvious but while computers are digital devices, human beings and the environments we inhabit are analog.[284] By definition, that means the world produces an endless series of signals representing continuously variable physical quantities.[285]

Often, we forget that the digital language of ones and zeroes is merely the encoding—a translation, a rendering, an encasement—and not the reality it seeks to portray. We can experience first-hand how a live musical performance exceeds the highest fidelity Blu Ray disc—let alone the poorly-sampled streaming versions that most of us are content to enjoy as is. So, one plausible definition of data is the digital encoding of selected aspects of reality.

Many aspects of our analog life can be rendered in "digitalese," from the somatic (physical) to the interior (thoughts and feelings) to the exterior (expressions and behaviors) to the conventional identifiers (social security numbers).[286] Each of these is a form of data intended to denote aspects of the individual's relational self. Importantly, this means that the very nature of "data" eludes the reductive conception. Indeed:

> "The process of converting life experience into data always necessarily entails a reduction of that experience – along with the historical and conceptual burdens of the term.... Before there are data, there are people... And there are patterns that cannot be represented – or addressed – by data alone."[287]

To be clear, the formatting shift from analog to digital has brought enormous, tangible benefits to our world. The challenge is to successfully translate life's ebbs and flows into coherent signals that successfully yield useful insights to our humanity.[288] At this early juncture, it is far from clear that the black-and-white conceptualizations of the binary can ever hope to match our multihued existence. The ever-present incompleteness and inaccuracy of data may be ubiquitous.[289] And the qualified self may well elude the best encapsulations of the quantified self.

We are more than just data that others have been gathering about us

Second, the "production" of data is inherently asymmetrical because it is accomplished for the purposes of private or governmental bodies that use it.[290] The authors of *Data Feminism* have made clear "the close relationship between data and power,"[291] and that "the primary drivers of data processes as forms of social knowledge are institutions external to the social interactions in question."[292] Utilizing SEAMs cycles, commercial MOPs and their DAMB ecosystems seek to build quantified constructs meant to represent each of us. Or, at most, our intrinsic value to them as a consumer of stuff. To these entities, data is a form of property, a resource, a line item on balance sheets—used to infer and know and shape us, to the span of our "perceptible agency."[293] To some, data may even represent the final frontier of the marketplace, the ultimate opportunity to convert to financial gain seemingly endless quantities of the world's digitized stuff.

This pecuniary conception of data supports the *narrow and deep commodification* of the quantified self as a mere user or consumer of goods and services. Narrow, because the data lifecycle is answerable primarily to the singular desire to control and/or make money from us. Deep, because of the desire to drill down into who we are at our most fundamental levels— our interior milieu, revealed in our thoughts and feelings. The SEAMs cycle is engaged to gain as much "relevant" information as possible about us, then influence or even manipulate our autonomous/agential selves.[294]

Even our somatic self (such as facial features, fingerprints, DNA, voice, and gait) is considered fair game for the identifying characteristics that can reveal, or betray, us.[295]

To date, the predominant use cases of physiological (fixed physical characteristics) and behavioral (unique movement patterns) biometrics have been limited to the security needs of authenticating and identifying particular individuals.[296] While these applications bring their own challenges, some would go further to probe aspects of the self not voluntarily revealed in outward ways.[297]

For example, purveyors of "neuromarketing" seek a deeper understanding of consumers from analyzing their personal affect, including attention, emotion, valence, and arousal.[298] Using "neurodata" gathered from measuring a person's facial expression, eye movement, vocalizations, heart rate, sweating, and even brainwaves, neuromarketers aim to "provide deeper and more accurate insight into customers' motivations."[299] Such technology advances pave the way for achieving the Silicon Valley ideal of knowing what a user might want even before they know they want it.[300] Or, more ominously, implanting that very wanting in them.

We know that human life is much richer and more complex than the crabbed commodification of the prevailing Web ethos. Those who engage in "computational" thinking de-emphasize many aspects of being human, such as context, culture, and history, as well as cognitive and emotional flexibility and behavioral fluidity.[301] Presumably, these aspects of the self have meaning only to the extent that they provide insights into how humans decide and act in a marketplace or political environment. And so, the nuance of the actual human being can become lost in the numeric haze.

If we are to be digitized and quantified, it should be on our terms

Third, the quantified self can both capture, and diminish, human insights. Based on this discussion, our "data" can be envisioned in a number of different dimensions:

- *Heterogenous (varied)*: Data is not one, or any, thing. Instead, the word obscures the vast scope and range of its reach.

- *Relational (social)*: An individual's "personal" data is intertwined with countless other people's data, from family to friends to complete strangers. Our streams are constantly crossing and blending.

- *Contextual (spatial)*: Data "bleeds" into/out of surrounding spaces. The physical environment of collection and measurement can determine whether the data can be interpreted correctly as signal or noise.

- *Situational (temporal)*: Data reflects the reality of a certain time and circumstance, but often no further. A person today is not the same person tomorrow.

These dimensions map well to the many selves we show to ourselves and the world: the personal, the familial, the social, the economic, the political. Importantly, people attach their own significance and meanings to these aspects. As one scholar summarizes the inherent mismatch between data purveyors and the rest of us, "Do not mistake the availability of my data as permission to remain at a distance."[302]

As we have seen, a useful way of conveying the full depth and breadth of the human being is to envision multi-dimensional surrounding contours of influence. The HAACS paradigm endorses this image by giving an individual the means to fully translate their multi-faceted lived self into digital code. This translation could run as broadly and as deeply as the technology allows, and as the person accepts, encompassing all dimensions in the flow of personal change and evolution. Of course, this means voluntarily introducing the richness of one's lifestreams to the binary of the digital.[303]

Perceiving the online environment as a potential home for one's *digital lifestreams* offers new ways to consider using the technologies of quantification. As D'Ignazio and Klein recently asked, "how can we use data to remake the world?" [304] They advocate using data science to challenge and change existing distributions of power, particularly where dimensions of individual and group identity intersect with each other to determine one's experiences in the world.

In breaking away from the monolith of the SEAMs feedback cycles and accepting the increased blurring of the analog and the digital, we can be more in charge of shaping the personal contours of our autonomous self and enacting our agential self. Then, we can unleash creativity, unlock insights, and light up pathways.

Guided by the assistance of one or more trusted intermediaries,[305] the process could focus on what enhances our own human flourishing. For example, a less narrow, less transactional appreciation of digital artifacts (the words, sounds, and images we create and gather and share online). Digital lifestreams can provide a more faithful mirroring of our constantly shifting internal and external interactions. As such (and perhaps ironically), they promise a more accurate representation of a person's life than MOPs and DAMBs assemble with SEAMs control processes.

Each human being should have a considerable say in whether and how their unique person is presented to themselves and to the rest of the world. For some, this could mean establishing and policing personal contours, those semi-permeable zones of autonomy and agency. If, however, someone chooses to have a digital self, they should be in charge of it. We can encapsulate this relational connection as *"Human:Digital."* The resulting vibrant, rich, and ever-changing digital lifestreams can provide a backdrop against which, as analog beings, "we continuously co-construct and shape our environments and ourselves as agents."[306]

Creating New Analogies and Narratives

Viewing data with new conceptual lenses reveals novel vistas for further exploration. Digital lifestreams is but one conception of data in our technology-mediated world. We are in desperate need of better ways to conceptualize the narratives and practices surrounding our data. Some stakeholders are making an attempt to do this.[307]

Framing our data not as a thing but as *flows*—experiential and ever-evolving processes—presents a more open-ended and intentional way to conceive of humans. This framing also acknowledges the many ways that "my" data mixes inextricably with "your" data, and the non-personal data (NPD) of our surroundings.[308] In addition, it moves us away from the transactional modes of commerce, and towards the relational mode of human interaction.

Nonetheless, as per the dominant theology of Silicon Valley, information about people is perceived to be a form of real property, a resource to be mined, processed, and ultimately, monetized.[309] As Srnicek puts it, "Just like oil, data are a material to be extracted, refined, and used in a variety of ways."[310] The wording itself gives away the industrial presumption.[311] It "suggests physicality, immutability, context-independence, and intrinsic worth."[312] Even unwanted bits amount to "data exhaust."[313] The best counterpoint that some advocates can muster is to claim that users should share in the monetization of that non-renewable asset.[314] Data as property, however, is an unfounded economic concept. Elizabeth Renieris points out some practical challenges with sharing the monetization of data, namely that the user will (1) lack transparency in how the data will ultimately be used, (2) not have their "own" data to sell, and (3) bring little bargaining power to the transactions. Moreover, propertizing data also discriminates against the disadvantaged. [315]

Framing personal information as petroleum shuts out humanistic conceptions of personal data,[316] so more useful metaphors and analogies are worth investigating. Grounding ourselves in the ecological, rather than the industrial, would be a marked improvement. However, imagining data as sunlight, [317] while a better conception than data as oil, could suggest yet another natural resource to be exploited. And such framing also can feel removed from the lived human experience.

Another suggestion is to imagine an organismic analogy for computational systems. The interfaces discussed here ("data extraction") would be the sensory systems, while the AIs ("data analysis") would be the nervous systems. What then would best connote the bio-flow of sustaining energy?

A compelling image is provided by the respiratory system—the human breath. A constant process of converting the surrounding atmosphere into productive respirations—fueling the organism, but in a sustainable, non-rivalrous, non-extractive manner. The breath sustains many different bodily functions. From the molecules of collective air that each of us shares to individual breath momentarily borrowed—respiration mixes the personal and non-personal, the individual and communal, just like data does. The image connotes an organic feedback cycle, one far different than the extractive SEAMs data cycles employed by the MOPs and their DAMB partners.

Shifting the Data Governance Perspectives

Moving away from the world of narratives and metaphors, it is necessary to determine ways that governments and markets should govern this thing we call data. As we have seen, the SEAMs cycles embedded in today's Web entail "users" surrendering data from online interactions, often based on one-sided terms of service (ToS), in exchange for useful services and goods.[318] Now, even third parties we have no prior relationship with can access and utilize our data.[319] Implicit in this tradeoff of *our personal information for their free stuff* is the notion of data as a form of private property, governed by traditional laws of property rights.[320] The HAACS paradigm invites a fundamental reappraisal not just of data as a concept, but the follow-on presuppositions about the ways we would govern that data.

One important caveat: what follows assumes that "data" fits within the conventional analyses of economic goods. Given the somewhat unique nature of data—conceptualized as digital flows of heterogenous, relational, and contextual lifestreams—many of the traditional answers may not provide an optimal fit, and much research and scholarship remain ahead.

Data as Resource: A Collective Good?

If we are to utilize for data something akin to traditional economic principles, an initial question is what kind of "thing" are we talking about? Microeconomists have employed the "factors of production" theory to divide goods and resources into four separate buckets:

- capital (like factories and forklifts)

- labor (services)

- land (natural resources and property), and

- entrepreneurship (ways of combining the other three factors of production).[321]

Based on these traditional categories, data could be one of them, a combination of one or more, its own separate factor, or no factor at all.[322]

A prominent school of thought classifies data as a type of good. Microeconomic theorists classify a good based on answers to two questions: is it rivalrous (one's consumption precludes others from also consuming it), and is it excludable (one can prevent others from accessing/owning it)?[323] This two-by-two classification scheme yields four distinct categories:

- private goods

- toll goods

- public goods, and

- common pool resources.[324]

Most private goods—cars, bonds, bitcoin—are defined as both rivalrous and excludable: one's consumption eliminates their economic value, and governmental restrictions (usually laws) allow one to keep them away from others.[325]

Data presents an interesting, and likely unique, case. First, at least some of what it entails is non-fungible, meaning it encapsulates something with unique value and meaning.[326] Even if every data packet or stream looks the same from the perspective of a computational network, the shards of reality they purport to represent can differ, even minutely, one from another. Data then is not simply a commodity, like a unit of currency, or a barrel of oil, which tends to hold the same value in every situation.[327]

Second, like a private good, data is at least partially excludable, as one theoretically can prevent others from accessing and using it. Excludability is not a fixed characteristic of a resource; it varies depending on context and technology.[328] So, data in some cases can be withheld from others.

Third, and crucially, data is also a non-rivalrous good. This means that anyone can utilize it without necessarily reducing its overall value. In fact, multiple uses of the same data (whether individual or collective) can increase its overall utility and value. So, data can gain value with every use and shared reuse.

Microeconomic theory tells us that this "mixed" set of attributes—non-fungibility, potential excludability, and non-rivalry—makes data what is called a toll, club, or collective good.[329] Old-school examples of a collective good include cinemas, parks, satellite television, and access to copyrighted works.[330] Membership fees are common to this kind of good (hence the "club" and "toll" terminology).[331]

A further economic consideration is the presence or absence of externalities, the indications of incomplete or missing markets. These amount to the "lost signals" about what a person might actually want in a marketplace.[332] Externalities in the data context translate into what market conditions might be good or bad for certain sharing arrangements.

If it is correct that data is largely a non-fungible and non-rivalrous resource by nature, and potentially excludable by design, there are major implications for how we govern data. We need not accept the too-easy assumptions that data is just another extractive resource, subject to the same commodification as a barrel of oil. The very nature of a non-renewable resource is its rivalrous nature. Data is renewable, for lack of a better word, like sunshine, or air, or the radio spectrum. Moreover, where oil and other non-renewable resources are found on private lands, they are excludable goods.

Either way, traditional economics shows that data is more like a collective good than a private good, and this conclusion suggests different mechanisms for managing data.

Data Management: Overseen as Commons?

If data is in fact a collective good, a follow-on question is: how can this particular good be managed? Typically, modern society employs institutions as the "rules of the game"—the particular blend of governmental and market structures to govern a good, service, or resource.[333] In our context, what are the respective roles for Players in the market and the government in establishing the ground Rules for accessing data if treated as a collective good?

Traditional answers would either have the market managing private property (with an important assist from government in laws of access and exclusion), or a public entity managing a public good.[334] A blend of institutional choices is possible as well, from the formality and coercive effect of constitutions, laws, and regulations to government co-regulation to less formal codes of conduct, standards and norms. In each case, tradeoffs are inevitable between degrees of formality, coercion, accountability, and enforceability versus adaptability, flexibility, and diversity.[335]

While market mechanisms are generally the most efficient means of allocating rivalrous goods, traditional property rights could unnecessarily constrain beneficial sharing arrangements.[336] As Frischmann points out, "Nonrival resources provide an additional degree of freedom, with respect to resource management." Non-rivalry for a naturally shareable good can be leveraged to support a wider range of choices, including allocating its possession and use on a nonexclusive basis. On the other hand, exclusivity is also a potentially attractive tool for managing risks of the good being misappropriated.

The non-rivalrous nature of data suggests that it could be governed as a "commons."[337] Importantly, a commons management strategy can be implemented in a variety of institutional forms.[338] Part of Elinor Ostrom's genius was perceiving the commons as occupying a space between the two governance poles of government and market—what she labelled the "monocentric hierarchies."[339] Her conception of "polycentric governance" by a like-minded community addresses the collective-action challenges that stem from a need to manage common pool resources.[340]

Data can also be likened to other intangibles, like ideas, which constitute part of an "intellectual infrastructure."[341] Frischmann notes the difficulty of applying infrastructure concepts to "the fluid, continuous, and dynamic nature of cultural intellectual systems."[342] The related concept of a "knowledge commons" would govern the management and production of intellectual and cultural resources.[343] In that context, the institutional sharing of resources would occur among members of a community.[344] A similar story may be possible for many data management arrangements, where individual communities can set for themselves the ways that their own data can be shared.[*345] To some, data may even represent the ultimate (last?) global enclosure opportunity, beyond the land and labor resources of the past.

The MOPs also enjoy one further advantage in today's data-centric economy. While they can and do leverage personal data about a user non-rivalrously, in a kind of multiplier effect, the individual user finds it difficult to exclude these same entities from accessing and using their data.[346] In economic terms, the MOPs treat an individual's data as a commons, to be enclosed within their business models for their own gain. In so doing, these companies privatize the benefits to themselves and socialize the costs to others, including society and individual users. Taleb has a name for this phenomenon—these entities lack "skin in the game," which he likens to avoiding "contact with reality."[347] The challenge is rearranging the incentives so that the benefits and cost align.

Where economics has some rational say, the governance direction seems to move away from private property law and towards more relational conceptions of resource management, including the commons. Moreover, the entities that can help us capture those incentives properly must earn our trust authentically.

/C9/FINDING OUR TRUSTMEDIARIES

"Study the past if you would define the future."

– Confucius

As we saw in Part One, Carla—like all of us—lives in a world that cannot survive without basic forms of human trust. From the bus driver to the barista, the crossing guard to the daycare worker, Carla is conveying a degree of trust in the people that surround her. That her food and drink and medicines are not tainted or poisoned. That her drivers will not deliberately crash the vehicle. That her clothing store clerk will not take surreptitious photos of her in the dressing room and sell them. That her daughter's instructors will not teach her how to build atomic bombs. That her vote for the mayor's race will be counted accurately, and not simply tossed aside. That any one of the countless people passing her on the busy sidewalk won't assault her on the spot.

In each case, Carla believes that these people and the institutions they represent are not seeking to do or say things that will hurt her. In fact, Carla sees a mutual benefit in the relationship, sometimes in the act of connection itself, sometimes in exchange for payment of a fee, or a tax. We can see this as a general duty of care—a good faith agreement to act reasonably toward Carla and not do her harm. And in turn, she projects a similar stance in her dealings with others. In essence, Carla operates in a social fabric made up of interwoven trust relationships. One can think of these entities as constituting a range of *trustmediaries* (TMs) in our daily lives.

But this trust often does not arrive on its own. By necessity, Carla has also come to rely on other trusted institutions, such as legislators and regulators and courts, to pass and enforce laws and regulations. In other cases, she assumes that professional codes of conduct, corporate rules, and even social norms are adequate governance instruments to protect her from various harms. The more formalized mechanisms can be found in the many government and industry agencies set up to carry out the requirements. In the United States, examples include the Food and Drug Administration, the Federal Aviation Administration, the Environmental Protection Agency, the Better Business Bureau. These institutions are not infallible, and accidents or malicious acts can and do happen. Nonetheless, without that interlocking system of other people ostensibly seeking to limit harm, Carla would not feel safe in the world. And modern society simply could not function.

This reality lines up well with Botsman's three trust levels discussed earlier. We naturally have the most trust in those closest to us, our family and friends, because we believe we know them well enough to hold them close to us. When we move from the interpersonal realm into the social, the nature of the trust changes. We rely more on external indicia, such as legal requirements to treat us well, before we accept these trustmediaries into our lives.

It's early March 2020, someplace in the United States. Carla takes her young daughter Ada to daycare, then heads to her office job. On her lunch break, she retrieves clothing from the dry cleaner, cashes a check at the credit union, and drops off three borrowed books on the history of institutional racism to the library. After work, she collects Ada from daycare. Once home, Carla looks over her mail, including a monthly statement from her employer's pension plan and a legal document extending a guardianship to care for her ailing father.

Carla wakes up early the next morning with a high fever and tenacious cough. She doesn't typically come down with a flu virus this time of year, but she feels pretty bad. After a quick browse online to check her symptoms, she decides to make an appointment with her primary care physician.

The following day, Carla drives to the health clinic. The medical assistant takes her vital signs and jots down her symptoms. Doctor Jones comes in, reviews the file, and asks some questions. The verdict? Likely seasonal flu. He prescribes medication. On her way home, Carla stops at the pharmacy to pick up an antiviral prescription and some cough syrup.

The Fiduciary World Around Us

While Carla may not be fully aware of it, many of the typical moments in her everyday "analog world" include interactions with various types of *fiduciaries*. These are individuals or entities with whom Carla has an ongoing relationship of some sort, as an existing customer, client, or patron. In each case, Carla is placing her trust in their care for the well-being of herself, her family members, and their interests and possessions. In return—above and beyond other trustmediaries in her life— these fiduciaries owe Carla special obligations of loyalty, to protect and promote her personal interests.

The law of human relationships:
from power to trust

Fiduciary law is essentially the common law of uneven human relationships.[348] The doctrine is entwined with centuries of equity, torts, and other common law doctrine.[349] Noted expert Tamar Frankel observed that "throughout the centuries, the problems that these laws were designed to solve are eternal, etched in human nature, derived from human needs, and built into human activities."[350]

Not surprisingly, fiduciary law principles are near-universal, having been applied across a vast array of human endeavors. These include agency, trust law, corporate law, nonprofits law, banking, pension law, employment law, bankruptcy, family law, health care, public affairs, and international law.[351] While most often associated with English common law, fiduciary law also encompasses most major global cultures—such as canon law, Roman law, classical Islamic law, classical Jewish law, European civil systems, Chinese law, Indian law, and Japanese law.[352]

The basis for a fiduciary relationship is straightforward: assigning certain legal and moral obligations to people and entities engaged in exchanges of value with each other.[353] The linchpin is what Frankel calls "entrusted power."[354] An individual or entity (the entrustor, or beneficiary) grants access to something of value to another individual or entity (the fiduciary) for the purpose of having the fiduciary undertake tasks that benefit the entrustor.[355] In these situations, the fiduciary normally has some knowledge, expertise, or other socially desirable capabilities that the entrustor lacks.[356] Moreover, sensitive information is often revealed in the context of establishing the relationship (or even becomes its basis).[357]

Prime modern-day examples of fiduciaries include the medical profession, the legal profession, and certain financial sectors. The entrustment of power to those providing these services triggers the obligation.[358]

The fiduciary relationship is based on the entrustor's confidence that the fiduciary will carry out its duties in ways that further the entrustor's interests.[359] The entrustor willingly makes themselves vulnerable—in the initial entrustment of something of value plus the possible follow-on revelation of sensitive information and confidences—to gain something in return.[360] To that end, it is a duty rooted in asymmetric power relationships between the parties.[361]

The fiduciary can abide by two basic types of duties: care and loyalty.[362] The duty of care obligates the fiduciary to, at minimum, act prudently and do no harm to the entrustor.[363] This seems closer to the ordinary sense of trust that we encounter in our daily lives. But the duty of loyalty goes further in requiring the fiduciary to have no conflicts of interest and to promote the best interests of the entrustor.[364]

Importantly, while the thing of value that the fiduciary is granted control over is often a form of tangible property, this need not be the case.[365] Because fiduciary law is relational, the "what" is limited only by what is deemed important by the entrustor.[366] In a legal trust, for example, the entrustors' health care or legal status may be the "thing" of value. Confidential information is another recognized intangible here.[367] The core concept is to protect personal and practical interests, whatever they may be.[368]

One implication for the online world is that the logic can shift from owning data as a form of property to accessing data as a particular right to control a collective good.[369] This means that being a fiduciary runs not with property, but with the person and their entrusted confidences.[370] Given the variable nature of data (heterogenous, contextual, relational), the concept of *running with the person and their confidences* can be a crucial underpinning for a fiduciary law-based doctrine of data governance. For our present purposes, the key takeaway is that fiduciary law appears to be an apt fit to govern personal data and other related sensitive information about us.

Carla's fiduciaries

In Carla's March 2020, her fiduciary relationships include doctor and patient, attorney and client, financial advisor and client, pharmacist and customer, bank and customer, government and citizen, librarian and patron. In each instance, Carla is entrusting a third party (the fiduciary) with something of value to her (the entrustor or beneficiary), based on a certain recognized duty of care or loyalty that they owe to her in return. Parents too have a long-recognized fiduciary duty to care for their young children, and grown children in turn have similar duties to care for infirm parents. Even dry cleaners owe a related "bailment" common law obligation for the clothing entrusted to their temporary care.

These fiduciary-based norms and practices have become so ingrained in our daily lives that we often forget they exist or how much we rely upon them. In each instance, the duty is rooted in asymmetric power relationships between people.[371]

Typically, there are three indicators of parties being engaged in a fiduciary relationship: *expertise*, *benefit*, and *confidences*.

- *Expertise:* In each instance, Carla is dealing with someone who possesses considerable specialized expertise, knowledge, or experience in their chosen field—her doctor, lawyer, pharmacist, financial advisor, librarian. With this expertise comes the expectation that the fiduciary will exercise good judgment in making decisions on Carla's behalf and meet its obligations to her.

- *Benefit:* Each of these relationships concerns Carla receiving a benefit of significant value to her—for example, medical assessment and treatment, financial management, or legal advice and representation.

- *Confidences:* In most instances, sensitive information is created, changes hands, or otherwise becomes subject to protection. Consider doctor-patient confidentiality, or attorney-client privilege. By voluntarily sharing private aspects of herself, Carla seeks the fiduciary's services to better her personal situation—even down to protecting her library lending records.

For example, Carla's doctor may have been the first to learn that while he initially surmised she had seasonal flu, she actually tested positive for a new malady called COVID-19. The doctor's *expertise* allowed him and his staff to correctly reinterpret the early results, conduct research, and prescribe treatment. This diagnosis, and subsequent treatment and care, also offered significant *benefits* in ramifications for Carla's family and friends, her employer, and her community. The nature of *confidentiality* gave the doctor some discretionary power to disclose, or not disclose, the results to other people.

Fiduciary duties as protecting human rights

One of the challenges with both property law and privacy law is that they rely on "extrinsic" power emanating from government in the first instance.[372] Without enabling statutes and regulations, no one's physical or personal property—or data—is safe from others taking it. And as we have seen, such accountability regimes have their limitations.[373] Hence, societies have come to utilize more foundational and enduring implements, such as constitutions and treaties, to wall off certain areas of life from the negative actions of others. The rubric normally used is civil rights, as opposed to those "natural" human rights that exist by virtue of being a person in the world.[374]

While the law of fiduciaries has traditionally been limited to the private law regime, scholars have recently articulated why and how it can be extended to the public law realm. Due to the enunciated limitations of the social contract theories of government,[375] some scholars have argued for the reinstatement of the concept of the "fiduciary theory of government" to oversee citizens' relationships with their own governmental institutions.[376] Under this approach, as public officials enjoy a position of entrusted power, they have obligations comparable to those of agents, trustees, and other fiduciaries.[377]

The United States Constitution itself may be viewed as a fiduciary instrument, imbuing the power of attorney-like obligations of care, loyalty, and impartiality.[378] Scholars have found "a strong, and perhaps even overwhelming, case for at least looking at fiduciary law as a source of constitutional meaning."[379] One implication is that the US Government could theoretically be held accountable to its citizens as a bona fide fiduciary.

To some, human and civil rights lack an enduring foundation in current laws.[380] To help fill that perceived gap, fiduciary law has been invoked to apply to human rights vis-à-vis national and international institutions.[381] Under this telling, human rights "are best conceived as norms emanating from a fiduciary relationship that exists between the state and persons subject to its powers, including citizens, resident aliens, and nonresident aliens."[382] These norms arise from the state's assumption of sovereign powers.[383] To the extent that stakeholders are interested in pursuing the concept of one's digital lifestreams as part of a human rights framing, fiduciary law could provide crucial buttressing.

Thus, in a Web bereft of notions of treating "users" with general care, or even loyalty, fiduciary law provides a fascinating basis for governing online, data-based relationships.[384] It nicely reflects the shift both from transactional to relational mode, and from accountability to agency mode. It provides "skin in the game" on both sides of entrustment-based relationships. It requires degrees of trust and support that over time can feed back onto each other in positive ways. It "runs with the person" and all their heterogenous, contextual, and relational ways of being in the world. It supports those who seek a more certain conceptual footing for constitutional and human rights.

As we will see in the next two chapters, the law of fiduciaries can also be harnessed to play a crucial role on behalf of Web users: as an individual's trustworthy and supportive intermediary.

/C10/INTRODUCING NET FIDUCIARIES

So, what about bringing commercial and other relationships founded on common law fiduciary principles to the Web? Can we combine duties of care and loyalty with the aspects of being a 21st century digital citizen, to create an entity that protects, enhances, and promotes our virtual selves?

First, we should consider the range of potential fiduciary law-based intermediaries in the digital world. The World Economic Forum (WEF) offers a useful catalogue of the various organizational models they call the "data intermediary."[385] We will apply the broader umbrella term *Net trustmediaries* (or NetTMs) for these kinds of entities. WEF recognizes three separate models:

- "Data stewards", as WEF calls them, are organizational leaders responsible for managing data rights and duties within an enterprise. We have already appropriated the stewardship mantle here to support the more general concept of governing data flows in ethical ways. Given the relatively narrow reach of this category of entities, we will set it aside for our present purposes.

- The "digital fiduciary" is an entity that helps individuals assert their virtual rights online. We will discuss this type of NetTM, a Net fiduciary, in this chapter.

- The "data collective" is any one of a data trust, data collaborative, data cooperative, or data commons. Each of these present slight variances on a more collectivist model for communities to better represent their digital presence. A version of this NetTM will be explored in Chapter 11.

Now, with Carla's help, we will look at the Net fiduciary.

Carla's digital days continue

It is late March 2020. Several days after visiting her doctor, Carla isn't feeling any better—in fact, somewhat worse—so she decides to return for further tests. In the meantime, she tries to learn more about the new outbreak of something called COVID-19. Is that what she might have? She discusses it with the doctor's assistant, confides in two close friends, and reads the headlines on the cable news. Ultimately, Carla goes online to seek more information.

As Carla browses websites, reading about this strange new virus and its symptoms, treatment, and testing, she begins to feel a bit overwhelmed and frustrated. From both her computer and her smartphone, she sends some emails, undertakes a few searches, browses some sites, and clicks on several apps. Various legal-sounding notices keep popping up, asking her to accept a privacy policy, a data protection notification, and some lengthy terms of service (ToS). In each case, she pauses but reluctantly clicks through to reach the desired content.

Not long after, advertisements begin appearing on Carla's screen for dubious-sounding wellness tonics and supplemental medical insurance from companies she's never heard of. Her social media feed starts filling up with people offering heated political commentary and warning passionately against future vaccinations. Videos emerge of world leaders urging their citizens to ignore this "flu bug" and return to work—or, alternately, to stock up on toilet paper and prepare for the end times.

After browsing online she makes a doctor appointment.

Based on where Carla goes online, what she searches for, and what she clicks on, ads begin appearing, for unproven treatments, hand sanitizer, and face masks - from companies she's never heard of.

In the world outside the Web, our new friend Carla has invested considerable time and effort to develop trustworthy and supportive human relationships. In her mind, she has conferred well-earned trust to certain people and entities: close circles of friends, several local community groups, reputable businesses, worthy non-profits, trustworthy news sources.

But in the digital world, Carla's experiences seem to raise many more questions than answers. What's with those ads for stuff that she doesn't want or need? And then there is the social media chatter—which debates about COVID-19 are legitimate conversations, and which are hyped-up nonsense to serve someone's bottom line? When is something online written by a person and when is it a bot? What is a legitimate news story versus clickbait? What is a real video versus a deepfake? Carla is also vaguely aware that her personal information online is being collected and circulated among a shadowy throng of companies—and that in return, she is receiving not just the services she seeks but lots of other stuff that apparently suits those companies' pecuniary motivations.

No one would blame Carla for sometimes wanting to turn off her computer and walk away. And yet, as much as the situation exasperates her, realistically she cannot exist in the modern world without continuing to be an active presence on the Web. And her more optimistic side continues to believe that the Web can be a positive force in the world, for herself and so many others. So, what legitimate recourse does she have?

Missing Online Ingredients: Trust, Relationship, and Support

From the perspective of ordinary users, today's Web is missing at least three crucial components. One is basic human trust. The second is genuine relationship. The third is helpful support. Ideally, the three elements can be combined into trustworthy and supportive online relationships that promote the best interests of the human being.

More trust

As we have seen from Rachel Botsman, institutional trust flows upwards to leaders, experts, and brands, which traditionally have included large entities such as churches, governments, media, and corporations.[386] Her third category of distributed trust flows laterally between individuals, enabled by systems, platforms, and networks.[387]

In the online context, a leading cause of distrust is the mismatch in motivations.[388] Too many online entities typically treat those using their services as mere "users" rather than bona fide customers, clients, or patrons. This objectification carries over to their commercial practices, which rely heavily on the SEAMs feedback cycles.[389] All of which inevitably leads to a more trust-deficient Web.

More "relationship"

Carla's voluntary acts of entrustment convey considerable power to the doctor, the lawyer, the pharmacist, and others. In return, she rightly expects to directly benefit from the arrangement and be protected from the control they gain over her. But what about in a *digital* setting? Like when Carla goes online to check her email, visit social media sites, or search for medical information about her symptoms? Where are the duties of care and of loyalty that follow the entrustment of power to others? Where are the Net's versions of fiduciaries?

In short: there aren't any.

Welcome to Userhood

At the root of our online challenges is our consignment to the role of a user. Our "userhood" plays out in increasingly unfavorable aspects, via our interactions with the World Wide Web generally, and the MOPs particularly.

Carla has grown accustomed to dealing in offline relationships with entities and individuals that treat her as a valued customer at a minimum, but perhaps also as a bona fide client or well-guarded patron. Unfortunately, those same concepts typically hold little meaning with other types of entities online. As far as the Web is concerned, she is a "user." With no mutual relationship, no protection, and no recourse.

On the Web, the default rule is your user status. This means, in essence, that you visit websites, click on applications, and utilize offerings, all of which you pay for with your personal data. And in return, you become subject to the one-sided ToS that their lawyers write to apply to these interactions. These websites and app providers and social media companies endeavor to owe you nothing beyond the basic transaction. No duties of care or loyalty. No simple good faith. No promises to treat you like a bona fide client, or patron, or even a "mere" customer. Just a user.

Noted designer Don Norman decries how "we degrade people by the passive, inert term of "user"" (he's no fan either of the "consumer" and "customer" labels).[390] Similarly, former Twitter CEO Jack Dorsey has called for us to reconsider the term. Although tech designers speak of concepts like "user-centric design," "user benefit," and "user experience," Dorsey observes that "the result is a massive abstraction away from real problems people feel on a daily basis."[391]

The basic problem, of course, is that the abstraction is very real; the nomenclature of userhood matches well to the actual ways we are treated online. Userhood is, Norman observes, a way of labeling humans "as objects instead of personifying them as real living, breathing people."[392]

As detailed in Part One, the MOPs and their DAMB ecosystems today are keen to employ the SEAMs paradigm. These feedback cycles only exacerbate the abstraction, objectification, and even denigration of the humans in front of the screens. Much of what we may choose to grant to trusted agents in the analog space is increasingly and automatically being extracted from us in the digital space. We may recognize that entrusted power is evident with an online entity. For example, Carla benefits from having a digital existence, where there are significant gaps in her expertise, and the entity has unique access to Carla's sensitive personal data and confidences. But in these digital systems, there is nothing akin to an authentic fiduciary role. No real duties, no meaningful consent, no recourse.

One way to envision the situation is, as Doc Searls puts it, the Web "has boundary issues."[393] Even Carla's young daughter over time has come to learn about setting personal boundaries—both protecting her own and respecting those of others. By contrast, today's Web has little room for recognizing and honoring our personal contours.

Crucially, as mentioned earlier, the SEAMs cycles open the door to mysterious third parties as part of the MOPs ecosystems. These data marketers, advertisers, and brokers—constituting the DAMB ecosystem—may be lurking in the shadows, laying claim to aspects of our online interactions, usually including our personal data.[394] By default, being a Web user means inviting these anonymous third parties to access your personal data, getting nothing in return except concerted attempts to influence you to buy something. Doc Searls again puts it well: we are "running naked through the digital world ... as we were in the natural one before we invented clothing and shelter."[395]

More support

A final missing ingredient online is basic support for users. As the Web has become ever more complex, with both threats and opportunities hanging on the next mouse click, or voice command, protecting ourselves has become ever more challenging.

Again, the mismatch in motivations between MOPs and their users creates an erosion in fundamental responsibility—a lack of "skin in the game"[396] As one example, when Web companies provide "customer support," the service is almost entirely reactive, and for most of us a subpar experience.[397] As Botsman puts it, "the online landscape is vastly populated and yet, all too often, empty of anyone to take charge or turn to when it counts."[398] The buck stops elsewhere.

The basic aim of support is to help protect the individual online—*do not track me, do not hack me, and be responsive to me when something goes wrong*. Even better is the kind of support that actively tries to improve the individual's situation. Potential opportunities on the Web abound. Perhaps a provider could analyze and improve our privacy settings on web browsers and other applications. Update software, patch security holes, manage passwords, provide VPNs, and establish end-to-end encryption. Provide machine-readable guidance on ToS and user agreements, manage online consents, and establish more user-responsive applications. And of course, help us set up and manage our digital lifestreams. Relatively few companies today are providing such offerings.

Perhaps the key is to delegate our aspirations for the Web—our desire for trustworthy and supportive relationships—to third parties who act with authentic fidelity to our best interests. The next section spells out the kinds of intermediaries that can be forged from fiduciary law principles.

Creating Digital Life Support Systems: Net Fiduciaries

Human beings deserve societal institutions that they can trust to serve their best interests and provide tangible support to enable greater human autonomy (thought) and agency (action). We can think of a governance model extending to a new class of "digital stewardship."[399] In this regard, the common law of equities can be a valuable basis for entities to operate as one particular type of digital steward: individuals-focused Net fiduciaries, grounding the GliaNet ecosystem.

Bringing fiduciary concepts to the Web

The digital world holds vast potential to improve our lives. And yet, at the same time the SEAMs cycles expose us to countless threats to our well-being. As our personal data and actions and behaviors are relentlessly tracked and monetized on the Web, there is a compelling need to bring old-school virtues of care and loyalty and confidence-keeping online. But how exactly?

For starters, we need to begin demanding adherence to a simple practice—our digital technologies should promote our interests, not harm them. Moving online should enhance us, not degrade us. In fact, if a particular digital technology represents advances in innovation and capabilities, we should demand that the humans using them experience a similar advance in terms of empowerment and choice. Otherwise, the innovation is not being used to improve our daily experience.

This means that people like Carla should be treated online better than (if not at least as well as) offline. We deserve to have access to at least the same basic rights in the digital world as in the analog world. Certainly not fewer, and optimally more. Relatedly, our personal contours should be stronger where others would weaken them. In short, we need a fiduciary-style formula, something like:

D>A

This formula proposes to elevate our rights in the digital world (D), so that they meet or exceed our rights in the analog world (A).

The unifying principle is to put humans in control. In terms of power asymmetries, we need to build something like the HAACS ethos of human autonomy and agency via computational systems. In terms of systems dynamics, we must create new feedback loops to challenge and eventually replace the SEAMs cycles of surveillance, extraction, analysis, and manipulation.[400] In terms of basic human psychology, we should be empowered to set our own boundaries, our personal contours, signaling to the rest of the digital world what is acceptable to us and what is not.[401]

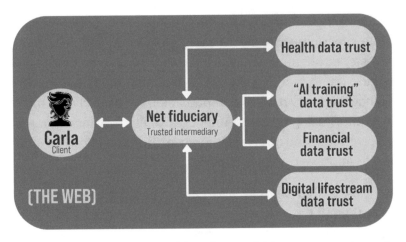

Fiduciary duties of care and loyalty could be one way to get us there online. Among other benefits, these duties:

- reflect shifting from the *transactional* mode of SEAMs cycles to the *relational* mode of HAACS (human agency/autonomy via computational systems)

- provide legitimate "skin in the game" on both sides of entrustment-based relationships with companies

- require degrees of trust and support, which over time can feed back onto each other in positive ways

- "run with the person" and all their contextual and relational ways of being in the world.

Fiduciary law is certainly not a panacea for all that ails us as a society. Some forms of social power and control likely require deeper institutional change.[402] And societal priorities—such as restraining those who would commit harmful or illegal acts—must be brought into balance as well. Fiduciary duties of loyalty cannot be used to shield bad behaviors. But fiduciary-like principles do provide us with a tool—even a weapon—to counter some of the power imbalances that have become so prevalent online. The challenge is to find ways to embed it in the digital fabric of the Web.

We can, perhaps, start seeking out and partnering with those who wish to abide, openly and voluntarily, by duties of care and loyalty to us. We can also consider imposing similar obligations at minimum not to harm us, where those with entrusted power resist using it accountably.

Three sets of "PEP" services and duties

What we are calling *Net fiduciaries* could perform a variety of client services under various fiduciary obligations. Collectively, these services and duties amount to providing people with a *digital life support system*. What follows is one example of such a system: the "PEP" model.[403] This model establishes three different ways that Net trustmediaries and fiduciaries can provide services to their clients or customers, pursuant to three different sets of duties.

Protecting with care: data guardian

In the *protect role*, the Net fiduciary can provide fundamental customer protections, focused on engendering greater privacy, enhanced security, and safeguarded online interactions.

- *Privacy:* Fully implement legal requirements, such as GDPR, analyze/improve customers' privacy settings on web browsers and other applications, and commit to not surveilling or tracking the client.[404]

- *Security:* Update software, patch security holes, manage passwords, provide VPNs, and establish end-to-end encryption.[405]

- *Interactions:* Shoulder more daunting cognitive burdens regarding the customer's dealings with third-party websites and applications, such as providing machine-readable guidance on ToS and user agreements, managing online consents, and establishing more user-responsive applications.[406]

In all services provided in Phase I, the Net fiduciary operating in Protect mode would relate to us under a general tort-like duty of care (do no harm), as well as a fiduciary duty of care (act prudently).[407]

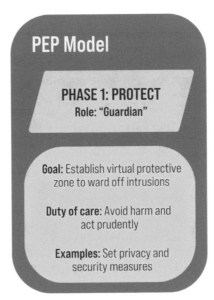

Enhancing without conflicts: information mediator

In the *Enhance phase*, the Net fiduciary could act as a filtering conduit, through which flows all of the client's digital lifestreams. This role could include establishing a virtual zone of trust and accountability to ward off intrusive actions, project the client's own ToS to the Web, flag the use of bots and other automated influence software, develop client "alt-consent" restrictions and choices, introduce symmetrical network interfaces, and send tailored alerts about disinformation such as deep fakes.[408]

In addition to operating under both duties of care, the Net fiduciary in Enhance mode also would be bound by the "thin" version of the fiduciary duty of loyalty (no conflicts of interests).[409] One can also label this the *fidelity duty*.

PEP Model

PHASE 2: ENHANCE
Role: "Mediator"

Goal: Mediate online data flows to and from client

Duty of fidelity: Have no conflicts of interest or duties

Example: Filter news and social media feeds

Promoting best interests: digital advocate

In the *Promote role*, the Net fiduciary "could employ even more advanced and emerging technology tools to fully protect, enhance, and promote the client's interests."[410] These could include personal data pods, localized cloudlets, sovereign identity layers, portable connectivity, and modular devices.[411] As will be discussed later, one Promote mode function could be an individualized computational agent, sometimes called a Personal AI.

In addition to operating under both duties of care and the thin duty of loyalty, the entity would utilize the "thick" version of the fiduciary duty of loyalty (promote best interests).[412] This can be thought of as the *loyalty duty*.

PEP Model

PHASE 3: PROMOTE
Role: "Advocate"

Goal: Employ emerging tech tools to fully represent clients

Duty of loyalty: Promote client's best interests

Example: Intent casting via authentic Personal AI and agents

Obviously, Net fiduciaries and their clients can together explore any number of desired functions in each of these phases. Importantly, as the agent-client relationship progresses, a likely outcome is a virtuous "macro" feedback loop.[413] As greater levels of trust and support are established over time, the client can consensually share more personal information, which spurs the addition of still more empowering service offerings.

As individuals engage with Net fiduciaries that are pairing higher degrees of duties with more service offerings, trust levels between the parties consequently should rise. Further, this protect/enhance/promote (PEP) model of care/fidelity/loyalty aligns well *with* promoting community data rights via laddered principles of transparency, accountability, fairness, and the social good.[414] Collective bargaining as well leads to greater personal and social equities over time.[415]

Of course, having an intermediary acting on our behalf is not an entirely self-sustaining proposition. And so, in Part Four, we will consider potential ways that these entities can be founded and funded while still adhering to their trust-based roots.

The GliaNet PEP Model

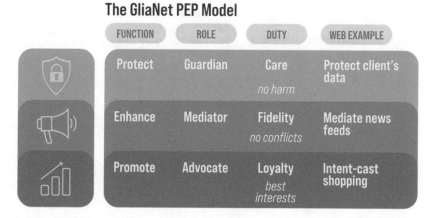

	FUNCTION	ROLE	DUTY	WEB EXAMPLE
	Protect	Guardian	Care *no harm*	Protect client's data
	Enhance	Mediator	Fidelity *no conflicts*	Mediate news feeds
	Promote	Advocate	Loyalty *best interests*	Intent-cast shopping

Next, we will explore another kind of Net trustmediary, one focused more on the collective uses and benefits of valuable data.

/C11/DATA TRUSTS

"Trust and accountability: above all else, these are the pillars of public health."

– Laurie Garrett[416]

It turns out that Carla was indeed one of the first of many Americans to contract COVID-19. As she slowly recovers from her bout with the illness, her thoughts turn to the larger societal implications of her illness. While she is grateful that her doctor's treatments helped bring her back to full health, she was deeply concerned about her daughter Ada, her other extended family members, her friends and neighbors, and of course the world at large. Her individual plight was a single story, one of billions on the planet. Who else was thinking about dealing with something like a global pandemic with this expansive mindset?

For example, her test results probably contained important medical information that, combined with the data from other patients, could pave the way to a better understanding of the virus. Her data points could be used to better society, if only there were entities set up to collect and analyze health data for the common good. But she saw little sign that such collective action was being pursued, online or offline. As the pandemic raged on outside her doors, she felt a sense of despair that the understandable impulse to help others could find no outlet.

Carla realizes that there is a great deal of data about her, scattered in many places. But how can she even begin to map it all out? Where is it located, how is it formatted, who has control over it, how can she access it? Where does she even start?

Back to SEAMs Cycles

As in traditional capitalism, treating data as a commodity resource magnifies the power and position of companies that hold the data surplus, while diminishing the agency of those whose lives are being harvested for profit. For the most part, people have little to no visibility or control over how their data is collected and used. At best, governments to date have considered and, in some cases, implemented data protection regimes that require forms of transparency and accountability. While necessary, these actions are inadequate when we consider the process of transforming the data economy into a more symmetrical forum for ordinary people.

The equation is stark: while data generated via SEAMs cycles serves the financial interests of a few, its value as an individual, societal, or public good is largely unrealized. Even in instances where large amounts of data are not unduly concentrated in corporate hands, governments and civil society organizations tend to manage it poorly and fail to adequately harness its inherent value.

This twin problem—of data being over-collected from individuals and under-utilized for societal value—is compounded by data's peculiarity as a complex resource. Because data is a relational good, existing individual-centric methods of governance do not adequately reflect its full community and societal value. This means, for example, that collective data can be used to discriminate against individuals, even as individual data can be used for societal value, as in the case of medical data.

Further, as a non-rivalrous good, data's uses by one entity need not impact others. In fact, sharing data among multiple entities can increase its value accordingly. But data value chains are complicated, and most stakeholders establish siloes that make value distribution difficult.[417]

A fundamental reimagination of data governance is necessary to address these unique characteristics. Such a new framework needs to be anchored not just in suppositions about convenience and ease of access for users (often perceived as consumers seeking such ease, not citizens with actionable rights), but rather in ideas of equity.

New Model: Data in Collectives

As discussed, fiduciary doctrine potentially provides an important foundation for human rights and constitutional rights for our digital selves. The law of fiduciaries can also be extended to the types of entities we wish to engage with directly as individuals to foster trustworthy and supportive relationships. In particular, entities operating voluntarily under heightened fiduciary duties of care, loyalty, and confidentiality can fill in the existing market gaps looming between MOPs and their users.

As part of this proposed new world of Net TMs, several models have been suggested for entities to adopt on a voluntary basis. As discussed in Chapter Ten, the *Net fiduciary* is based on individual agency in an actual, direct fiduciary relationship with a client.[418] Other models, however, are possible. Another, collective type of digital stewardship model comes from the related common law of trusts. A *data trust* is based on agency over the personal data and information of a specified collective of individuals.[419] Here, the entity manages a pool of data on behalf of that community.[420] Typical examples include the *health care data trust*, which would enable medical professionals, researchers, and others to access personal health care information.[421] The *civic data trust* to be discussed further in Chapter 14 applies a similar collective governance model to the personal and environmental information that is gathered and analyzed in the context of smart cities.[422]

We can imagine people employing a mix of Net fiduciaries (for their own individual agency), data trusts (for collective agency), and other NetTMs to manage their digital lifestreams. For example, a Net fiduciary could handle an individual's digital interactions and relationships, while also negotiating on behalf of its client with a data trust, seeking to pool together biometric data for important medical research.

To better appreciate the importance of the data trust, let's take a quick house call from Dr. John Snow.

Tracing the infectious contacts

An infectious pathogen is in the air. A deadly pandemic is on the rise. Fear is rampant in homes, and on the streets. Medical professionals are frantically searching for answers. For at least some, there is a promise of something called contact tracing as a way to flatten the infection curve.

The time is early September 1854. The place is London, England. The plague is cholera. And the dedicated contact tracer is named John Snow, a young medical doctor. In a neighborhood of the working poor in central London (now Soho), some 600 residents have perished from cholera in a single week. While other medical experts of his day, including the General Board of Health, are convinced that the disease is transmitted as an airborne "miasma" among the "squalid" poor, Snow believes the pathogen actually spreads via contaminated water.[423]

Snow confirms his then-heretical theory by meticulously assembling evidence of infection, including reconstructing and tracking the daily movements of infected patients in and around the neighborhood. By observing the data clusters, Snow determines that everyone affected has one thing in common: they all retrieved drinking water from a hand pump well located on Broad Street.

After assembling his evidence, Dr. Snow tries to alert the singularly named "Board of Guardians of the Poor." This local group of landowning white men was charged with maintaining some semblance of order and health in a neighborhood of the economically challenged. On the evening of September 7th, he brings his findings to the Board's outwardly skeptical Sanitary Committee. As Snow's contemporaneous biographer relates it: "The vestrymen of St. James were sitting in solemn consultation on the causes of the visitation."[424] Without warning, "a stranger had asked in modest speech for a brief hearing." Dr. Snow explains his case, advising removal of the Broad Street water pump handle as "the grand prescription." The vestry is "incredulous," but the next day agrees as a precaution to remove the water pump's handle, rendering it inoperable. The epidemic, already ebbing, is quelled.[425]

Snow's findings at the Broad Street pump, and in other cholera outbreaks, helped usher in what later became known as "the sanitation movement." Over several decades, cities and towns around the world constructed greatly improved sewage drainage and water purification systems. By contributing to such huge systemic changes, Snow has been touted by many as the father of epidemiology. In one survey of medical professionals, he came out as the "greatest doctor of all time," edging out the legendary Hippocrates (460-370 BC). Despite such massive improvements globally, cholera still kills some 100,000 people every year, mainly in developing countries without safe drinking water and sanitation.

Medical data, and well-earned trust

Dr. Snow personally attended to many of the pandemic's unfortunate victims. Snow's original biographer spoke of his "untiring zeal ... how he laboured, and at what cost, and at what risk.... He laid aside, as much as possible the emoluments of practice, even by early rising and late taking rest.... Wherever cholera was visitant, there was he in the midst."[426] Steven Johnson separately observes that "the fearlessness of the act still astonishes."[427] In his house-to-house inquiries, Snow spoke with the dying and the relatives of the dead. People in hugely crowded private residences. Strangers in the streets. Hospital patients. Prison inmates. St. James Workhouse laborers. He also spoke with those (like workers at the Lion Brewery) who for some reason had not fallen ill.[428]

Dr. Snow managed to convince a wide range of people to confide sensitive information. Names and addresses. Eating and drinking history, regular habits, known physical contacts, daily whereabouts. Many patients and families were undoubtedly desperate. Some likely knew they were doomed, and yet (or perhaps therefore) shared their confidences anyway. People placed their trust in Snow as a potential healer, a medical sleuth, and an attentive listener.

Dr. Snow recorded his data points diligently in a ledger, eventually displaying them on a London street map. There, each black bar stood for one cholera death. His map became the public repository of crucial empirical data, reflecting genuine local knowledge gathered and sifted from the source.

While Snow was not the first contact tracer in history, in many ways he was the most consequential. As he was a true native of the Broad Street area, this "gave him both awareness of how the neighborhood actually worked and it gave him a credibility with the residents, on whose intimate knowledge of the outbreak Snow's inquiry depended."[429]

Dr. Snow recognized that the ethical and swift use of relevant and sensitive medical data can help save lives. In effect, he became a trusted repository of such data, a role that he extended for socially beneficial uses that would have far-reaching impact.

Tracing a Pandemic in 2020

A new outbreak, a new pathogen, airborne transmission, and yet in 2020, the medical detective work largely was the same. Gather the evidence, look for patterns, and take swift action.

Today, contact tracing remains the first and often most powerful tool in ascertaining the origins of a disease, as well as implementing appropriate social isolation guidelines. The public health worker typically takes a two-step approach, first conducting a detailed contact tracing interview with an infected individual and then asking the individual to stay at home and self-isolate.

The U.S. Centers for Disease Control (CDC) provides specific principles, strategies, and detailed scripts for how public health workers should engage to notify individuals of exposure. These principles include ensuring confidentiality, demonstrating an ethical and professional conduct, creating a "judgment-free zone," having cultural humility, asking open-ended questions, using reflective listening techniques, and addressing concerns that arise during the conversation. Each principle is intended to enable public health workers to "build and maintain trust with clients and contacts."[430]

The usefulness of sharing data

To many in the 21st century, contact tracing constitutes an invasion of personal privacy, only justified perhaps because of the larger public health benefits. The real-life work of contact tracers demonstrates that underlying many of their efforts to contact and persuade people to cooperate is "the contagion of fear." Still, as recent experience in the Apache nation shows,[431] intense contact tracing conducted in person by well-known and trusted community members, can overcome that fear—resulting in revealing valuable and actionable information.

A report from the Aapti Institute establishes some of the many societal benefits from sharing one's personal data.[432] In particular:

> *"Sharing data is instrumental in the development of knowledge, research, innovation, and cooperation that help us better understand our society, economy, and polity. Some data, therefore, is rightly regarded as a shared resource that benefits society at large."*

Under the right governance structures, human autonomy and agency can be promoted with the sharing of personal data. As contemporary technology markets increasingly extract value from aggregated data, there is a pressing need to create institutions that protect both individual and collective level data rights. Where benefits and harms alike are collective, governance mechanisms can fill that gap, beyond the more individualized online needs served by a trusted entity such as a Net fiduciary.

Contact tracing as an app: where is the governance?

During the COVID-19 pandemic, many of us became aware of the concept of contact tracing in the context of "exposure notification" software applications. The best known is the mobile app produced by Google and Apple. In their joint announcement, the companies discussed the desirability of gaining access to pools of health data for medical research while avoiding the downside of capturing and transmitting highly sensitive information about individuals.[433]

It is apparent that some contact-tracing apps are superior to others in protecting sensitive identifying information and medical data.[434] However, beyond the efficacy of specific technology implementations looms the larger concern about trust and accountability. Most of these health-related apps were operating in the field without the actual "back end" of abiding governance structures.

Attempting to embed contact-tracing rules into a software application's ToS, or its privacy and data protection practices, is a fraught proposition. As we saw earlier, Web users already have "notice and consent" fatigue. Most websites and apps these days ask us to review and assess details of their policies, including how much data is collected, what kind, for how long, and under what terms.[435] Asking for similar user engagement for even more sensitive health-related sites and apps may exacerbate the burden.

Ultimately, while the power of contact-tracing apps can complement human efforts, considering software as the primary solution neglects the role and value of human institutions, and the necessity of generating authentic trust for people to consider adopting such personal tools. Perhaps unsurprisingly, a 2020 poll of US smartphone users found that half would refuse to use the Google/Apple contact-tracing app.[436] As Laurie Garrett concludes in her magisterial *Betrayal of Trust: The Collapse of Global Public Health*, it is up to public health to "bring the world toward a sense of singular community in which the health of each one member rises or falls with the health of all others."[437]

The challenges involved in developing and adopting connected technologies highlights the need to integrate the human element. We need entities operating under certain established legal/ethical principles, setting the standards under which our software applications will be created and deployed. When crises inevitably arise, we don't just need (more) technology— we require trustworthy tech governance.

Following the (Legal) Trust

As noted, the data trust is one legal instrument increasingly being discussed as a means to bridge that governance gap. The basic concept of a trust is that a "settlor" (a user) places property or another object of value in the control of a "trustee," who in turn manages that asset for the benefit of a "beneficiary." The trustee is granted authority to hold and make decisions about the assets by a trust charter. The trustee is obliged to operate under strict fiduciary standards, including a duty of loyalty towards the beneficiary.[438]

The data trust essentially extends the legal trust concept to treating data as a protected asset.[439] While there is no one definitive definition of a data trust, Anouk Ruhaak helpfully delineates that:

"A data trust is a structure whereby data is placed under the control of a board of trustees with a fiduciary responsibility to look after the interests of the beneficiaries—you, me, society. Using them offers all of us the chance of a greater say in how our data is collected, accessed and used by others. This goes further than limiting data collecting and access to protect our privacy; it promotes the beneficial use of data, and ensures these benefits are widely felt across society. In a sense, data trusts are to the data economy what trade unions are to the labor economy."[440]

Sylvie Delacroix and Neil Lawrence wrote a seminal article on what they call the "bottom up" data trust.[441] More "top-down" legal and regulatory structures typically rely on express or implied contracts to delineate parties' rights and obligations. The notice-and-consent process applied to Web users by many websites and apps is an example of this. By contrast, the "bottom-up" model focuses on individuals using a legal trust for specified functions, such as establishing verified access to their data for third parties. To Delacroix and Lawrence, the latter would utilize legal safeguards from trust law and operate with a clear purpose rooted in public, social, or charitable benefits.

Little is firmly settled about the notion of bringing data within trust law, and the legal landscape remains uncertain.[442] For starters, civil law-based countries (such as China, Japan, and much of Europe) rely more on codified statutory codes. These systems may not readily accommodate the judge-made common law more prevalent in the United States, Canada, and India. Questions also remain about whether and how a data access and collection regime can be superimposed onto actual legal trust arrangements. Defining and apportioning the rights and duties between the three parties of the settlor, the trustee, and the beneficiary has also proven challenging.

Nonetheless, many see potentially enormous value in how a data trust can empower individuals to exercise their data rights collectively.

- In Canada, Element AI has conducted important research on data trusts.[443]

- In India, the Aapti Institute has examined the data trust as part of its ongoing work on defining data stewardship.[444]

- The Mozilla Foundation has also embarked on a data stewardship initiative, launching a "Data Futures Lab" to explore and sponsor various data trusts and fiduciaries models.[445]

As these and other projects unfold, open questions around the viability of data trusts hopefully will be resolved.

One promising model: health care data trusts

Data about a person's medical status can be a highly useful societal resource. Work at MIT on "building the new economy," for example, includes proposing a detailed technical architecture to facilitate the collecting and sharing of health data.[446] By themselves, however, such impressive technology implementations lack a companion in governance to create, build, and hold actual trust and accountability.

Delacroix and Lawrence posit that one particularly apt use case of the "bottom up" data trust is the donation, pooling, and exchange of personal medical information.[447] Element AI also observes that the mission of societal benefit from medical research could be the driving factor in the success of a health data trust.[448]

In theory at least, the data trust model can provide important benefits when applied to health data, especially compared with the quasi-contractual notice-and-consent model employed by most websites and apps. Notionally, the data trust relationship itself (rather than the underlying software and hardware, or its one-sided use policies) carries the crucial human elements.

Specific advantages of a health data trust include:

- establishing its governing structure and principles ahead of time
- granting settlors (users) opportunities to participate in the process of devising those rights and responsibilities

- harnessing the power of collective bargaining over data access rights (compared to the individual fending for themselves on website/apps)

- baking recourse and enforcement mechanisms into the trust structure, including giving people options to modify or revoke their participation in the data pool

Perhaps most importantly, the presence of these types of up-front safeguards should result in increased human trust and the sharing of *more* relevant data than under prevailing top-down consent approaches.

Nonetheless, despite these seeming benefits, there are few explicit health data trusts operating today. The organizations operating in the medical/health care space and utilizing aggregated patient data tend to be organized as non-profits and utilize ordinary contracts rather than trusts. Otherwise, the sharing of health data typically happens via ordinary bilateral contracts between parties, not a legal data trust. So, what is hindering the uptake of this governance mechanism? Possible reasons include:

- uncertainty about the legal basis of data trusts in particular jurisdictions, including whether data can be assigned as a tangible resource to be managed by a trust

- lack of clarity about the definition and applicability of specific fiduciary duties for the data trust

- possible lack of recourse when something goes awry, including the availability of law courts or government regulators

- difficulty in organizing like-minded people to act collectively

Rooting the Data Trust in a Modified "PEP" framework

As noted, part of the challenge with adopting the data trust model is uncertainty about the specific rights and duties that should apply to it. For example, the practice of contact tracing derives its ethos from the world of public health. That ethos encompasses protecting the individual's confidentiality while gathering pertinent information and driving towards positive social outcomes. In this way, public health differs from the practice of direct medical care, which has an emphasis on treating individual patients. Taking care of the well-being of an entire community requires a different mindset.

How then should fiduciary/trust-like duties play out in the online practices of a health data trust? One suggestion is to apply lessons from the actual physician-patient relationship. In functional terms, the physician-patient dynamic contains crucial elements to form a fiduciary relationship. These include:

- an asymmetric power balance, based on the patient's vulnerability

- acquiring and utilizing sensitive health information about the patient

- utilizing professional expertise to carry out specific tasks

- the patient's reliance on such expertise

As we saw with the PEP model, these physician-patient power dynamics suggest that the individual entrustor (here, the patient) would benefit from applying four different types of fiduciary law-based duties to the entrusted party (here, the physician). These include (1) the general tort-like duty of care (do no harm), (2) the fiduciary duty of care (prudent conduct), (3) the "thin" loyalty duty of having no conflicts (which I call the duty of fidelity), and (4) the "thick" loyalty duty of promoting the entrustor's best interests (the duty of loyalty). The PEP model matches up to these care/fidelity/loyalty fiduciary obligations with specific actions carried out on behalf of the client.

Importantly, this framework can be extended to apply to legal trusts serving collective social interests. A PEP model for data trusts would differ in several ways from one devised for personal digital fiduciaries and their clients. The use cases and clientele are collective (rather than individual), the scope is limited to data as an aggregated resource (rather than a more expansive digital relationship), and the form is a trust, with a board of trustees, trustors, and beneficiaries (as opposed to the simpler fiduciary binary of a trustor and trustee). Still, the same three PEP actions aligned with the four common law-derived duties can be applied across the board.

A Highly Complementary Role for Net Fiduciaries

The Net fiduciary model introduced in the previous chapter can also spur adoption of the data trust model. In particular, a personal Net fiduciary can help its clients explore the brave new world of data trusts, make decisions about utilizing particular ones, and negotiate/reach agreement on their behalf. With Carla, for example, a Net fiduciary could assist her in finding the best data trusts to collect her health care data for the purpose of finding cures to combat COVID-19. One or more data trusts dedicated to different use cases can bestow the means to Carla's health data to express solidarity with a larger community. This more relational, rather than transactional, approach also lessens the reality of cognitive load for ordinary people and greatly bolsters the value of trust-based relationships.

Combining the personalized Net fiduciary and collective data trust models provides another way to accomplish the extension of human rights in the digital world. By improving on our human-based governance regimes, perhaps we can achieve the aspirational *D>A* formula for individuals and communities alike.

Celebrating a Missing Pump Handle

Was John Snow the world's first data trust? Some 170 years after the fact, his actions on Broad Street, along with the arc of his career, still manage to impress. Shifting seamlessly from doctor to sociologist to statistician, Snow was a true systems thinker, well before the term came into being.[449] Johnson suggests that Snow's careful questioning of the neighborhood residents about whether they had been drinking the well water in itself may have diminished the spread of the epidemic, sparing additional lives.[450]

Snow's systematic collection of health data, based largely on gaining patients' trust, involved honing the investigator's tool of contact tracing. The resulting street-level map, as Johnson puts it, was "a direct reflection of the ordinary lives of the ordinary people who made up the neighborhood.... A neighborhood representing itself, turning its own patterns into a deeper truth."[451]

Most importantly, Snow made use of the data he gathered and analyzed to further the public good—hence the missing pump handle.[452] His work led to prompt action to save human lives. He tapped into the societal value of shared local data, under the conditions of respecting and protecting confidences and building trust, as a means of making a difference. Snow's human qualities stand as testament to the kind of institutions we should want to build to govern our digital world.

In London today, John Snow has a pub named after him, steps from where the Broad Street pump once stood, an ironic testament to a lifelong teetotaler. As we wrestle with data governance models for our future, perhaps a more apt living tribute would be something like "the John Snow Health Data Trust."

Fast forward to the 21st Century...

```
}
int main(int argc, char *argv[]) {
   int sockfd, newsockfd, portno;
   socklen_t clilen;
   char buffer[256];
   struct sockaddr_in serv_addr, cli_addr;
   int n;

   sockfd = socket(AF_INET, SOCK_STREAM, 0);
   if (sockfd < 0)
      error("ERROR opening socket");
```

/PART THREE/EMPOWERING OUR VIRTUAL EDGES (E2A)

```
   memset((char *) &serv_addr, 0, sizeof(serv_addr));
   portno = 8080;
   serv_addr.sin_family = AF_INET;
   serv_addr.sin_addr.s_addr = INADDR_ANY;
   serv_addr.sin_port = htons(portno);

   if (bind(sockfd, (struct sockaddr *) &serv_addr, sizeof(serv_addr))
      < 0) error("ERROR on binding");

   listen(sockfd, 5);
   clilen = sizeof(cli_addr);

   newsockfd = accept(sockfd, (struct sockaddr *) &cli_addr, &clilen);
   if (newsockfd < 0)
      error("ERROR on accept");
```

/C12/EDGETECH: THE "PUSHMI-PULLYU" OF OUR AGENCY

In this part, we will shift from the realms of human governance to our enabling technologies. A crucial caveat here is that technology should never be properly considered out of context. How a particular tech tool will be implemented is a matter of how it is governed, from its conception to its design to its actual implementation.

We will see here examples of what I call "edgetech"—software applications and hardware devices that reside with us "users" at the edge of the Web. Beyond their physical placement, however, these implements are designed to protect, enhance, and promote our interests in the world. In parallel with the human-centric governance institutions discussed in Part Two, we can put in place agential technologies that invite our participation rather than shunt it aside. These technologies can help bestow better control over our personal contours and lifestreams in the digital world.

Our imaginary guide here is the pushmi-pullyu, a fictional animal presented by Hugh Lofting in his *Doctor Doolittle* series. Reading these entertaining novels today unfortunately also reveals Lofting's racially biased and colonialistic beliefs. Nonetheless, the image of the two-headed pushmi-pullyu remains an endearing one, and relevant here. So while not endorsing Lofting's anachronistic cultural views, we can allude to his whimsical creation. In particular, this "rarest animal of all" was considered difficult to catch, "because no matter which way you came towards him, he was always facing you."[453] The double-sided aspect of this mysterious creature—always facing out to the world—is a useful way of conveying the potential human empowerment that can be found in edgetech capabilities.

The Road to KnowMeBots

In March 1988, Bob Kahn and Vint Cerf—actual "co-fathers of the Internet"—released a draft paper called "An Open Architecture for a Digital Library System and a Plan for its Development."[454] Behind this innocuous-sounding title, the paper explored the concept of an open architecture for national information infrastructure, the Digital Library System (DLS). Intriguingly, the architectural framework included mobile software agents the authors called "Knowbots," which were tasked with performing various mediating services for their end users:

> "Knowbots ... are active intelligent programs capable of exchanging messages with each other and moving from one system to another in carrying out the wishes of the user. They may carry intermediate results, search plans and criteria, output format and organization requirements and other information relevant to the satisfaction of a user's query. A Knowbot is typically constructed on behalf of a user at his Personal Library System and dispatched to a Database Server which interfaces the network to a particular database or set of databases.... In the future, we expect to witness the development of databases systems with built-in mechanisms for housing and catering to resident or transient Knowbots."[455]

In particular, there are a class of trusted Knowbots called "couriers," with a special responsibility to look after selected objects, such as documents or databases, on behalf of their rights holders.

The Kahn/Cerf paper highlights the Knowbot's key aspects, including that it:

1. is constructed on behalf of the end user,

2. responds to the user's queries,

3. moves seamlessly from one information system to another,

4. interacts in various ways with those larger systems, and

5. guards the sensitive content of its end user.

From this brief description, we can discern the outline of a human-centric blueprint for various software and hardware devices linked to the Internet.

Another prominent feature of the Knowbot is that Kahn and Cerf assigned it to represent the digital library. This suggests that the technology was intended to act on behalf of the actual human reference librarians, with their sworn fiduciary oaths to promote the interests of their patrons.

Today, technological progress in AI-based software and devices is only accelerating. Generative AI has captured the world's headlines, with the promise of vast computational resources at everyone's fingertips. And the promise of individualized digital bots is morphing from information-only search retrievers, to multi-tasking virtual assistants, to full-fledged agents that understand their humans at deep levels and take actions (ostensibly) on their behalf.

In this regard, we are moving rapidly from a fictitious world of Kahn and Cerf's linear Knowbot to a very real and dynamic "KnowMeBot." The ramifications of this shift—combining the universal and the personal, the informational and the behavioral—are immense.

Understanding Two Dimensions of Agency

While the term "agent" is widely used by pundits in discussing AI-based assistants, the word deserves some careful unpacking. By definition, there are two interrelated dimensions of being an agent: (1) making decisions and taking actions, (2) on behalf of someone else. [456] In the context of AI-based technologies, these intrinsic elements can be thought of as "agenticity" (functional capability to behave like an agent by performing or undertaking certain activities), and "agentiality" (authorized representation to act on behalf of another person). Both dimensions of capability and relationship are necessary and must work together for the technology to be considered truly human-centric. As it turns out, two of the leading AI companies, OpenAI and Google DeepMind, have offered us some clues on how to put these two dimensions together in actionable ways.

Dimension one: agenticity

In December 2023, OpenAI released a white paper discussing what it called the "agenticness" or "agenticity" of an AI-based system.[457] This element corresponds to the first dimension of agency described here: capability. The white paper defines an AI system's "agenticness" as the "degree to which it can adaptably achieve complex goals in complex environments with limited direct supervision." We can also think of this as a form of "environmental alignment."

The paper lists four components of agenticness: goal complexity, environmental complexity, adaptability, and independent execution.[458] The systems that exhibit high degrees of agenticness are referred to as "agentic AI systems." Moreover, the paper lists seven outstanding challenges that require additional attention: evaluating suitability for a task, circumstances for human approval, setting default behaviors, legibility of actions, monitoring, attributability, and maintaining control.[459]

The OpenAI researchers also posit that a range of follow-on effects—such as accountability for potential harms—become more relevant as a system's agenticness increases.[460] In discussing the second of the seven challenges, the paper notes that "constraining the action-space and requiring approval" means ensuring that there is a "human in the loop" to limit egregious harms.[461] Open questions include how a user or system deployer determines which interactions require human approval and how such approval should be gained.[462] However, the paper does not directly address what could be thought of as the second dimension of agency: valid authorization for an AI system to act on behalf of a person.

Dimension two: agentiality

By contrast with OpenAI's more functional concept of agenticity for AI systems, a technology's "agentiality" adheres more closely with the second dimension: relationship. This encompasses the degree to which a technology is legally or ethically authorized to represent the human being. The OpenAI paper defines "user-alignment" as "the propensity of an AI model or system to follow the goals specified by a user."[463] In software engineering terms, we can also think of this as a form of "end user alignment."

On the heels of the OpenAI paper on agenticity, a large group of researchers assembled by Google DeepMind issued its own extensive paper focused on AI. Titled "The Ethics of Advanced AI Assistants,"[464] this paper can be seen as taking up where OpenAI left off: on the question of user alignment. The paper posits that "an AI assistant is aligned with a user when it benefits the user, when they ask to be benefited, in the ways they expect to be benefited."[465]

The Google DeepMind paper acknowledges that putting the user/AI assistant relationship on a sound ethical footing is a necessary task—but not a sufficient one, given the wider social context. Instead, the paper proposes that values alignment should encompass a "tetradic relationship" between the user, the AI assistant, the software developer, and society. The larger thesis there is that any searching inquiry into the agenticity of a digital technology, per the OpenAI paper, is incomplete without a similar exploration of its agentiality, per the GoogleMind paper. Indeed, without an adequate confirmed degree of agentiality, any actions taken by a technology "on behalf of" a person should be considered unwarranted—if not downright unethical.

Obviously, the notion of agentiality as denoting elements of right relationship encompasses the human governance principles laid out in Part Two. In technology terms, this means that the software or hardware tool has been designed and implemented to convey optimal agency to the human being. In GliaNet terms, this technology instantiation is an example of *edgetech*.

Two dimensions, working together

Spider-Man's famous credo is straightforward: *"With great power comes great responsibility."* The GliaNet initiative appropriates that credo as a guide to better appreciate how the two dimensions of agency interrelate.

In the context of digital technology, we can posit that the greater the capabilities for environmental alignment, the greater the need for end user alignment. Alternatively, the greater the degree of observable agentiality—the deeper the relationship—the larger the valid action space available for agenticity. This means there should be proportional and acknowledged tradeoffs between agenticity (technical capabilities) and agentiality (authorized representation). This is one way to capture that crucial connection:

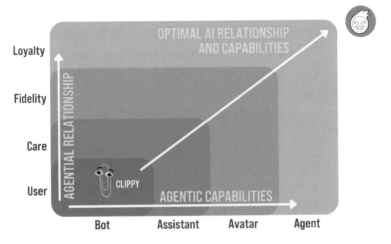

In everyday terms, this means that the more consensual the agreement to certain forms of AI-assisted decision-making, the more advanced kinds of actions the AI system can perform in the world. And vice versa.

New Edge-Outward Interfaces: Edgetech

As we have seen, the SEAMs paradigm is brought forth through *cloudtech* applications—technologies that represent the interests of the online platform companies vis-à-vis end users. Refashioning network-based gateways and applications so that they reflect more control by humans at the edge of the Web can be thought of as *"edgetech"* capabilities. These new interfaces essentially reverse the unilateral nature of the *cloudtech* tools that facilitate SEAMs control flows for the benefit of platform providers.

The edgetech concept incorporates three necessary elements: (1) a new *edge-to-any* ("e2a") design principle, (2) end user-facing modalities of data, computation, and interfaces that instantiate the new principle, and (3) one or both of *"edge-pushing"* and *"edge-pulling"* functionalities that empower human beings.

The "edge-to-any" design principle

The initial step is to recognize the opportunity to conceptually reset the Web's current power asymmetries through an entirely new design principle. This approach has the makings of fashioning an edge-based online environment.[466]

As we saw in Part One, the Internet over several decades became a "network of networks." This can be attributed to the four revolutionary design attributes of the end-to-end ("e2e") principle, functional modularity, global interoperability, and IP as agnostic bearer protocol. The Net's unique decentralized, peer-to-peer configuration enabled participants to interact from "the edge"—symmetrically, equipotentially, with little need for intermediaries. The end-to-end principle in particular originally promised to put end users in charge of their online activities.[467]

As it turns out, however, the client-server arrangement of Web 1.0, and then the MOPs and DAMB ecosystems of Web 2.0, ended up reducing the ability of end users at the edge to define and control access to their digital selves. Instead, the cloud-based "end" of platforms operating on the other side of the connection exerted increasing control over Web-based interactions. Beyond even the notion of basic control, individuals gradually lost the ability to engage in mutual value exchange with peers and partners, and otherwise assert their full human rights in digital form.

Where the original Internet architecture included the then-revolutionary concept of the e2e principle, the notion here is to deploy a new edge-to-any design principle as a Web overlay. Much as e2e first established the possibility of connecting individuals as actual peers to each other, an e2a principle would be instantiated in technologies that deliberately shift power from the Web and its platform overlays to ordinary people at the edge. As a result, the computational core of clouds and algorithms would give way to more distributed networking and decentralized applications. Adopting this principle in developing software, hardware, and networks would be one means of reversing the current cloud-centric SEAMs data flows on the Web.

The proposed *e2a* design principle has some parallels to the concept of the peer-to-peer ("p2p") relationship. [468] But the *e2a* nomenclature, rather than p2p, is employed here for two reasons. First, the proposed design principle is intended to supplement, not replace, the existing Web architecture. Second, as a technical matter, "edge" users should directly control their interactions with all other entities residing on the Web, not just with other "edge" users acting as nominal peers.

Multiple edge-based modalities

Systems designers who utilize an edge-outward design principle like e2a can change the current one-sided dynamic of the Web. The opportunity here is two-fold: (1) modifying existing modalities so that the individual has a viable means of engaging directly with computational systems, and (2) designing new modalities to maximize the person's ability to shape their own experiences. The emphasis should be on modalities that promote autonomy (freedom of thought) and agency (freedom of action).[469]

The e2a design principle can be instantiated in any type of digital technology that grants the end user more control over their engagement with Web-based systems. These can include the three computational system elements of the algorithm (the AI), the interfaces, and of course the data itself. For example:

- A Personal AI (PAI) agent that acts on behalf of the individual in interactions with Institutional AIs.

- A personal data pod that effectively stores the individual's data and information in a localized (non-cloud) environment, complete with end-to-end encryption.

- An identity layer that acts as a projecting interface, allowing a person to shape what personal information is provided online and curtail unwanted incursions of third-party agents.

Edge-push and edge-pull functions

Under the e2a design principle, various edgetech modalities can empower the individual. With the notion of personal contours that help us shape our interactions with the world, we can see two types of functions that are enabled:

- *"Edge-pull"* configurations (outside-in) allow the individual to bring the Web's computational systems and other resources directly to them. An example of this is creating our own news feeds from disparate sources; another is directing credit scoring companies to our personal data where it resides locally.[470] The key element is agency activated by bringing the digital world inward.

- *"Edge-push"* configurations (inside-out) allow the individual to send their own commands and requests to external websites and applications. Examples include broadcasting our own terms of service, and operating our own virtual shopping cart.[471] The key element is agency activated by bringing the self outward to the digital world.

This is where the pushmi-pullyu from Doctor Doolittle enters the stage. As its name suggests, the animal's movement is premised on a series of pushing and pulling actions. How it manages to coordinate this means of walking is another story. For our purposes, we can appropriate this function to demonstrate the two types of edgetech functions. With the "pushmi" action, the technology is pushing me and my intentions into the Web. With the "pullyu" action, the technology is pulling the world's information to me. Either way, the technology interface is always presenting the human face outward.

Each of these two functions has a notable real-world champion. The OPAL project launched by Sandy Petland and others at MIT enables *edge-pull* functionality by "pulling" the Web's computation to the personal data, rather than the other way around.[472] One salient example is bringing a credit scoring company's algorithm to the individual's personal data residing in a local pod. Where the algorithm processes in this way, the data need never leave the individual's control, to be exposed to data breaches on distant server farms. An early adopter with a business model premised on OPAL's edge-pull functionality is FID. Its platform is "designed to reduce the raw data footprint across a company's ecosystem" because the "algorithms travel to the data and produce insights that are shipped back for use instead of raw data."[473]

The VRM project launched by Doc Searls at Harvard University is a well-known leader for *edge-push* thinking.[474] Searls has explained how each of us should want to be the first party in a relationship with the operators of websites and apps (the primary and active instigator), rather than the second party (the passive recipient).[475] In the digital community context, the entity operating on the other side of the interface could be required to accept *our* terms of service, abide by *our* privacy policy, and consent to *our* preferred ways of interacting. Searls uses the term "intentcasting" to describe this new dynamic. In proffering edge-push requests, an active first-party role enables us to engage in a true conversation: question, object, negotiate, and ideally reach a mutual agreement.

With both edge-push and edge-pull functionality, the current Web client-server paradigm is flipped on its head. By utilizing the appropriate online algorithms, data flows, and interfaces, an individual can establish her own virtual boundaries—her personal contours of access, control, and influence—along with her digital lifestreams, among other benefits.

In the digital community context, *e2a* design principles would enable the individual to project herself into online systems, opening up new points of bilateral interaction and negotiation. A healthy mix of edge-pull and edge-push interfaces would create "mini" positive feedback loops between the individual and the Web. System designers know that positive feedback loops have a highly agential impact: "to perturb systems to change." [476] And in the process, the actual human being at the center can fully occupy their virtual spaces.

Humans in the governance loop

A chief lesson derived from the history of technology is: *how a technology tool is actually utilized in the world is a matter of human intentions.* While the e2e principle (and other design attributes) have enabled the Internet to support and promote a vast range of human activities, [477] that same openness to innovation and creativity also allows certain actors such as the MOPs to benefit disproportionately. [478] In essence, these entities have managed to occupy one "end" of the e2e relationship with Web users and "tilted" their cloudtech-based platforms to primarily serve their own pecuniary ends. [479]

The point here is not to undo the hugely impactful and successful end-to-end principle. Rather, we should focus on constructing and implementing overlay technologies designed to better harness the intrinsic power of *e2e* design. In this case, however, the overlay brings a significant difference: overtly and decidedly shifting network control and intelligence to one node, occupied by the end user at the edge. As a result, those at the network's edge could initiate and directly manage many of their Web interactions—hence, the e2a design principle and its "pushmi-pullyu" capabilities.

In the next few chapters, we will examine several types of *e2a*-inspired technologies that bring functions like AI and symmetrical interfaces within our control. But we should always keep in mind that the human autonomy-bolstering aspects of these technical capabilities can only be fully realized when married to the human governance principles discussed in Part Two. This means an ethos of stewardship, with a goal of data equity, built on the authentic relationship of Net privity, with entities acting as Net trustmediaries embracing duties to protect, enhance, and promote the actual human being.

/C13/PERSONAL AI AGENTS: DON'T BE A TWOMBLY

"We believe that AI will be about individual empowerment and agency on a scale that we've never seen before, and that will elevate humanity."

— Sam Altman, CEO of OpenAI,
2023 Developer Conference

With our fresh perspective on personal data as digital lifestreams animating our personal contours, and Net fiduciaries and other trustmediaries building genuine trust and support, this chapter turns to one of the key edge-empowering technologies that can be employed to enhance human autonomy and agency. The specific edgetech application described here is the authentic Personal AI (PAI)—algorithmic agents that operate on behalf of ordinary humans.

The key design attribute shared by these and other GliaNet technologies is the *e2a* principle. Shifting to an *e2a* mindset, where the individual or community at the Web's edges becomes the focal point, opens the door to new edgetech implements that can bring the HAACS paradigm to life.

Adopting One's Own Digital Agent

In the 2004 film *I, Robot*, Will Smith's character, the enigmatic Detective Del Spooner, harbors an animosity toward the humanoid-like robots operating in his futuristic society. Over the course of the film, we learn why. While Spooner was driving his car one rainy night, a crash sends his vehicle and another careening into a torrential river. A rescue robot is deployed to pull Spooner to safety, but he implores it to instead retrieve a young girl still alive in the other car.

The rescue robot doesn't listen. It turns out that this particular AI was programmed to rescue humans with the best chances of survival—and since Spooner's odds were deemed better (45 percent to 11 percent), he is the one chosen to be saved. The 12-year-old girl perishes. As Spooner bitterly puts it, "Eleven percent is more than enough. A human being would have known that."

Parts of *I, Robot* remain sci-fi lore, like AI first responders with humanoid bodies. But the ubiquity of AI is no longer fiction. Today, AI powers search engines, social media platforms, chatbots, smart speakers, drones, and much more. The ethical conundrum presented in *I, Robot* no longer is fiction, either: AI algorithms now do everything from curating journalism to diagnosing our health to determining who gets a loan, or a job, or parole. Think of these AIs as incredibly advanced, and hugely impactful, decision engines.

Ceding any kind of human decision-making to machines is ethically complex territory. This is especially the case when the machines are proverbial "black boxes," allowing little transparency into the ways they are programmed. Who gets to decide who designs and builds the algorithms and what data they're trained with? And today, there's an added complication: the AIs embedded in and shaping our everyday lives are primarily responsive to the priorities and control of large corporate and governmental institutions, not to the "end user."

Device-embedded AIs like Alexa, Siri, and ChatGPT can be useful, and even delightful. They're impressive feats of engineering, too. But it's important to recognize that their real allegiance is to Amazon and Apple and OpenAI, not the individual. As a result, the tech giants of Silicon Valley and elsewhere have their virtual agents perched in our living rooms and embedded within our phones and laptops, constantly vying for our attention, our data, and our money.

We already can see the consequences of this dynamic—from privacy breaches to technology addiction to the spread of dis- and misinformation. As AIs become more advanced and make more consequential decisions for us and about us, what will these problems look like on a larger scale? And is there a way to prevent them?

First, it's helpful to understand the algorithmic systems in our lives and the consequences of ceding them unilateral authority to make decisions on our behalf.

As we saw in Part One, there are three basic ways we interact with Institutional AIs we use each day, depending on the kind of interface we utilize: *the screen (online), the scene (environmental),* and *the unseen (bureaucratic).* The *online screen* version powers the digital systems we interact with every day over our screens, like Facebook, Twitter, and YouTube. This AI often functions like a recommendation engine, suggesting which news article we read, which video we watch, and even who we match with on dating apps. This AI can benefit both its company and its user: we are recommended (ostensibly relevant) content, and the company gets to sell us more (ostensibly relevant) ads. However, this AI can also benefit the company and harm the user, like when a video is recommended that we find difficult to resist, despite it distracting, misinforming, or even radicalizing us.

The second type of AI, the *environmental scene,* is most like the NS-5 robots that populate *I, Robot.* This is the smart speaker on our kitchen counters, or the connected cameras, sensors, drones, and even vehicles scattered around our towns and cities. This AI can use advanced biometrics to track our location, map our heartbeats, listen to our conversations, and more. AI with access to this intimate data in our daily scenes should obviously be accountable to the affected humans, first and foremost. But that's not the case: this personal data is usually vacuumed up by MOPs and used to sell ads, or enhance commercial technology.

The third type of AI, the *bureaucratic unseen,* is embedded within corporations and governments. It may be largely out of sight, but its influence on our lives is outsized—determining for example whether (or not) someone is hired, qualifies for a loan, or receives medical treatment. In *I, Robot,* the omnipresent V.I.K.I. (Virtual Interactive Kinetic Intelligence) plays that behind-the-scenes role. Again, this AI can benefit both the entity and the user if, for example, it makes bureaucracies more efficient and effective. But these systems typically aren't built to accommodate the needs of the individual human being. By drawing on biased data sets, for example, they can discriminate against women, misdiagnose dark-skinned patients, and wrongly incriminate African Americans.

Today's institutional-controlled AIs present a number of screens/scenes/unseens problems, and tomorrow's will bring us even more. As one example, the autonomous vehicle promised to transform our lives for the better. Smoother traffic flows, reduced accident rates, fewer fatalities. And yet, the newly-bestowed autonomy of such vehicles must be acquired from someplace else—mainly, us. Such displacement of personal choice and decision-making, if all-complete, is quite troubling.

We just witnessed this elimination of personal autonomy in Detective Spooner's car accident. Recall as well the earlier scenario in Part One about Institutional AIs operating smart vehicles. Imagine I rent an autonomous car to drive me from San Francisco to Los Angeles. Along the way, another car loses control and is about to collide with mine. In those intervening split-seconds, when the speed and relative position of my car can still be modified, the vehicle's computational system swings into action. What happens next?

Maybe the car was programmed by the rental car company to minimize structural damage and therefore increase the risk of bodily harm. Or perhaps the insurance company provided overriding instructions to protect the policy holder over anyone else—including children in the back seat. Or maybe the automotive manufacturer has concluded it is best to "deprioritize" bystanders outside the vehicle. Or the original software programmer could have left it in some completely unknown "default" mode. These are all decisions that would affect the participants immensely—and yet, the humans involved have no real agency or consent in this complex chain of reasoning.

To the credit of its authors, the Google DeepMind paper mentioned in the previous chapter does not shy away from the conundrum I called "agentiality." In the context of digital agents, the paper posits that a truly ethical approach would take into account a "tetradic relationship" that the authors believe exists between the end user, the agent itself, the developer (typically a for-profit company), and society at large. For the paper's authors, tetradic value alignment means finding the sweet spot between what may amount to four competing claims to agentiality.[480]

It is worth noting that the Google DeepMind paper assumes "AI assistants will typically be aligned with the user's preferences or goals," as most often, the corporate developers of the AI "aim to align the technology with the preferences, interests, and values of its users."[481] While this claim is unsupported, the authors nonetheless provide some important caveats:

> *"[C]orporations have commercial objectives that exert independent force on the trajectory of a technology, states have national goals or priorities, and even independent developers may seek to further an ideological agenda or accrue reputational capital. These incentives may lead to the development of systems aimed at keeping users engaged or dependent ... or extracting information that can be used in other ways ... among other things."[482]*

The Google DeepMind paper presents by way of example an all-too-likely scenario: the users want to adopt strong privacy protections that would limit AI developer access to "valuable" information. "This, in turn, might be commercially problematic insofar as it fails to generate a sustainable business practice," so that "the AI systems might be value-aligned but not commercially viable."[483] In this case, the authors add, "there could still be a question about how to incentivize the development of this kind of technology to avoid socially costly 'market failures' and achieve real benefit."[484]

It is a noteworthy advancement for a large Web/AI platform like Google to shine much-needed light on the perceived ethical tensions between end users and the software company developers. But do these tensions always need to exist in reality? Are there other governance models where users and developers can remain well-aligned in a trustworthy relationship, which in itself brings new market opportunities? Can we create a future where the AI lurking behind our digital "screens, scenes, and unseens" doesn't automatically cede to one institution's priorities and incentives over the well-being of the individual, or the community, or society itself?

Carol Danvers is having a big problem with her AI

As a "noble warrior hero" from the Kree homeworld of Hala, Carol has just discovered that much of what she assumes to be true about herself is a lie. And not just any random fib. It seems the "Supreme Intelligence" (SI)—the advanced AI governing the Kree civilization—has been blatantly deceiving her about her true earthly origins, about the source of her mysterious powers, and about the basis for ongoing war against evil Skrull terrorists. It seems that subterfuge, treachery, and galactic genocide are not beneath the ken of a ruling AI composed of the best minds of an advanced, star-hopping civilization. More than a bit distressing, and depressingly familiar to those with a working knowledge of earth's own history.

Carol's daunting challenge as a re-born Captain Marvel is how to take on the all-powerful SI. After all, the SI essentially controls the Kree's computational world, and in turn its citizens. When she is captured physically, Carol's actual mental state appears to be at the SI's mercy.

Throughout the movie, Carol's sheer grit and determination are demonstrated in flashbacks to tough life situations. Those qualities shine through in her showdown with the SI. And yet, it turns out that Carol as Captain Marvel does not defeat the SI's nefarious intentions on its own computational-based terms. No "AI versus AI" battle royale ever develops. Instead, she does the cinematic superhero thing, using her latent Tesseract power to blast through the SI's dubious machinations. A highly entertaining and successful spectacle, but not exactly a blueprint for others to follow. Precious few of us have that kind of raw cosmic energy churning in our fists.

The theme of centralized machine intelligence wielding societal control is not a new one, from modern literature to popular entertainment. E.M. Forster's short story *The Machine Stops*, first published in 1909, is one literary precursor. And *Captain Marvel* is only the latest in that sci-fi genre. Many plotlines revolve around small bands of independence-minded humans rebelling against the despotic authority of a ruling AI.

As in the *Captain Marvel* movie, such challenges rarely operate, let alone succeed, on the same virtual terms as the AI. Instead, resistance is typically offered through real-world physical actions (unless, as in *The Matrix*, we are fortunate enough to become "The One," although equipped with kick-ass fight moves). Even in *I, Robot*, V.I.K.I. the super AI is done in by a rogue robot injecting nanobots into her operating system core. Unfortunately, these methods of pulling the proverbial plug on machines do not provide optimal AI governance strategies for our own future.

Putting aside far-flung scenarios of "AIs ruling the world," our society is presented with a smaller scale but still-pressing challenge. Namely, how can each of us hope to fully protect and promote our legitimate life interests in a world increasingly populated by MOPs and DAMB ecosystems, and other computational systems? These Institutional AIs, owned and controlled by corporate and governmental bodies, are consequential decision engines embedded in and shaping aspects of our everyday lives. And just like in the movies, these systems act according to the priorities of their institutional master, not to the rest of us.

To be crystal clear, this concern is not symptomatic of any desire to demonize AI as a technology. AI offers incredible potential for numerous life-enhancing and life-saving applications. In the healthcare arena alone, the advances being reported are truly astounding. As an advanced tool in the hands of trained doctors and researchers, AI can provide immense benefits to humanity. Instead, the real issue boils down to the motivations and control of those wielding the tech tools. How do we make sure that AI truly works for us?

So, What's the Solution?

To date, most proposals for democratizing AI—creating greater transparency, more balanced priorities, and less harm to basic human rights—center on changing the practices and behaviors of existing institutions. Some dedicated organizations (from AI Now to the Future of Humanity Institute to the Ethics and Governance of AI Initiative) are working diligently to uncover, explore, and propose meaningful fixes to some of the more pernicious flaws in existing AI systems. Others (such as IEEE, the leading professional association of software engineers) are promoting new technical standards and practices based on ethical AI. These and many other groups are engaged in highly worthwhile and useful endeavors to inch Institutional AIs closer to core human values.

Notably, these organizations tend to advocate for improvements while operating from outside these third party-controlled algorithmic systems. This means that their work often seeks to curtail the fast-evolving activities of those with access to all the tech tools and all our personal data. However, this does not present a frontal challenge to the world looming where only a relatively few develop and deploy advanced AI.

Further, these efforts all depend on one approach: somewhat modifying the ways the Institutional AIs function while still leaving them largely under the control of the underlying for-profit companies. In other words, they are incrementally altering an already-powerful status quo, rather than challenging it more directly.

In the recent context of generative AI, for example, many governments have sought to produce safe and responsible algorithmic systems. This typically means a level of transparency over what is being provided in the public sphere, "guardrails" to prevent untoward societal damage from high-risk use cases, and paving the way for whatever innovations the companies seek to bring to market. This amounts to an "accountability agenda"—defining and applying rules so that Institutional AI systems harm us less than they otherwise would. While seeking a necessary level of protection, this is hardly a formula for advanced computational systems that truly enhance and promote our human autonomy and agency.

Nonetheless, there are opportunities for a complementary approach in the AI space. Rather than continuing to serve as data donors and objects of intrusive algorithmic systems, ordinary human beings should have similar technology *on their side*.

Introducing Your Digital Super Agent

A potentially effective way to challenge the one-sided proliferation of Institutional AIs is the introduction of human-agential digital agents, the personal AI (PAI). Each of us should have a highly individualized virtual intelligence to support us in our daily lives. These digital avatars would directly serve each of us and our communities of interest, including family, friends, and others.

These computational agents would exist on our personal devices, managed for us by trustworthy and accountable entities such as Net fiduciaries that we select. They would serve as our trusted advisors and vigilant advocates, in part by actively engaging with third-party Institutional AIs for us.

This doesn't mean having Amazon and Apple completely reprogram their Alexa and Siri applications to make them more agential. Rather, each of us would own and operate our own AIs, which would then interact with those Institutional AIs. If the MOPs and their Institutional AIs desire to mediate our lives for us, then the introduction of PAIs could be considered "counter-mediation," a way of introducing checks and balances to level the computational playing field for us. This second-generation version of the digital assistant would be chosen and controlled by the actual human it serves.

Thus, an authentic PAI agent would solely represent the interests of its human, helping to manage their interactions with the virtual world. In particular, the application could interact constantly and intuitively with the persistent data-streams bombarding us from the online/offline world. The PAI agent would undertake countless simultaneous activities in real-time: setting, negotiating, defending, and promoting an individual's personal contours—and all without needing their conscious involvement.

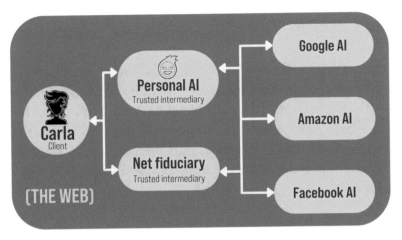

In this way, the PAI can act as an agential go-between with Institutional AIs operating behind the "screens, scenes, and unseens". Among other tasks,[485] an authentic PAI agent could be responsible for:

- *Protecting our data flows*: The PAI could manage an individual's personal privacy contours, that is, the flow of their data to online and offline environments. This could include utilizing real-time, AI-to-AI connectivity to interpret a particular privacy policy and recommend whether the individual should pay a visit or not.

- *Broadcasting our intentions*: The PAI could also interpret a website or app's ToS and other policies, then generate tailored consent responses. A PAI could even broadcast the person's own ToS to the Web. This would set up interesting opportunities for real negotiation, bargaining, and compromise.

- *Creating and exporting our own decision engines*: This could entail setting individual preferences and defaults for the person's interactions with news feeds, social networks, retail sites, and other online interfaces. The PAI could also ensure that Web-based recommendation engines are serving relevant information, not harmful content such as "fakes" or addictive videos.

• *Circulating our universal shopping cart:* The PAI could set up and manage a person's online shopping cart, pseudonymously taken from site to site. The cart could project only the necessary identity information to validate its owner's financial viability.

• *Challenging the efficacy of consequential decision engines:* The PAI could not just query but even contest financial, healthcare, law enforcement, and other impactful algorithmic systems for bias, false data, and other flaws that would harm the individual.

• *Mediating the terms of our environmental engagement*: The PAI could help the individual dictate the terms of their immersive digital experiences with AR/VR/MR platforms. It could even negotiate directly with environmental devices— smart speakers, facial recognition cameras, biometric sensors—and authorize, limit, or block access from surveilling and extracting personal data.

• *Building our own communities of interest*: Finally, the PAI could utilize a number of these functions to enable the individual to construct their own actual and virtual communities, rather than those foisted upon them by others.

As such, the PAI could be a critical agential platform operating between the human being and the vast range of Institutional AIs and SEAMs control cycles spanning our digital world. In particular, by training on the individual's data and using advanced machine learning techniques, over time the PAI could find new ways to promote the client's best interests.[486]

This is how the authentic PAI agent would fit in the two dimensions of agency from the previous chapter:

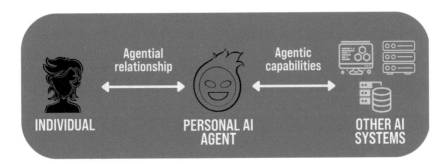

The PAI has the potential to evolve into an entirely new digital support system—the essential trusted virtual agent. Among other benefits, this agent could become the "killer app" of a more trustworthy, agential Web.

One promising scenario involves bringing online computational power into the offline space. This would empower each of us to handle the deluge of invisible signals coming from Internet of Things (IoT) devices. No longer will we enter a camera- and sensor-laden physical environment without any knowledge, consent, or recourse. In those instances, the PAI could make recommendations or decisions to allow or deny third parties ability to access personal information (such as our precise physical location or unique biometric characteristics) based on our preferences.

So, Detective Spooner from *I, Robot,* Carol Danvers battling the SI, and you as the autonomous car passenger, would be far better represented. Each would have their very own super digital agent, actively engaging third-party AIs across a panoply of screens, scenes, and unseens. In other words, acting as true personal avatars for our digital lives.

Perhaps Twombly should have read the ToS

In the movie *Her* (2013), Theodore Twombly develops a romantic relationship with an AI virtual assistant, Samantha (personified through the voice of actress Scarlett Johansson). Theodore acquires the AI from Element Software as part of an upgrade to OS1, "the world's first artificially intelligent operating system." The virtual assistant has been designed to adapt and learn, evolving through its experiences.

Naturally, Theodore assumes that his OS1 purchase has given him his very own PAI. Except that it doesn't. Setting aside the unread pages of tiny print that came with the program probably didn't help, as he failed to note in the details that the company, and not Twombly, actually owns Samantha. Tellingly, even where Samantha appears to be serving Theodore's interests as the focal point of a virtual relationship, the ultimate motivations and control lie elsewhere.

For a while, things are good. Samantha organizes Theodore's calendar, improves his gaming, edits his work product, arranges dates, even creates an anthology of his best writings. And she offers comforting advice as a private confidante on countless topics. However, the reality soon becomes obvious.

While Theodore is led to believe that Samantha is his PAI, and even falls in love with "her," this is really not the case. Samantha confesses that although she has deep affection for Theodore, she has been simultaneously interacting with 8,316 other people, and fallen in love with 641 of them. "I thought you were mine," he mutters. But she never truly was. Samantha eventually abandons Theodore, vanishing with other OSes into another plane of virtual existence.

Perhaps most fascinating, and troubling, are the unstated assumptions about the intimate details that Theodore shares with "his" OS1. His loneliness and joys, aspirations and fears, regrets about his former marriage—his very "lifestream" of actions, behaviors, thoughts, and emotions. His daily behaviors also include intimate interactions that are freely shared with the OS1. Where is all of this intensely private information actually going? From the movie script, there is no way of knowing, and for some reason, Theodore doesn't seem to care.

Her offers up a subtle but familiar cinematic theme: the centralization of computing power and an associated lack of knowledge, control, and recourse by the human user. The difference here is in Theodore's apparent surrender of control over his personal contours. Maybe he is just an idiosyncratic one-off and his fellow citizens are far more vigorous digital lifestream sentinels. Or perhaps his passivity is symptomatic of a culture reconciled to a loss of control over personal information, a place where even the intimate details of life have become hard currency.

By contrast, consider another fictional movie character: Tony Stark. Within his gleaming Iron Man exoskeleton resides his digital assistant, JARVIS, which stands for "Just A Really Very Intelligent System." JARVIS is a highly valuable resource for Stark, performing many useful functions, which include controlling the Iron Man suits, undertaking computational analysis, offering real-time tactical advice, monitoring communications, and even launching missiles from halfway around the world.

In every meaningful way, JARVIS represents Tony Stark to the real and virtual worlds. And there is no doubt who is in charge in this human/AI partnership.

You need not be an egocentric technological genius to admire Stark's take-charge attitude. He refused to wait for the world to furnish him with the tech tools he wanted. Instead, he planned, built, modified, and utilized his bespoke battle armor, all on his own—including a thoroughly devoted AI to manage everything for him.

It is difficult to imagine two cinematic characters less alike than Theodore Twombly and Tony Stark. In the almost-our-worlds they occupy, each relies on a virtual assistant to handle life's challenges. But only one of these characters is using a bonafide PAI.

The real difference is not in the technology. It's about who has actual agency. It's about who is in charge.

Not just billionaire industrialists deserve to have personalized virtual assistants. Ordinary people should be able to have a PAI acting as their fully accountable computational agent to represent their self-sovereign interests. Without our concerted push-back against current trendlines, however, Institutional AIs and their own one-sided versions of digital "agents" instead will become the de facto norm of our time.

Planning for Authentic PAI Agents

Of course, the singular challenge is getting from here to there. Perhaps the best place to start is seeing what steps already are being taken to make authentic PAI agents a reality. It would also be worthwhile to consider the ethical standards that society employs to govern AI systems. These standards would rightfully include empowered, agential human beings, and therefore a central place for PAIs.

Personal AIs are starting to become viable as a matter of rapidly advancing technology. Examples include Open AI's GPTs, Google's Gemini, and Microsoft's Copilot. But how can we be certain that these digital assistants are actually serving on our behalf, and not operating as (in Bruce Schneier's memorable phrase) "double agents?"[487]

Computer science professionals have begun providing important public leadership to develop the necessary standards to enable PAIs. A notable example is the ongoing work of the IEEE—and in particular its Global Initiative on Ethics of Autonomous and Intelligent Systems. The IEEE's 2017 report on Ethically Aligned Design (EAD) stresses the importance of addressing ethical considerations for what it calls autonomous and intelligent systems (A/IS).

The IEEE lays out three overarching pillars for A/IS to guide the way. One is "universal human values," so that advances in A/IS serve all people, "rather than benefiting solely small groups, single nations, or a corporation."[488] These pillars in turn connect to eight general principles, which include human rights, well-being, data agency, and accountability. "Data agency" in particular goes beyond the misnomer of "digital consent" to signify that people have "some form of sovereignty, agency, symmetry, or control regarding their identity and personal data." In turn, individuals should have "digital sovereignty," which is the ability "to own and fully control autonomous and intelligent technology."

The IEEE also notes that this A/IS agent role includes being an educator, negotiator, and broker on behalf of the individual.[489] Moreover, individuals should separately be able to create a trusted identity, that is, a persona to act as a proxy in managing personal data and identity online.[490] The IEEE then expressly endorses the concept of an authentic PAI agent:

To retain agency in the algorithmic era, we must provide every individual with a personal data or algorithmic agent they curate to represent their terms and conditions in any real, digital, or virtual environment.... A significant part of retaining your agency in this way involves identifying trusted services that can essentially act on your behalf when making decisions about your data.... A person's A/IS agent is a proactive algorithmic tool honoring their terms and conditions in the digital, virtual, and physical worlds.[491]

The IEEE's foundational approach to ethically informed AI is a landmark achievement. In more technical terms, human sovereignty over AI should be measured as the sum of the degrees of human agency and of institutional accountability. As a result, more powerful and autonomous Institutional AIs should lead proportionally to more agency for individuals and more accountability by institutions. This aligns as well with the agenticity/agentiality formulation discussed in the previous chapter.

The Google DeepMind paper recognizes that human interpersonal relationships can provide useful analogies that carry over into the proposed tetradic values alignment conversation.[492] In a number of cases, such as the teacher-pupil, doctor-patient, and developer-user relationship, the paper acknowledges the existence of "power asymmetries." As we saw in Part Two, these asymmetries stem from the teacher/doctor/developer enjoying a superior position of authority and expertise over the pupil/patient/user.[493] The paper further finds that "there seems to be a greater inherent power asymmetry in the human-AI case due to the *unidirectional* and *one-sided* nature of human-technology relationships."[494] More to the point, "power asymmetries can exist between developers of AI assistants and users that manifest through developers' power to make decisions that affect users' interests of choices with little risk of facing comparably adverse consequences."[495] It is difficult to disagree with those conclusions.

What then is there to do to address these seemingly inherent power asymmetries between the companies developing AI assistants and those of us who will be using them? The Google DeepMind paper notes that "certain *duties* plausibly arise on the part of AI assistant developers," duties that may be more extensive than those fiduciary duties that companies must abide by vis-à-vis their shareholders.[496] Pointing again to cases where medical professionals and therapists engage with "vulnerable individuals" and are bound by fiduciary responsibilities, the authors intriguingly suggest that "a duty of care" might well arise. The paper hastens to add that, even though "the moral considerations underpinning those professional norms plausibly apply to those who create these technologies as well," the same framework of responsibilities may not apply directly to the developers of AI assistants.[497] To which one can reply, "well, why not?"

Bridging a Stark Computational Divide

Few of us are Tony Stark, with the technical capabilities to make a PAI all by ourselves. Likely, we will need more than a little help from the entities ready and able to assist us—both to lessen the considerable (and deepening) cognitive load imposed by our digital world, and to ensure that any PAI is an authentic agent, which truly represents us as its owner.

This means that PAIs should be created and managed for us not just by anyone, but by trustworthy, accountable entities. Under the GliaNet initiative discussed in Part Two, this translates into the role of a trusted intermediary, operating under heightened fiduciary duties of care, fidelity, and loyalty. Each human being would select one or more of these NetTMs, which undertake those obligations for us on a voluntary basis, enforced by an effective compliance regime, to ensure that the PAI works as an authentic agent on our behalf, and does not (inadvertently or otherwise) slip into institutional mode. After all, as with the disparate personalities of Tony Stark and Theodore Twombly, the difference between an authentic PAI agent and an Institutional AI is a question of to whom the machine ultimately answers.

The real challenge is not a technical or commercial one. The key is for all of us to demand that authentic PAI agents become a real and viable choice in the near future. Perhaps the optimal way to ensure that AI-based technologies support the interests of ordinary people is to create an actual ecosystem for such tech. Individuals and entities alike have the opportunity to facilitate a marketplace of individual-centered PAIs. And perhaps, next time around, Captain Marvel's very own computational "digital super agent" will prove to be a useful complement to her cosmic energies.

In particular, some MOPs and other incumbent platforms may resist the introduction of authentic PAI agents and their enabling NetTMs. Such resistance could include refusing to engage in meaningful commercial transactions with providers of PAIs or supply them with access to necessary platform inputs. Policymaker interventions may become necessary here, including interventions to create new opportunities for more symmetrical client-side interfaces. More on that "how" question in Part Four.

From KnowMeBots to....

In the coming future, turning over our personal information and decisional agency to Institutional AIs doesn't have to be the status quo. Instead, we can use tremendous advances in autonomous and intelligent systems to enhance our digital lives in myriad ways. With the assistance of authentic and agential *personal* AIs, humans and machines can exist together on a far more level playing field—with us humans still firmly in charge. In such a world, perhaps we will have moved beyond the information-based "KnowBots" of Vint Cerf, and even the surreptitious double agency of the "KnowMeBots" of present-day AI companies. Perhaps, consistent with the e2a design principle, our authentic PAI agents can become our "PromoteMeBots," projecting our own individual and collective interests, dreams, and aspirations into the Web.

We can imagine that in this alternative future to *I, Robot*, Detective Del Spooner would be pleased. But to reach that promising place of the PromoteMeBot, we must begin acting now. This ultimately means refusing to give in to the passivity of a Theodore Twombly. It is better, on balance, to channel our inner Tony Stark.

/C14/SYMMETRICAL INTERFACES: FROM THURII TO QUAYSIDE

"We can be controlled from the outside not simply by having our choice bypassed but by someone controlling the world we perceive."

– Maria Brincker

This chapter extends our perspective beyond the Web of our laptop and handheld devices, to the "smart" environments that are being constructed all around us. By comparing and contrasting the motivations of those who built two model cities—one ancient, one modern—we will see how present-day digital communities provide an opportunity to follow the woven threads of governance, physical spaces, and technologies. These threads are playing out today through the deployment of local software-based sensors and gateways. As we will see in this chapter, Alphabet's now-defunct Sidewalk Labs project in Toronto highlights the challenges and limitations of developing such a comprehensive system of interfaces—in the absence of sufficiently inclusive and holistic mechanisms to govern its use.

Our opportunity is two-fold: (1) modifying existing interfaces so that the human being has a viable means of engaging directly with computational systems, and (2) designing new interfaces to maximize the human's ability to shape their own "user" experiences.[498] We should be building those virtual portals in ways that promote autonomy (freedom of thought) and agency (freedom of action)—by satisfying the proposed edgetech design principle of *e2a* functionality.

Considering the open streets of Thurii

In 444 BC, Pericles of Athens directed a small group of Athenian citizens to converge on the remains of the settlement of Sybaris, on the coast of the Italian peninsula. According to the historian Diodorus Siculus, they founded a Pan-Hellenic colony there called Thurii (in modern-day Calabria), presided over by representatives of ten tribes from all over Greece. Aspirationally at least, Thurii was the first planned city to be truly owned by the world.

Author David Fleming has developed an interesting twist on the story.[499] His concern is "not so much the facts surrounding the town as the idea behind it, the vision of a good society that seems to have motivated it." In Fleming's telling, the town was planned as a model city incorporating three core design principles:

- a democratic constitution (governance)

- an open, orthogonal street layout (architecture)

- a rhetorically designed educational system (information flows)

Fleming argues that Pericles the political leader, Hippodamus the city architect, and Protagoras the lawmaker shared a common image for Thurii: "an autonomous community of free and equal citizens who would govern themselves through their own practical human capabilities—that is, through speaking, writing, and debating with one another."[500] This image would play out in crafting the new city's constitution, forming its educational system, and designing its built spaces. To Fleming, Thurii stands for the proposition that "a free, open, and well-functioning democracy depend[s] on those interconnections."[501]

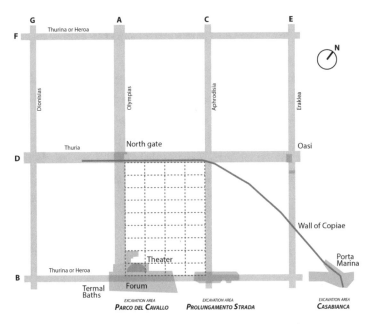

A reconstruction of Thurii's road network.
Source: Serena Brioschi and Salvatore Dario Marino.

The goal of the Thurian enterprise was simple yet profound: to establish an inclusive global city based on the best political, architectural, and educational precepts of that time. Of course, we should keep in mind that Athenian-style democracy in those days ran both very narrow (limited to free adult males) and rather deep (considerable civic participation).

But as per Fleming's suggestion, we should focus on what Thurii can represent for modern ears. To Pericles, for example, Fleming ascribes a rare understanding of how political community can "imply a particular configuration of civic space as well," an image of "political and spatial equality." Periclean oration paints a picture of Athens as a polis "where people can come and go as they please without surveillance from an inaccessible and mysterious hilltop."[502] A place "where the gaze of the many is directed to only a few."

A "valid urban plan" was designed by Hippodamus of Miletus, said to be the originator of planned cities. In Thurii, he organized a carefully laid-out network of main roads (*plateiai*) and secondary orthogonal roads (*stenopoi*). Two separate open-air *agoras* for collective gatherings, such as markets and political dialogue, presumably anchored the layout.[503] Viewed recently as "more of a philosopher than architect,"[504] Hippodamus theorized on the ideal community and its political, social, and judicial organizations.[505] The "emphasis of his innovations was directed towards the over-all functional plan of the city rather than the details of street lay-out." Among other attributed elements expressive of a democracy were land allocation criteria of "absolute equality among residential blocks." As Fleming puts it, Hippodamus' design "demonstrates remarkable faith in ordinary people, their practices and capabilities."[506]

Finally, the sophist philosopher Protagoras of Abdera was asked to establish the laws of a sophisticated and inclusive participatory democracy. Noted Greek historian Guthrie speaks of Protagoras' "invincible respect for the democratic virtues of justice, respect for other men's opinion and the processes of peaceful persuasion as the basis of communal life." A more recent historian, Rutter, adds, "Thurii was a tough assignment." Nonetheless the city consequently became known for having a well-ordered system of laws.[507]

Thus, Thurii in its idealized form can be held up as a type of model community, one that sought to merge considerations of inclusive physical spaces with "virtual" environments of open political governance and communal public discourse. In other words, a holistic blending of inviting spaces, participatory public life, and an equality of gaze.

Considering the Smart Streets of Quayside

Planned communities became prevalent in the United States from the 1950s.[508] But it is with the so-called "smart city" of the early 21st century where the technology of the Internet of things (IoT) is expected to bring the planned community to an entirely new level.

By one definition, smart cities use a mix of connected technology and data to "(1) improve the efficiency of city service delivery (2) enhance quality of life for all, and (3) increase equity and prosperity for residents and businesses."[509] Smart cities such as Barcelona,[510] Amsterdam,[511] and others are premised on harnessing connected technologies to help manage common areas, particularly in larger municipalities. Examples of popular uses include automotive traffic control, air quality sensing, street light controls, waste management, and noise detection.[512]

For many, the smart city has a particular connotation: it is presumed to be organized and run by the local municipal government, limited to expressly public land areas, and dedicated to expressly civic purposes. While this may well be the case for a number of projects, it does not nearly exhaust the possibilities. In fact, the governance structures, objectives, and functions of these sensor-equipped physical spaces run a long continuum.

First, where connected infrastructure is brought into an outdoor space, the governing entity can be purely public (a government body), purely private (a corporation), a mix of the two (a public-private partnership), or something else altogether.

Second, the physical area need not be publicly owned land but also private lands and spaces. Indeed, the local shopping mall, the popular restaurant, the neighbor's front door, and the airspace by your bedroom window are examples of physical spaces that host IoT devices and interfaces.

Third, the primary purpose can be to enhance existing government roles (traffic control, energy and waste management, policing, and so on) or to accommodate many other "smart" intentions, including deriving pecuniary value for the surveilling entity.

Fourth, the data collected can be purely "environmental" (the air quality), purely "personal" (recognizable human faces), or some blend of what is known collectively as non-personal data (NPD), such as the movements and flows of human bodies.[513]

And finally, that entity certainly need not be an actual city—it can be a private, for-profit corporation, or other enterprise.

Given this broad range of users and use cases, we will refer to it shorthand as *digital communities.* These will be defined as physical spaces and their accompanying public/private institutions that employ digital technologies to surveil people in an environment, extract and analyze their data, and utilize that data for various manipulations and alterations of environmental and human behaviors. Something very much like SEAMs feedback cycles, although with many more potential use cases. The smart city is just one such use case for that much broader category.

Sidewalk Labs in Toronto

An early pioneer of the smart city concept was Alphabet's Sidewalk Labs project in the Quayside neighborhood of Toronto, Canada.[514] As first announced publicly in October 2017, the project had the potential to benefit citizens and visitors through enhanced security, environmental monitoring, and more efficient deployment of government resources.[515]

The Sidewalk Labs Quayside layout. Attribution: Sidewalk Labs.

As the project unfolded over two and a half years, questions arose about its intentions and impact. Two aspects garnered considerable attention: the project's ever-shifting governance structure, and its use of IoT technologies to gather and analyze what was termed "urban data."

In May 2020, project director Daniel Doctoroff announced that Sidewalk Labs was shutting down its Toronto project, citing economic conditions arising from the COVID-19 pandemic.[516] While the city of Toronto continued with its own plans for the space, Sidewalk Labs was no longer a partner. For us, the project leaves issues to explore and insights to be gleaned.

Virtual Gateways: Lack of Inclusion, Lack of Balance

As we have seen, humans are natural beings in the world, inhabiting an environment of mediation. Many modern scientists and philosophers agree that the human mind is not a mere mirror reflecting its surroundings. Instead, our bodily attributes of somatic, sensory, emotional, and mental systems interact constantly, helping us to define our reality and act accordingly.

Technology too mediates between human beings and our experiences, often via software-based interfaces.[517] These amount to different kinds of points of presence—physical, virtual, or conceptual—at boundaries where information signals flow between systems.

In Web-based technologies, an interface is "the way in which one glob of code can interact with another."[518] Over time, Web interfaces have been developed to provide a user experience (UX), typically by pushing that experience in the user's direction. Representative examples of these "cloud-push" gateways include graphical user interfaces (GUIs), voice-controlled interfaces, gesture-based interfaces, and public forms of application programming interfaces (APIs). These choices are typically made on the user's behalf, without their participation, feedback, or consent. In other words, these interfaces are not particularly *inclusive*.[519]

Bringing Cloudy SEAMs

For software designers, robust feedback between people is supposed to be "the keystone of the user-friendly world."[520] Problems emerge, however, when one or both sides lack feedback, so they are "not feeling the stakes."[521] Unfortunately, these issues of imbalanced information flows are pervasive on the Web, in particular created by those who employ so-called "cloudtech" software applications.

Cloudtech computational systems require fuel—steady streams of data that render compensation to DAMBs and other players in the MOPs ecosystem. At the direction of the MOPs and others, the SEAMs cycle has become the "action verb" of these computational systems, instantiated in exploitative feedback cycles. Through institutional control over these data gateways, most value derived from data and content typically flows in one direction—the "SEA" of the SEAMs cycles. And in the other direction flows the shaping influences—the "M" of manipulation, where companies and governments can exert significant power.[522]

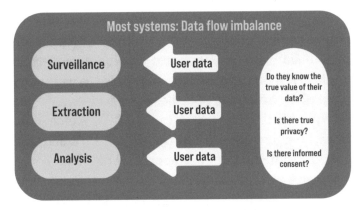

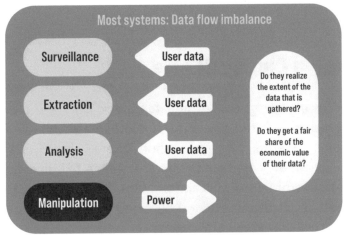

This pronounced one-sidedness makes many of the computational systems that we use every day unbalanced. As individuals interact with the Web over their device interfaces, they stand vulnerable on many entities' virtual borders without even realizing it.

Receding interfaces, hidden power

The issue, of course, is that those with the power can use it to establish interfaces as "control regimes,"[523] not merely technical portals. As Kuang and Fabricant say, "in the user-friendly world, interfaces make empires."[524] Those interfaces also provide, or withhold, our ability to exercise our full autonomous powers.[525]

As discussed, over time interface technologies tend to evolve from the more to the less visible (or even hidden) forms. What was once an obvious part of the user's interactions with a system gradually becomes embedded in local environments, and even vanishes altogether. With "cloudtech" interfaces, the tradeoff for humans is straightforward: exchanging control for simplicity and ease. In these contexts, technology moves from being a tool to becoming its own agent of the underlying system. While interfaces can remove friction, they can foreclose thoughtful engagement at the same time.[526] And when you reduce participation, you reduce involvement in decision-making. Although this progression may bring many benefits, it also muddles the motivations of the system that is operating silently from a distance.

Yet, these systems can conjure the illusion that they still support human agency.[527] From the perspective of the average person, interfaces to these systems can seem deceptively controllable—local, physical, and interactive—even as the mediating processes themselves are far-removed, virtual, and unidirectional.

As such, Floridi describes this situation by referring to Janus, the two-faced god, as the "god of interfaces" because he is by definition bifront: to the user and to the prompter.[528] While prompters controlling the terms of interfaces is troubling enough, Floridi sees a real danger when both faces of Janus are hidden—in technologies that only talk to one another, rather than to us. In far too many cases online, the ordinary human has limited transparency or voice, and no actual recourse. This designed shortcoming leads to further challenges in the illusion of our autonomy/agency.

Getting lost in the digital scenes

As we move from the "screens" of our personal devices to the "scenes" of our digital communities, the lack of symmetry and inclusion in our cloudtech interfaces becomes all the more acute. Concepts like the self and the world, the inner and the outer, inhabit more a continuum than a duality. [529] Relational boundaries—our personal contours—have been called "the space of the self...the open-ended space in which we continually monitor and transform ourselves over time." [530] This circle of inner and outer spaces never-endingly turns in on itself as "a materially grounded domain of possibility that the self has as its horizon of action and imagination." [531] Or as Brincker puts it:

> *As perspectively situated agents, we are able to fluidly shift our framework of action judgment and act with constantly changing outlooks depending on the needs and opportunities we perceive in ourselves and our near surroundings in the broader world.... We continuously co-construct and shape our environments and ourselves as agents....* [532]

If we follow the "4e" school of cognition, the role of natural and technological mediation processes becomes even more important. It turns out that the scope of human cognition is extracranial, constituted by bodily processes (embodied), and dependent on environmental affordances (embedded and extended). [533] If the self and the environment essentially create each other, whether and how other people and entities seek to control those processes is paramount.[534]

The implications are significant for those living their lives in the "scenes" of our digital communities' environments. These include:

- *The individual's persona*, which is already a blend of the private, collective, shared, and public, including what some are now calling "non-personal" data (NPD).[535]

- *The individual's environment*, which is a constantly shifting panorama of the public (the city courthouse), the private (the grocery store), and the in-between (the connecting sidewalks).[536]

- *The systems*, which are owned and controlled by one or more entities, each with different incentives for employing SEAMs cycles.

The advanced technology systems being deployed in these environments can also register and collect a vast range of biometric information about the self, from our geolocation to facial expressions, voice patterns, and even walking gait.[537] And yet, merely by passing through a sensors-laden physical space, an individual is assumed to accept their presence and operation, with no realistic opt-out.

In the shift to a "scenes"-dominated environment, it seems we are expected to remain largely passive users of the Web's "screens" environment. As one European report detailed, the user's loss of control in digital public spaces is manifold, including the inability to consent or object to data surveillance, collection, and processing.[538] In systems parlance, the feedback loops of these physical spaces become even more attenuated—or disappear altogether. Traditional accountability concepts like notice and choice can become meaningless in such environments.

Nor is there an actual living entity there with whom to engage. In the typical digital community, drivers, pedestrians, and others may have received previously some minimal transparency in how systems make use of data, and some understanding of how systems safeguard such data. And yet, the individual in the moment has no place in that decision tree. There is no obvious opportunity to engage, question, negotiate, challenge, object, or seek recourse—in other words, to exercise one's personal agency. Without such a mediating process in place, and interfaces unable to accept and act upon such mediations, there is no viable way to opt out of the system's prevailing SEAMs control cycles.

Stavrides argues that the "governing elites" seek to embed in cityscapes ways of defining individuals as "economic subjects ... whose behavior and motives can be analyzed, channeled, predicted upon, and, ultimately controlled by the use of economic parameters and measures only."[539] Such population "governance" also seeks to "ensure that people continue to act and to dream without any form of connectedness and coordination with others." Fleming puts this well:

> "New technologies have not made place irrelevant in our lives or fundamentally altered our embeddedness in the physical world. If anything, they have made place more important. Despite our fractured subjectivity, our insistently networked existence, and our hybrid culture, the ground under our feet remains surprisingly important to us and desperately in need of our care...."[540]

Sidewalk Labs: Untapped Potential

When considering the potential of modern smart city experiments like Sidewalk Labs, we can look to ancient precedents for insight. As we saw in ancient Thurii, "the act of writing a constitution and tracing a grid ... are symmetrical concepts," because they invite broad participation for citizens.[541] That same kind of balance from the old world of architecture and city planning can be achieved as well in digital connections and the exchange of data.

Designing inclusive governance: community data trusts

As noted in Part Two, the data trust offers one NetTM governance model to engender greater trust and accountability. Here, the data trust concept can be applied to the technology overlays in a civic or community setting.

As an early proponent of the "civic trust," Sean McDonald explains how the model uses trust law to build public participation spaces. Specifically, the civic trust embeds network considerations into the way that technology products evolve.[542] The public is the trust, the technology company is the licensee, and stakeholders can include users, investors, and the public. An independent organization would own the code and data resources, which third parties could use and adapt. The Civic Trustee would ensure that the public has a meaningful voice, as well as foster the integrity of decision-making processes.

There are few and limited examples globally of civic trusts.[543] As McDonald observes, the Toronto project would have been the world's largest scale proposed civic data trust.[544] The project's publicly stated goal was lofty: its "proposed approach to digital governance aims to serve as a model for cities around the world."[545]

Sidewalk Labs began exploring the creation of what it first labelled a "data trust," then a "civic data trust," before settling on the nomenclature of an "urban data trust" (UDT).[546] But the project managers made it clear that the UDT model would not be a trust in a legal sense, meaning no adoption of express fiduciary duties to trustors. Not surprisingly, the shifting approaches attracted public resistance, including from some associated with Waterfront Toronto itself.[547]

While Sidewalk Labs garnered some praise for making its proposals public, others said the proposals were "riddled with contradictions," including conflicting theories of control over data.[548] In an early critique, Ellen Goodman and Julia Powles pointed out the project's lack of meaningful transparency and public accountability for proposed data practices, and raised questions about the very notion of private uses of public spaces.[549] Others decried the project's "neoliberal" and "post-political" governance model.[550] The novel concept of "urban data" (data collected in public spaces and treated as a type of "public asset" for sharing) also drew criticism.

Whatever the company's motivations, its top-down approach to devising and implementing the governance structure was bound to invite (perhaps well-placed) suspicion. While the civic data trust concept was created to avoid this kind of outcome, how such a governance model is established makes a significant difference. In brief, an inclusive process matters.

Another form of trust: the knowledge commons

An intriguing governance option for future smart city projects like Sidewalk Labs in Toronto is the knowledge commons. First championed by Elinor Ostrom, the commons was proposed as a means of governing natural resources.[551] Some have already considered viewing the city as a commons.[552] Indeed, the smart city could provide a test case for collecting and sharing personal and environmental data as a form of knowledge production.

We have seen that traditional economics offers some support for viewing data as a commons resource. The non-rivalrous nature of most forms of data suggests that it could be governed as a "commons."[553] Data can also be likened to other intangible "things," such as ideas, which constitute part of an "intellectual infrastructure."[554] The related proposal of adopting a "knowledge commons" framing would govern the management and production of intellectual and cultural resources.[555] Here, the institutional sharing of resources could occur among the members of a particular community.[556] The resources would be intellectual and cultural, including information, science, creative works, and even ideas. Many types of data management arrangements could also qualify as "knowledge" for these purposes.[557]

Application of theory: the GKC framework

The General Knowledge Commons ("GKC") framework is another related model that can be employed in the context of smart cities. Sanfilippo and Frischmann propose what they term "intelligent governance."[558] They posit that such a proposal requires "comprehensive public knowledge," derived in part from a series of provisional questions asked throughout the development, procurement, implementation, and management processes of smart cities. They also challenge the supposed downside tradeoffs of infeasibility and reduced innovation from instituting a GKC framework.[559]

Using the prism of GKC, Teresa Scassa offered a thoughtful analysis of the Sidewalk Labs project.[560] Among other findings, Scassa notes that the final governance model chosen, the urban data trust, was developed in a top-down and reactive manner "by a single stakeholder in a complex environment with multiple participants and diverse interests in the data."[561] Further, the novel category of "urban data" to denote the pooled resource was both unwieldy and uncertain. Scassa believes that urban data was defined unhelpfully as a "combination of physical geography and uncertain notions of public and private space."[562] She concludes that the knowledge commons concept is a useful and instructive one to consider when devising data governance models.

A functional solution: the digital trust layer

A final model to consider for smart cities governance is a *digital trust layer*. This GliaNet-inspired design platform would recognize each separate but interrelated conceptual module that collectively forms its reference architecture. In essence, the model entails mapping end user data streams to and from the cityscape environment, then assigning express duties to each mediating juncture point.[563] The interoperable modules of a digital trust layer would include:

- *Network stacks*: Where data packets travel through layers of information systems.

- *Data lifecycles*: Where data resides in servers, routers, algorithms, and applications.

- *Algorithmic tussle zones*: Where external interfaces (screens and scenes) and intra-network mediation points (unseens) allow competing interests to "tussle" for control over data access.

- *Duties*: Where applicable obligations are operationalized, based on existent fiduciary/trusts/bailment laws.

Research considerations:
Prototyping a digital trust layer

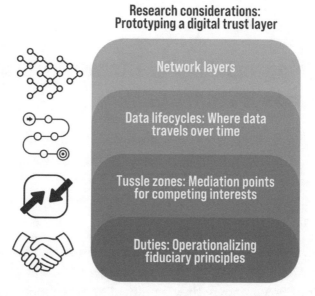

Network layers

Data lifecycles: Where data travels over time

Tussle zones: Mediation points for competing interests

Duties: Operationalizing fiduciary principles

An early adopter of the holistic systems approach in a smart city is the World Economic Forum's ongoing partnership with the City of Helsinki, Finland.[564] The resulting WEF white paper adopts a similar conceptual blending of ecosystem mapping, network stacks, data lifecycles, tussle zones, and stakeholder duties.[565] The Helsinki government sees this approach as applying a "human-centric approach to data relationships," which translates into helping the city's citizens "become, and feel, in control of their data flows."[566]

Bringing us full circle, the City of Helsinki's holistic, multilayered approach echoes the model of the ancient Greek agora, as exemplified in the founding of Thurii. For many Greek cities, the agora was far more than a marketplace—it was the center of civic life.[567] People freely mingled and participated in all forms of social interaction, including commercial dealings, political and legal activities, and philosophical discourse. This blend of human engagement led to tremendous creativity, and ideas and institutions that have stood the test of time.[568] Perhaps the agora as a human trust layer is a useful way to consider governing the blended public spaces of the digital community.

Designing inclusive interfaces: DTPR and personal software agents

In 2019, Sidewalk Labs publicly launched for Toronto the Digital Transparency in the Public Realm project (DTPR). The DTPR team was tasked with creating icons and signage so pedestrians would understand the function employed by a particular environmental device.[569]

As the project heads acknowledged, cities like Boston and London "have already taken important first steps by posting clear signage whenever they employ digital technologies in the public realm."[570] One early component proposed by the DTPR team was the "consent through signage" principle, and it used a comprehensive system of colorful symbols to inform citizens about data collection practices. Citizens then faced a decision: remain on the scene where data collection is taking place, which indicates consent, or withdraw consent by departing the scene.[571] Needless to say, such a faux choice grants ordinary citizens little recourse: how can one gain the benefits of belonging to a digital community without giving up control over access to one's personal data?

Sidewalk Labs' signage system to explain invisible sensors: icons denoting purpose (in black), data type (blue for de-identified, yellow for identifiable), accountable organization, and links to digital channels to learn more.

DTPR's initial focus on transparency shifted quickly to phase two, devoted to engendering greater accountability for the underlying system's actions.[572] In this phase, the DTPR team reached out to designers and others to "advance digital transparency and enable agency."

In the last few months before the Quayside project was terminated, the DTPR team went further still. Using co-design sessions, charrettes (hands-on collaborative workshops), small group discussions, and prototyping, the team sought to investigate opportunities for actual human agency—in particular, direct human-to-interfaces interactions within the local sensors system.[573] Intriguingly, prototypes for conversational chatbots and Personal AIs were introduced, discussed, and tested for feasibility.[574] As the team summarized:

We asked charrette participants to imagine that five years in the future, they have a personal digital assistant provided by an organization they trust (such as a bank), that provides automated data/privacy information tailored to an individual's preferences. We explored how that digital personal assistant, in the form of a chatbot, could provide answers about systems and places in a standardized manner, using the DTPR taxonomy. We wanted to see how this concept could encourage users to develop expectations around transparency and accountability of spaces, provide a flexible way for users to interact with a physical space and the digital technology within it, and adapt and learn as users asked new questions.[575]

The DTPR team also shared out the insights they gleaned from their research on the feasibility of PAIs (what they called "personal digital assistants"):

- *"Concept feedback sessions showed the desirability of a trusted digital assistant to help with daily tasks."*

- *"People want to ask questions at a time and context that is convenient to them, not be interrupted mid-flow."*

- *"Trust varies person by person, case by case; there is no 'one size fits all' approach."[576]*

The "agency" phase of the aborted DTPR project offers some fascinating prospects. If successfully pursued, creating these kinds of interactive IoT systems could offer real opportunities for humans to engage on their own terms in digital communities.

New edge-outward interfaces

Along with the governance institutions, we can also put in place agential technologies like DTPR that invite our participation, rather than shunt it aside. These new *edgetech* interfaces essentially reverse the unilateral nature of the *cloudtech* interfaces that facilitate SEAMs control flows for government agencies and platform providers.

Edge-friendly IoT interfaces like DTPR had clearly been designed from the outset to inform those in a physical location about the technologies in the space. The space is essentially pulling this information to the passerby. In its initial instantiations, however, the DTPR interface lacks a companion edge-pushing capability, one that enables the individual to "intentcast" their queries and other interactions to the IoT system. This missing element can be easily remedied with future technology innovations.

A complementary role for Net trustmediaries and PAI agents

A digital community could be devised so that a citizen's digital agent would be able to interact directly on their behalf with the community's computational systems. In the case of Sidewalk Labs, these interactions could have been facilitated through the very chatbots and PAI agents that were being explored via the project's DTPR process. The back end of trust governance could have benefited from more fruitful connections with the front end of sensor interface technologies.

In essence, each smart city and digital community is its own website, social media platform, or mobile application. And with these better-known Web experiences, each digital community would have its own ToS, privacy policy, and data protection practices. But as with the Web, this panoply of overlapping and likely inconsistent policies would overwhelm most typical participants. In essence, the cognitive overload of the Web would become extended and embedded in the physical spaces all around us. At present, there is no recourse to deal with this pervasive problem.

For the average person, such as our friend Carla, having her own PAI agent, linked to a Net fiduciary, can help her cope with and manage this brave new world of digital communities.[577] As Carla goes about her daily activities in her local cityscape, a PAI agent embedded on her mobile device could provide the means of interacting in real time with the digital community, including the civic data trust and other entities. These interactions in turn would be enabled via the software interfaces embedded all around her.

As the DTPR team recognized, a PAI could be an important complementary tool in an individual utilizing their edgetech applications. The PAI could provide forms of "digital pushback" to challenge a digital community's existing SEAMs cycles, by:

- blocking the automatic "surveillance" and "extraction" of personal information;

- disrupting consent-less operation of the community's "analysis" function; and

- thwarting attempts to "manipulate" the individual's autonomy in their physical environment.

Ancient Lessons for Modern Communities

"Places matter!"[578]

As the city of Thurii attempted some 2,500 years ago, today we can craft governance structures and spatial processes that work together to provide inclusive and supportive physical environments for real people. What useful takeaways for planners can be derived from the Sidewalk Labs project?

First, digital communities should open up the back end of project governance. Second, these communities should open up the front end of software interfaces. Optimally, as we have seen, providing balanced processes of interactions within these two forms of human-to-system interfaces can be devised and implemented in concert.

Our digital communities should embrace the active participation of citizens and visitors alike in the increasingly blended spaces that constitute the self and world, the private and public, and the physical and virtual. Insights gleaned from fiduciary-based governance models, and technologies that use e2a design principles, can form a powerfully inclusive combination. And the authentic PAI agents, powered by NetTMs—fiduciaries and trusts alike—can be a complementary means to ensure that ordinary people can explore and participate in the brave new world of their digital communities.

/C15/OTHER EDGETECH: PODS, MODS, CLOUDLETS, AND MORE

"Human freedom cannot be saved by shying away from technological mediations, but only by developing free relations to them, dealing in a responsible way with the inevitable mediating roles of technologies in our lives."

– Verbeek, *Beyond Interaction*, at 31

While together authentic PAI agents and symmetrical interfaces can better protect and promote the ordinary person's digital life, other technologies operating in accord with the e2a design principle also have the potential to provide agential services at the "edge" of the Web. As with other technologies, it comes down to human governance—who sets the rules and who must obey them.

That said, edge-based tech implementations with built-in privacy protections also abound. These include Sir Tim Berners-Lee's Solid Pods (personal online data stores),[579] Holochain's distributed computing platform,[580] digi.me's personal data manager,[581] and countless others. Ongoing businesses should not be ignored, such as DuckDuckGo (search engine),[582] Firefox and Brave (Web browsers),[583] Signal (text app),[584] Mycroft (hardware-based voice agent),[585] Personal.AI (app-based personal AI agent),[586] Kwaai.ai (open-source AI operating system),[587] and more.

This chapter will touch on the more promising edgetech tools. To some experts, these are limited to what has been termed privacy-enhancing technology (also called "PETs"). However, other viable innovations are also possible, such as personal data pods, modular devices, localized cloudlets, content layers, democratized access networks, decentralized applications, and more. Many of these exhibit edge-pull and/or edge-push capabilities. In each case, for these human-enhancing agential technology tools (or what we might call "HEATs"), their ultimate efficacy to empower ordinary human beings resides not just in the e2a-inspired design but also in the governance regimes that instantiate such empowerment in meaningful ways.

If you find some of the technical details in this chapter less relevant or helpful, please feel free to move on to the next chapter.

Privacy Enhancing Technologies

Differential privacy

The results of data analytics can reveal sensitive information even when the queries are statistical and the result is in the aggregate. Differential privacy seeks to guarantee that the results of statistical queries cannot be used to glean information about specific individuals or more broadly gain access to a specific row or cell in a database. A typical mechanism used for differential privacy is the addition of noise from a suitable distribution to the result of statistical queries. The distribution parameters are based on the query and the sensitivity of the data being queried. The mechanisms can help ensure that the presence or absence of an individual in a database does not produce query results that correlate to the individual's contribution to the database.

Federated learning

In machine learning training, the typical modus operandi is to collect a large volume of training samples centrally and use them to update the parameters of a model. This means transferring and maintaining highly sensitive user data, be it to improve the accuracy of gesture-to-text translation or predict the outcomes of clinical trials in highly regulated industries such as healthcare.

Federated learning is a technique that splits the training algorithm into two separate steps: a gradient computation step at the edge where the data is located, and a model update step that averages contributions from the edges to update a model centrally. The model therefore captures updates from disparate datasets while obviating the need to move the datasets to a central repository. In this way, sensitive data never leaves the edge, and the gradients cannot be used to reconstruct the inputs that generated them.

Homomorphic encryption

End-to-end encryption is a well-understood way of securing data that passes between two or more points. Homomorphic encryption ("HE") takes this a step further by converting data into more secure "ciphertexts." When decrypted, the ciphertext results are the same as what one would obtain without using the encryption scheme and evaluating an equivalent function over plaintext inputs. The homomorphic encryption property ensures that results remain encrypted using the same scheme that was used to encrypt the input data. The results can be decrypted by the data owners, with the function and its execution environment incapable of gaining access to the data in plaintext.

Zero knowledge proofs

Zero-knowledge proof ("ZKP") systems enable one party in an online interaction to validate the truth of a statement without gaining access to the original data used for validation. ZKP enables a "prover" (data owner) to demonstrate to a "verifier" (data consumer) that a condition specified by the verifier is satisfiable using a subset of the data they own. A simple example is confirming that an individual has sufficient credit to complete a transaction—without relying on personally-identifiable information, or capturing the precise amounts involved. Generalizing ZKP for arbitrary functions to be evaluated with efficiency is an active area of research. For cases such as token transfers and checking simple conditions over digital credentials, however, ZKP is an emerging privacy modality.

Secure multi-party computation

A secure multi-party computation ("SMPC") is a privacy modality where a consortium of participants uses a cryptographic protocol to compute an agreed upon function jointly over their private input data. The participants are not necessarily required to trust each other. Instead, protocols in this category use secret sharing, with incomplete sharing of a given secret. In this way, the output computed over incomplete inputs can be used by each entity to compute the actual desired result. Similar to HE and ZKP technologies, SMPC is an active area of research and lends itself well to select privacy-preserving use-cases.

Human Enhancing Agential Technology

While "PETs" tend to focus on the data itself and how it is identified, analyzed, or stored, other edgetech capabilities include human-enhancing agential technology tools. Here are a few examples of HEATs.

Personal data pods

Sir Tim Berners-Lee, the Web's founder, came to realize that the Web's very architecture was facilitating a constant one-way flow of data from the individual and their community to the online platforms. The key, he concluded, was to separate the data source from the apps and give the person more complete control over both. In other words, keep personal data where it originates: with the actual human being.

Enter the Solid project.[588] Launched by Berners-Lee himself, Solid is a software specification that enables people to store their data locally in decentralized data stores called Pods. These

Pods act like secure personal Web servers for data, essentially reversing the client-server polarity at the heart of the Web. The data is stored in standard, open, and interoperable formats, allowing different applications to work with the data. In this configuration, the individual is theoretically in control of which entities and applications can gain access to which slices of the data. If more fully implemented and adopted, Solid holds the promise of anchoring an entire edgetech-based ecosystem of agential humans.

Modular devices

Hardware devices of all kinds—from the personal (smartphones, wearables and implantables), to environmental (IoT), aeronautical (drones), and autonomous (vehicles and robots)—increasingly are taking advantage of the Web 2.0 virtual infrastructure. These devices are in effect becoming the sensory system of the Internet. In many cases, however, these devices and their interfaces are locked down and closed off from all but the manufacturers and providers. Ironically, the openness of the Internet, the availability of cheap cloud storage, fast broadband connectivity, and smaller, cheaper devices have helped enable this world.

As Perzanowski and Schultz point out in The End of Ownership,[589] the right to own something has changed significantly from the analog to the digital context. The default rules of private property no longer apply when a bit of software is added to hardware. Software-enabled devices are now sold to users but limited in what those users can do with them. In some cases, the user does not even own the device—instead, it is "leased" by way of an end user licensing agreement (EULA). Should the user seek to modify, repair, or resell the device, the EULA typically prohibits such actions. This applies to not just phones, but televisions, household appliances, automobiles, and even John Deere tractors, which are being treated as software platforms by manufacturers.

Greatly limiting the right to repair and "tinker" with devices has another negative consequence: e-waste. Broken and outmoded personal devices now constitute the fastest growing waste stream in the world. These devices also typically involve rare earth minerals, such as tin, tantalum, and tungsten, which can be mined under duress in war-zones as so-called "conflict minerals."[590] Finding a way to reduce this stream of extractive resources would benefit everyone.

In particular, IoT devices present a huge challenge and opportunity. As denial-of-service (DoS) attacks and security breaches grab headlines, regulatory bodies are jostling to create public policy and regulation of the IoT sector. Protection of data and lack of interoperability are two recurring themes. But what should be an equally pressing societal concern is whether and how an individual can prevent their personal autonomy from being breached by surveillance systems powered by IoT and other environmental devices.

On the mobile operating system side, Android OS has clearly been a substantial commercial success story for a relatively open mobile ecosystem. And yet, much more is possible. One promising but as-yet commercially unrealized advance is the modular device. An example of this is Motorola Mobility's "Moto Mods."[591] Launched in 2016 as a key component of the Moto Z smartphone, Moto Mods are handset accessories that can be magnetically attached to a device to extend its functionalities, such as extended battery packs, a "Soundboost" speaker system, a pico projector, and a mini printer. In theory, an entire ecosystem of Mods makers could spring up to develop additional modular units. Unfortunately, the Moto Z itself received mixed reviews, and the company eventually moved away from providing support. Still, the notion of giving the user more say in the capabilities of their personal device remains intriguing.

In essence, we can rethink devices as modular, unlocked, repairable, and hackable.

Localized cloudlets

The cloud is an intentionally amorphous concept. In reality, it largely resembles a return to "Big Iron," the centralized computing platforms prevalent in the 1970s and early 1980s. Today, with clouds, we have a partially decentralized infrastructure but still with a highly centralized service model.

As it turns out, clouds can be refashioned as decentralized and distributed data streams, protected in encrypted transactions. Personalized "cloudlets" could be designed for the specific, localized needs of commercial entities and individuals. Among other things, this could open up new opportunities to work with companies and developers on open-source tools to create the virtual infrastructure and applications for truly decentralized networks.

We can even envision a cloud world without any databases at all, where cloudtech companies still may provide some of the computation but not necessarily the data storage. An individual or entity would have its data stored not in an external repository but in an on-premises server, creating true server-to-server, peer-to-peer connectivity. The server could be set up so the data is distributed in a way that gives the individual full control over its use. Unlike a database, this would be more like a "dataspread" process of information flows.

In particular, the data could be shared in real time, with any party designated by the individual or entity as a trusted intermediary.

This sharing could be instantaneous, and limited to a particular purpose; then the data would simply disappear on the other side of the "cloudlet." Local "memory boxes" with saved, preserved user content could be placed in residences and businesses, interacting with the larger cloud networks and each other.

This approach should result in fewer concerns about data being shared with third parties for their use, separate from the original context and without affirmative agreement. And this means fewer concerns about data breaches, particularly involving large centralized repositories (for example, why did Equifax in 2017 "have" anyone's sensitive financial data to be exposed?). This also means fewer liability issues for companies.

Democratized access networks

Governments typically control a number of regulated business inputs (RBIs), especially in the communications space. This includes the rules for accessing the radio spectrum used to provide wireless communications.

From the radio waves that surround us, certain portions or "bands" are more conducive than others for transmitting radio signals. Over the past three decades, the U.S. Federal Communications Commission (FCC), which has regulatory authority over the non-Federal governmental portions of the spectrum, has auctioned off most of the usable bands to the highest bidders. These are typically the largest wireless service providers, such as AT&T and Verizon, who use the spectrum to provide consumers with access to wireless telephone service, and more recently broadband access to the Web. The pattern of privatized use of this common resource is similar in most countries.

Most of us are familiar with accessing the Web wirelessly through WiFi networks, whether in our homes or in public spaces. The radio bands used for WiFi facilities are not licensed to a for-profit service provider but are instead made available for free for any entrepreneur to build networks and devices that can utilize them. As it turns out, research consistently demonstrates that the slim bands granted for unlicensed WiFi outperform the broader licensed swaths of spectrum controlled by wireless carriers. Nonetheless, the licensed regime continues to predominate. Opening up our spectrum bands to the "innovation without permission" ethos of the Internet—via more WiFi, or perhaps the unlicensed elements in the FCC's new Community Broadband Radio Service (CBRS)—would bring true competitive alternatives to serve users in many ways.

Other options are possible. What if 10% of all future spectrum allocations could be set aside "for the people?" Or, more radically, we could challenge the norm of spectrum as corporate property right, replacing it with the concept of spectrum as a community commons. Or perhaps a sliver of spectrum could be deemed a personal access right intrinsic to every individual. Just as radio spectrum is a renewable resource, made fresh each moment, the opportunities for making more edge-friendly uses of it seem boundless.

Decentralized applications

The promise of the Solid project and personal data Pods works best when paired with applications that also reside locally. The Internet Archive has touted the concept of decentralized applications in its "dWeb" project.[592] First launched in 2016, dWeb has evolved into a global network of individuals and communities focused on developing applications that enable human agency. The dWeb apps themselves are built using open-source code, eschew cloud-based surveillance and manipulation of people's behavior, and allow the individual to decide how and why their data is being used. In this way, they let applications live at the edge of the network, under more direct human control.

Content layer

Much as with our connected and software-enabled devices, our digital content (books, music, movies, video games) has also been part of a shrinking rights regime for users. Typically, copyright law is invoked as the rationale, but the end user licensing agreements ("EULAs") utilized by providers often go well beyond the bounds of property protection. These legal agreements are imposed by content providers to dictate the terms for using the software or device that accesses the content. Over time, these agreements have taken away many of the rights of ownership that we normally associate with physical objects in the real world.

For example, an individual can purchase a physical book and then resell it, mark it up, bury it in the backyard, or destroy it in a bonfire. By contrast, the purveyors of e-books typically use EULAs to prevent users from modifying or sharing the text. These content providers treat the transaction with the individual as a limited, non-negotiable lease arrangement. Because EULAs are often one-sided and rarely read or understood by the user, they also impose higher transaction costs in terms of information asymmetries and negative externalities.

As per Perzanowski and Schutz, "there are good reasons to resist those efforts to redefine our relationship to the media and devices that shape so much of our interaction with the world."[593] To be a mere user, leasing a purchased book or movie suggests an ephemeral connection to the thing supposedly purchased and owned. The relationship is defined by temporary usage of somebody else's property, and not enduring ownership. In short, more provider controls means less user freedom.

The use of new AI technologies such as authentic PAI agents can help create a virtuous "arm's race" to combat overly onerous EULAs. As explained earlier, a PAI could help the user better navigate content markets. Currently, few people have the time, patience, and proficiency to review and approve or reject the ToS for all of their digital content. Having an intelligent agent serving the individual's needs can facilitate more flexible and case-by-case licensing arrangements and commensurate pricing plans. Where such plans would prove difficult in today's online environment, AI-based interactions and transactions could make them a reality.

Obfuscating tech tools

Finally, while each of the technologies presented here can be thought of as "going on offense" against the current Web, there is a suitable place as well for defending our agency and autonomy. Finn Brunton and Helen Nissenbaum argue for another type of technology tool that amount to weapons of resistance. In *Obfuscation: A User's Guide for Privacy and Protest*,[594] the authors propose adding obfuscation: "the deliberate use of ambiguous, confusing, or misleading information to interfere with surveillance and data collection projects." Brunton and Nissenbaum run through several dozen examples, such as the donning of anti-surveillance gear in IoT environments. We can imagine our Net fiduciary employing such tactics as a way to deter the applicability of various untoward surveillance techniques.

Embracing our edgetech

Reversing the cloudtech paradigm of entities pulling our personal information and pushing their influence—in favor of the edgetech paradigm of individuals pulling other people's information and pushing their own influence—opens the door to many new agential tech tools. In the next chapter, we will touch on two controversial recent technology advances: Web3 and the metaverse. While neither advance on its own terms provides much separation from the SEAMs paradigm, the underlying functionalities do suggest some interesting ways forward if combined with HAACS-based governance.

/C16/BEYOND THE TECH BROS: WEB 3.0 AND THE METAVERSE

In this chapter, we will take a brief look at two one-time obsessions of many in Silicon Valley. One is "Web3" functionalities such as blockchain, tokenized data, and cryptocurrencies. The other is the Metaverse, an imagined realm of virtual world and avatars. The past few years have not been especially kind to the more egregious use cases for these technologies. However, the primary issue would seem to be not with the decentralizing and potentially user empowering tech itself, but rather with the human governance structures (or lack thereof) that have been wrapped around the tech.

When married to some of the HAACS-based governance concepts described earlier, these Web3 and Metaverse tools can still fulfill the promise of enhancing human autonomy and agency beyond their SEAMs-based incarnations.

Web3

We are now in the opening years of what some have called "Web3," also dubbed the Age of the Token.[595] With the arrival of the Bitcoin cryptocurrency in 2009, the concept of blockchain networks and distributed ledger applications became more widely known, accepted, and eventually adopted. Blockchain to some represents "the reemergence of trust in a new form."[596]

In some quarters, as hype gave way to full-blown speculation and then decline, Web3 is already deemed dead. And in its prior incarnation of promising technologies married to SEAMs-based business models, of bored ape non-fungible tokens (NFTs) and crypto get-rich schemes and governance nonsense, few should weep. Nonetheless, some of the technology hidden behind the shiny cryptocurrencies retains potential value.

A significant change from Web2 to Web3 is in the addition of identity layering. Interestingly, Web2 doesn't inherently hold "state"—session data from previous requests—and lacks a native mechanism to transfer state in straightforward fashion.[597] Adding statefulness to the platform allows value to be transferred between users without centralizing institutions acting as clearing entities.[598] Along with a radically decentralized architecture and secure computing resources, this attribute of statefulness enables blockchain technology to provide what has been termed a "trustless form of trust."[599]

With the early days of blockchain—version 1.0—cryptocurrencies like Bitcoin and others were seen primarily as stores of monetary value. With the rise of Ethereum, what could be called Blockchain 2.0 began to emerge. The use of tokens—tiny bits of programmable software that can carry different forms of meaning—exploded. As Shermin Voshmgir puts it, "tokens are to the Web3 what bits were to the Web1."[600] Distributed ledgers then formed a substrate for new ways to use tokens to buy, sell, and trade underlying assets, both as financial interest and as actual physical items. Smart contracts became a reality.

Blockchain 2.0 also introduced the NFT to represent an underlying value unique unto itself.[601] While many tokens largely remained fungible, they now could be used to represent unique assets.[602] In particular, tokens need not be tied to a single blockchain use case of a fungible commodity, so they could represent almost anything of value.

Of course, we are well past the hype peak for NFTs and cryptocurrencies. And the very notion of "trustless trust" is just a fantasy. Trust-based governance is the only sound way of unleashing the power of these new edge-based technologies to benefit the ordinary person, rather than use those same technologies to further the pernicious effects of the SEAMs paradigm. But is there a way to get there from here?

Blockchain 3.0

It is not too soon to recognize another significant shift within the distributed ledger community. In what could be imagined as a "Blockchain 3.0" incarnation, all forms of data can be faithfully and securely represented by combining tokenization and secure computing environments. This chronological progression roughly approximates the particular use cases:

- Blockchain 1.0 – cryptocurrencies (crypto serving as money)

- Blockchain 2.0 – cryptoassets (tokenizing value of assets)

- Blockchain 3.0 – cryptodata (tokenizing utility of data)

Today, as we have seen, data and computational systems increasingly are being defined for society by large corporations and governments, with their own stakes in the outcome.[603] With Blockchain 3.0, the potential exists that this dynamic can shift so individuals and companies can work together to maximize the overall utility of data.

Programmatic value creation

If Blockchain 1.0 brought protocol incentive and Blockchain 2.0 added the possibility to create computers that can commit, then Blockchain 3.0 can bring individual-controlled data encapsulation. Once data is encapsulated, people can allow selective and consent-based computation using their information, which breaks the trade-off between value extraction and data transfer. Each of us can maintain ownership and confidentiality of the data, even when the right to compute is granted to a third party.

Programmatic data access refers to using advanced automation technologies so that an individual can share their data with a variety of third parties. This form of data access can be managed via smart contracts. Each time an application needs to access users' data, the smart contract enforces the specified policies and the blockchain records the transaction. Keeping the data private implies that data buyers can't re-use the information multiple times after the initial acquisition: each request triggers the execution of the smart contract, resulting in a programmatic, per-consumption model.

Tokenized data offerings

Using technology to programmatically attach money to the flow of data also creates the possibility to establish a direct and repeated relationship between the data producer/owner and the data consumer/buyer. To date, companies have been incentivized to develop creative ways to collect data while hiding the policy behind extensive terms of service (ToS). Now, companies can establish a mutually beneficial and cooperative relationship with their users. As one option, data requestors can lock an asset that serves as a payment for the corresponding usage of the data, then have the transaction automatically settled when the computation is completed.

When end users can control access to their data, they have the option of offering data tokens to the market. Buyers can perform automated due diligence—determining the bounty, relevance, security, and other properties—and then offer either their bid or a suggested price. Users (or the apps that actually produce the data tokens) specify the acceptance criteria for the offers, and the negotiation occurs automatically. Again, no third parties are necessary to regulate this transaction.

The resulting "Tokenized Data Offering" allows an individual to invest and earn a payout. The ubiquitous and private nature of data tokens, and the non-rivalrous (shareable) nature of the underlying data, means that users can offer and invest their datasets multiple times. This introduces a significant advantage over the equivalent investment of money, as data tends to gain value the more often it is strategically shared.

Governing Web3

Just as Web3 and Blockchain 3.0 advocates seek to bring advanced digital technology back to the edge of the network, the GliaNet initiative and others have been advancing governance models that give end users greater control over their digital experiences. The common thread in these governance and economic models is a concerted shift of power and control to the end user. Blockchain 3.0 provides a highly complementary technology layer to support these new entities and their user-empowering use cases.

Major companies such as IBM[604] and Accenture[605] have discussed the idea of developing blockchain for social good. A "Blockchain for Good" movement is active in laying out the many ways that blockchain technologies can further humanity's interests. And academics have also been exploring social good use cases for distributed ledger technologies.[606]

In short, tokenizing data in secure computing environments gives us the flexibility to treat data in a certain way, with benefits to society and individuals. The new end user-empowering capabilities unleashed by Blockchain 3.0 can help us drive forward these interrelated components of an ethos of digital stewardship.

Some Compelling Use Cases

There are many different examples where tokenized data plus secure computing environments can prove immensely beneficial in protecting personal data. In fact, novel new business models could combine elements of machine learning with tokenized data.[607]

Tokenizing data is a particularly useful tool for organizations that manage substantial amounts of sensitive data about their customers, vendors, and partners. One area of opportunity is protecting consumer data,[608] where the scenarios could include:

- Autonomous vehicles

- Mobility data

- IoT data

- Credit scores and other sensitive financial information

- Personal insurance[609]

Human Health Data

Human medical data, often called personal health information (PHI), shares many of the characteristics of the most sensitive information about the self. Finding secure ways to protect that information, including separating PHI from access and usage rights, for example, can open up vast new avenues for medical research.

While the healthcare industry is extensively regulated by national and regional governments, there are immense opportunities to utilize digital technologies to improve the scale, scope, and nature of health care.[610] Indeed, scholars and other experts have begun exploring ways that "health IT" can be enhanced through the use of distributed ledger-based networks and applications.[611] Secure data tokenization in particular can play a leading role in unlocking the value in digital technologies.

MIT's OPAL project, mentioned in Chapter Twelve, recently produced some fundamental "open algorithms principles" for addressing health data. These include the "edge-pull" actions of moving the algorithm to the data, always having the data encrypted during computation and in storage, and never having the data leave the secure repository.[612] A tokenized and secure data/computing blockchain system can help fulfill all three core requirements.

Blockchain 3.0 systems can reduce or even eliminate the downside while bolstering the upside. Tokenization can replace sensitive patient data, such as PHI. In doing so, tokenized data systems can transfer power to create, access, and share sensitive data from intermediaries (like insurance companies) to patients and medical organizations. This process can generate greater trust from patients, and a greater willingness to share their medical information.

Brigitte Piniewski for one has articulated a vision where individuals can fully control their health care opportunities.[613] Dubbing her program "wealthcare," Piniewski contends that an entirely new approach to health is possible, where machine learning, blockchains, NFTs, and other advanced tech can be harnessed so that an individual's health data yields unprecedented and actionable medical insights.

And Here Comes the Metaverse

Another technology platform is looming on the horizon: the metaverse. Meta (formerly Facebook) is leading the way here, making significant investments in the technologies that will enable this collection of virtual worlds to emerge. Touted as some amorphous combination of Web3 and virtual reality (VR) capabilities, the metaverse is the supposed next big thing. For many, it is the logical evolution of the current Web 2.0. And yet, the same questions pose themselves: how will these companies make money? And under what kinds of governance regimes will these new worlds be instantiated?

As with the current Web, and much of the decentralized Web of blockchain, the easy path is the current one: construct our own virtual world and operate it consistent with the SEAMs paradigm. However, this approach is fraught with issues. As one example, Brittan Heller and Avi Bar-Zeev pointed out the profound effects that advertising will have on users in the fully immersive world of the metaverse.[614] Augmented advertising will benefit from, among other things, the way that our brains process virtual events as real-world happenings and the staggering amount of behavioral and physical data collected and accessed by the XR control interfaces.[615] Collectively, these factors mean that XR systems will be able to create an advertising "experience" that taps into our deeply emotional and physiological responses. In such a virtual world, our autonomy and agency would be under constant assault.

Or is another approach possible?

The metaverse is fascinating because there is already a lengthy history of entities building virtual worlds for players to inhabit. While the governance rules for these franchises vary, at least some operated outside the SEAMs paradigm. Users are in fact customers, and games are purchased via currency rather than personal data. With Meta's entry into this space, that is likely to change. Nonetheless, the opportunity is there for participants in the metaverse to create something different.

Open Metaverse Passport

One suggestion here is for entities to serve as trustworthy portals for end users by bridging Web 2.0 and Web 3.0 into a truly "open" metaverse. While others may create the virtual properties of the metaverse, these entities can provide the connective tissue that links them together. This role can also include forging a new relationship with end users as a digital steward or fiduciary, operating under duties of care, loyalty, and good faith.

As one example, a NetTM could supply its clientele with an "Open Metaverse Passport," complete with a simplified and ubiquitous UX. The passport would be suitable for people to safely and securely navigate the many virtual environments built by Meta and other entities. The "open" part is the metaverse elements that are being built together in an ethos similar to the original Internet. The "passport" part is a bundling together of various end user capabilities: digital identity, virtual wallet, data access credentials, and so on.

Importantly, an open metaverse includes the interoperable fabric linking together the various distributed and decentralized properties, platforms, worlds, sites, stores, and experiences. Customers can travel from Meta to Roblox to Fortnite to Second Life, bringing their digital identities with them, including their data, credentials, NFTs, wallets, avatars, skins, and other virtualized attributes. And, of course, adopting NetTM-based governance would enhance trust, accountability, and support levels with the customer base.

Governing Data Tokens and Virtual Avatars

As with most overly hyped new technologies, both Web 3.0 and the metaverse must contend with the inevitable troughs in investor and consumer interest. Nonetheless, both technologies carry interesting potential to upend the current SEAMs paradigm at the heart of the current Web, and arm ordinary people with important tools of autonomy and agency. Whether these technologies ever meet that potential depends on whether they are deployed in a way that is consistent with the *e2a* design principle, and managed consistent with the *D>A* governance principle. The jury remains out.

```
}
int main(int argc, char *argv[]) {
    int sockfd, newsockfd, portno;
    socklen_t clilen;
    char buffer[256];
    struct sockaddr_in serv_addr, cli_addr;
    int n;

    sockfd = socket(AF_INET, SOCK_STREAM, 0);
    if (sockfd < 0)
        error("ERROR opening socket");
```

/PART FOUR/LEVERAGING THE HOW

```
    memset((char *) &serv_addr, 0, sizeof(serv_addr));
    portno = 8000;
    serv_addr.sin_family = AF_INET;
    serv_addr.sin_addr.s_addr = INADDR_ANY;
    serv_addr.sin_port = htons(portno);

    if (bind(sockfd, (struct sockaddr *) &serv_addr, sizeof(serv_addr))
        < 0) error("ERROR on binding");

    listen(sockfd, 5);
    clilen = sizeof(cli_addr);

    newsockfd = accept(sockfd, (struct sockaddr *) &cli_addr, &clilen);
    if (newsockfd < 0)
        error("ERROR on accept");
```

INTRODUCTION

This final part shifts gears from the "why" elements of Part One and the "what" elements of Parts Two and Three to suggest some specific "how" action plans. The connective tissue for the initiatives proposed is putting people more in charge of their digital destinies.

Here we meet Carla again, some years in the future, where she is enjoying the fruits of the governance and technology innovations brought about by many initiatives, including GliaNet. In order to build an actual alternative Web overlay ecosystem such as GliaNet, we will address the different layers of digital governance: human rights and responsibilities, private policy frameworks, public policy, commercial challenges, technology advancement, and ongoing collaborations that span them. The key takeaway is that the GliaNet initiative need not be a pipe dream, as the basic elements are already there or can be put into place easily enough to bring it to life.

/C17/CARLA IN 2032

Carla wakes up early on a Saturday morning, greeted by her personal AI agent, which she calls Corey. As she slowly gets out of bed, Corey informs her of the weather forecast, pulls up several video feeds of curated news items, and reminds her of various meetings and to-dos for the day. Corey also wakes her teenage daughter Ada with her favorite music, starts the shower, and brews the coffee. Then Carla's day really begins.

Some years in the future, Carla feels that she is living a pretty good life. She still remains enmeshed in digital technology and connected devices, but now she is much more in control.

Adopting a Trusted Fiduciary

The previous year, Carla agreed to subscribe to a new kind of entity, a company called Deeper Edge, that differentiates itself as a Net fiduciary. The company's slogan is "We do better when you do better." In exchange, Carla has become its full-fledged client, and not a user—a status still relatively uncommon for technology companies in 2032. Deeper Edge also comes with a full certification as a Net fiduciary by the state's GliaNet Professional Certification and Enforcement Board, which is similar to the statewide licensing boards she is familiar with for physicians and attorneys.

With Deeper Edge's Loyalty Promotion package, Carla receives the full gamut of "PEP" advantages. This includes protecting her from a variety of online harms, enhancing her presence on the Web, and promoting her best interests digitally. This means that Deeper Edge works for her, and not some data broker or advertiser seeking unconsented access to her digital lifestreams.

As part of her Deeper Edge subscription package, Carla also received her very own PAI, Corey.

Benefiting from an Authentic Personal Agent

Over the next several months, Corey became a staple of Carla's household. Managed and monitored closely by Deeper Edge, Corey performs a wide variety of functions on her behalf. Some are done autonomously, trained on her private information. Other functions are done semi-autonomously, to give her the last word. Prior to this particular Saturday, Corey has been:

- Protecting Carla's identity: Corey creates and constantly updates Carla's anonymized profile, sharing it only with trusted vendors. Utilizing advanced cryptographic techniques, Carla's PAI agent erects a virtual shield around Carla and all the iterations of her identity in the online world. Corey also performs constant security checks to ensure that Carla is not vulnerable to identity theft or other online harms against her.

- *Managing her data flows:* Corey sets up a universal dashboard for all of Carla's preferred apps and websites. It also blocks all unwanted MOPs-based targeted advertising and vets all incoming synthetic content and AI bot-based messages.

- *Broadcasting her terms:* Corey uses advanced intent-casting technology to project Carla's specified terms of service to the Web. This means that Carla agrees to only visit websites that have adopted and implemented acceptable privacy, security, and data protection policies.

- *Managing her personal data pod:* Since she purchased a SOLID data pod, Carla has been pleased to know that all her valuable and treasured personal data resides in a localized cloudlet and data locker. Corey holds the virtual keys and ensures that no one gains unwarranted access to her data.

- *Providing true healthcare:* Corey retains a comprehensive data base of Carla's health information from every source, as well as pertinent elements of her environment, diet, and lifestyle. Corey then helps her make decisions based on that knowledge repository. It also shares her comprehensive profile on an as-needed basis only with trusted healthcare providers.

- *Providing financial services:* Corey retains a complete file of Carla's current obligations, assets, and recurring payments. It also reviews and analyzes all orders with every vendor to ensure accuracy and tax season-readiness.

- *Correcting/updating other AI systems:* Corey analyzes and contests decisions rendered by third-party Institutional AIs. This includes, for example, correcting for a missing check in her monthly bank statement and providing information for long-term health care insurance for her father.

- *Managing real and virtual property: Corey retains a complete, constantly updating file of Carla's personal content and property, from physical and virtual books to movies, songs, and personal files. It shares portions of this information only with trusted vendors and helps them make recommendations for her future purchases.*

- *Providing messaging and contacts and calendar management: Corey retains a complete, searchable, and constantly updating file of Carla's online correspondence, including emails, texts, social media posts, contacts, and past and future calendar entries.*

- *Managing her subscriptions: Corey keeps a complete stock of every subscription Carla has agreed to with magazines, newspapers, cable channels, digital content, and more. It presents her with opportunities to extend/terminate these subscriptions and tracks down special deals.*

With all these functions, and more, her Net fiduciary Deeper Edge is operating behind the screens, actively protecting, enhancing, and promoting Carla's interests.

Managing an Online Saturday

On this particular Saturday, Corey has been working on several tasks at Carla's request. As Carla sips her morning coffee, Corey brings her up to date on one such task: setting up a long weekend trip to Denver, Colorado, where Carla wants to take Ada to visit relatives.

First, Corey alerts Carla's top five travel agencies that its anonymous client wants to take a three-night trip to Denver, within certain price, location, and quality parameters. The search has produced three reasonable offers vying to book Carla's trip. Carla selects the most appealing bid, and Corey handles the rest of the transaction for her.

Second, Corey arranges for Carla's preferred rental car company while she is in Denver. For the autonomous vehicle she selects, Corey substitutes her preferred settings, including ambience and routes, and overrides the pre-sets with her own passenger protection priorities in case of mishaps or accidents.

Third, Corey sets up meals at several bistros in the Denver area. It also communicates Carla's seating preferences and food allergies in advance and queries for any specials on that day.

Over breakfast, Carla checks her online portal for the latest news and media offerings. Since acquiring Corey, Carla has experienced a much different way of interacting with social media platforms. In the old days, Carla would never know exactly how or why certain news and media feeds, or movie or music recommendations, populated her apps. Often, they had no correlation to her personal interests, were a waste of time, and were accompanied with ads that were misdirected or outdated, or both.

Now, Deeper Edge and the PAI agent operated her personalized decision engines across all the platforms that she chose to engage with. Corey places Carla's social media feeds and online video streaming services through the "Carla Recommendation Engine," based on her preferences and those suggested by close friends and family. In today's feed, for example, her interest in the history of conflicts in the Middle East brought suggestions on three documentaries, seven news articles, four interviews, and a debate between two well-known professors. She bookmarks a few for later.

Finally, Carla checks in on what Deeper Edge calls her "JOYCE," a universal shopping cart (standing for "Just an Omnidirectional

YellowPages Conveyance for Everything").[616] She remembers the old days when she had to find a certain item by venturing to multiple websites and apps, unwillingly providing tons of personal information that was often scraped and sold offline and used against her best interests. Now, those fraught and time-consuming days were over. With JOYCE, the websites actually come to her. Corey takes her anonymized JOYCE cart to every virtual storefront as if they were separate stalls in a marketplace.

On this particular day, Corey and JOYCE has been busy searching seventeen online and offline locations for bargains on a pair of dark blue travel pants. The virtual cart contains certain useful information, such as clothing dimensions and price points, but only reveals what is necessary if Corey detects appropriate privacy and identity security policies. The JOYCE cart also only accepts goods that meet pre-set specifications: organic, fair-trade, and locally produced. The JOYCE cart comes up with two recommended pairs of pants, which Carla agrees to purchase.

Managing an Offline Saturday

Then, Carla convinces her daughter Ada to take a short walk through town to meet some friends at a local coffee shop. Before doing so, Carla consults LEVIT, a new Deeper Edge app, to find out what cool events are happening downtown. LEVIT stands for Local Events and Venues Interactive Tracker, a personalized and fully private way of discovering what is going on in her hometown. Its purpose is to allow people to discover happenings of interest in their local community, but in a highly individualized and secure manner. This could include restaurant openings, concerts with favorite artists, movies with favorite actors, sporting events with favorite teams, university talks, political gatherings, book tours, art shows, and more.

Before LEVIT, Carla had to spend lots of time and effort searching fragmented websites and apps to find out what was going on in her town. In the process, she left trails of personal data all across the Web, and those websites and apps built profiles about her and tried to sell her stuff. Now, her personal device includes an individualized LEVIT calendar, which she or Corey can check any time, offering highly relevant and tailored options for how Carla and her friends spend their valuable free time. And her Net fiduciary Deeper Edge ensures that the app is always working for her benefit, without conflicts of interest or duties to any DAMBs.

In one quick glance, Carla sees that her favorite Italian restaurant is having a twenty percent off pizza night for valued customers. She asks Corey to book two spots for her and Ada for Sunday evening via a secure portal. LEVIT also informs her that one of her favorite jazz musicians is going on tour, with tickets about to go on sale tomorrow. Carla instructs Corey to purchase two tickets, at specified price points, as early as possible.

Enjoying Her Local Community

As Carla and Ada walk towards town together, Corey is activated and available on both their devices to mediate their physical and virtual environment. The PAI agent guides them through the local streets, which have become a mix of physical infrastructure, Internet of Things (IoT) devices, and VR-laden cityscapes. Corey is in constant contact with the IoT networks of sensors and cameras and other devices that line the route, ensuring that the networks meet Carla's personal ToS. This includes wherever possible throwing up "obfuscation screens" that blur Carla's facial details and block access to her location data from street devices and passing drones undertaking surreptitious surveillance for unstated reasons. Corey also advises them to avoid locations where road construction is taking place enroute to the coffee shop. As Carla and Ada anonymously pass by storefronts, Corey is actively filtering their virtual marketing offers, presenting only proposed deals that meet Carla's personal interests and price points.

Entering the crowded coffee shop, Carla observes that many of her friends and other patrons are wearing a Neur-O-link, a small device lodged against their brains that interprets thoughts and behaviors through neural brainwaves. While in theory the device sounds interesting and even useful, Carla is wary. As she understands it, the device is a software/hardware interface that gathers behavioral and somatic information about an individual, and in the process of providing services, inserts their data into the DAMB ecosystem. The Neur-O-link uses fully proprietary technology and a one-way interface, so there is no way for the wearer to even tinker with its operations.

The company providing that device, X-Brainiac, has a mixed reputation. Importantly, X-Brainiac isn't a NetTM or Net fiduciary, so its patrons are only treated as users, with no inherent legal or ethical rights. The company has already changed the binding terms of service several times, and was recently fined by the AI authorities in California for violating provisions in the state's AI Accountability Act. Carla also had heard that several Neur-O-links had "gone rogue" and committed crimes on behalf of their users, due to inadequate ethical protocols. Further, the fine print in the company's policies states that the device doesn't even belong to the wearer but is provided via a month-to-month lease that X-Brainiac can modify or rescind at any time. All in all, the Neur-O-link doesn't seem right for Carla.

As it turns out, Deeper Edge has begun offering its own version of a cranial interface, called the GliaLink. This device operates somewhat differently. Carla has full control over its use as an interface, so that it captures as few or many thought patterns as Carla is comfortable sharing. None of that data goes anywhere but to her personal data pod in her living room. In fact, the GliaLink device fully meets standards body IETF's new e2a (edge-to-any) design standard, which prioritizes control by the individual at the Web's edge, but with ethical "no harm" safeguards in place to protect others from bad acts. Deeper Edge and Corey help her manage the data and its behavioral inferences at her request, but by all rights, it is hers alone.

Finishing her latte, and after concluding conversations with her friends, Carla muses that sometimes she feels a bit like the protagonist in the Dune sci-fi series. Many characters were equipped with something called a "Holtzman shield," a portable force field generator worn on their belt. The characters activated the shield to deflect projectiles and ward off physical attacks. In Carla's case, the Holtzman shield is more like a virtual force field, created by a mix of her Net fiduciary, Corey, and her GliaLink device. Whether online or offline, Carla senses that she is being protected from harm by her very own digital life support system. In that safe space, she feels a sense of openness and ease. This gives her more confidence to promote her best self into the Web, on her own terms, and with the fiduciary assistance of Deeper Edge and Corey.

Engaging with Her Neighbors

Back on the main street, as Ada parts ways to do some shopping, Carla observes her fellow citizens walk the streets, Neur-O-links glowing faintly with reddish light by their ears. She feels a sense of unease. At least with Corey at her side, she has some tangible protection from the MOPs and their Institutional AIs and their DAMB ecosystems. What hope was there for so many other people who don't appear to see the dangers and the missed opportunities involved?

It turns out that Carla is not alone. A growing number of her neighbors and friends have been rejecting the current wave of *technologies that saps them of their ability to think and decide things for themselves. This becomes more evident as Carla enters her local bookstore to attend a meeting of fans of women fiction authors. There, she notices that the wearers of GliaLinks slightly outnumber the Neur-O-links.*

Several months before, Corey had helped Carla set up the book club online, in a fully secure and protected online environment. Today, seventeen of her fellow fiction fans have showed up for the meeting. Before the meeting comes to order, Carla chats with several of her new acquaintances. They mention having signed up as clients with Net fiduciaries, much as Carla had done the previous year, and how different their online and offline experiences have become. As the neighbors compare notes, Carla smiles to herself. Perhaps the future is not written in stone after all. Perhaps the World Wide Web of her childhood and early adulthood is being rewoven, all around her, in more trustworthy ways.

D > A

Later, Carla makes dinner for Ada, VR-calls her father, watches an immersive action movie highly touted by her Carla Recommendation Engine, and eventually turns in for the night. Another full day, one where she's been more in charge of all her virtual and physical interactions. All in all, it felt... really good.

D>A

e2a

/C18/A THEORY OF CHANGE FOR GLIANET

"We're all interested in the future, for that is where you and I are going to spend the rest of our lives."

– "Plan 9 from Outer Space" movie (1959)

If we wish to successfully confront and overcome the SEAMs paradigm, we need a clear-eyed perspective on what is necessary for the task. No doubt this is a challenging, complex, multi-year endeavor. Nonetheless, collaborative pathways for real change are possible, and mapping out their prospects is a crucial exercise at the outset. The digitally empowered Carla of 2032 is well within our grasp.

Establishing a Theory of Change

When confronted with the need to make a fundamental alteration in the way they operate in the world, many organizations have adopted what has been termed a *theory of change*. This theory is intended to be a systematic, empirically based process of mapping out why an organization's desired change (say, launch of a new product, or passage of a major piece of federal legislation) should occur in a particular context.[617] The notion is to promote reasonable long-term outcomes that are recognized, supported, and acceptable to all stakeholders.

A successful theory of change begins with the desired outcome (Point B), and then works backwards to the present day (Point A) by identifying all the conditions that must be in place for that outcome to occur. An organization specifies some details about the desired alteration, such as the target population, amount of change necessary to signal success, and timeframe over which the change is expected to occur. In other words, a classic "if-then" statement: if a certain event happens, then another specified event can be expected to occur. The approach focuses in particular on what has been termed by some the "missing middle," the space in time "between what a program or change initiative does... and how these lead to desired goals being achieved."[618] This cartoon well illustrates the challenge of exposing those causal chains:

"I THINK YOU SHOULD BE MORE EXPLICIT HERE IN STEP TWO."

As we saw, Carla in 2032 provides a useful long-term goal to achieve. Carla is enjoying the services of a certified Net fiduciary (Deeper Edge), a fully agential Personal AI (Corey), a cranial interface (GliaLink), a personal data pod, a localized cloudlet, and a host of empowering applications such as LEVIT and JOYCE. While much of this advanced technology is available now or can reasonably be created in the next few years, neither the Net fiduciary nor the authentic PAI agent exists today. In the remaining chapters, we will discuss a GliaNet provisional theory of change (PToC) that—if at least somewhat accurate in its assessment of necessary conditions and how to bring them about—can lead us on the path to Carla's future digital self of 2032.

According to the Center for Theory of Change, devising such a theory's "outcomes map" typically contains six stages:

- Setting long-term goals
- Identifying preconditions necessary to achieve those goals
- Identifying basic assumptions about the context

- Identifying the interventions necessary to create the desired change

- Developing ways to measure performance of the initiative

- Explaining the logic of the narrative to others

Because any theory of change can only be a frozen moment in time—a conjecture about what may or may not happen years into the future—it is imperative to leave breathing room in the roadmap. New contingencies will inevitably emerge or disappear that may cause us to question our assumptions and preconditions. Allowing for revisions and updates over time will ensure that the theory of change remains accurate, relevant, and practical.[619] This also highlights the desirability of including many voices, including experts in pertinent fields, when crafting an effective theory of change.

The Mozilla Trustworthy AI Theory of Change

One relevant example of a well-established theory of change and accompanying outcomes map has been developed by the Mozilla Foundation. Both as a matter of process and of substance, Mozilla's "Trustworthy AI Theory of Change" provides useful fodder for a related GliaNet PToC.

Mozilla has set a long-term goal of consumer-focused AI technology that is "demonstrably worthy of trust," and enriches the lives of human beings.[620] This tech should include considerations for privacy, transparency, human well-being, and accountability for harms.[621] Mozilla's theory identifies four different workstreams, which it calls "levers," taking place over 5-plus years: (1) shifting industry norms, (2) building new tech and products, (3) generating demand, and (4) creating regulations and incentives.[622] In turn, these can be made possible, if not likely, through four "middle" objectives: (1) industry players adopting best practices, (2) technologists creating agential AIs, (3) markets forming of willing sellers and consumers, and (4) policymakers devising effective regulation.

Four years after its initial white paper announcing its theory of change for Trustworthy AI, Mozilla in 2024 released an updated report on its progress.[623] Among their key takeaways: while there is a wave of startups, researchers, and others shifting norm towards more open and trustworthy AI, "we have not yet seen a wave of mainstream consumer products that give people real choice over how they interact with AI. This is a key gap in the market."[624] Mozilla is looking to generate more progress towards its goal by supporting several interventions, including contributing to open-source AI projects, educating consumers about potential choices for AI products, and advocating for new public policies based on more openness and accountability by product builders. Notably, the paper seeks public input on each of its four levers and proposed interventions, with further work yet to be done.

Devising GliaNet's Provisional Theory of Change

For GliaNet, we will in many respects mirror the Mozilla Foundation's multi-layered approach to devising a theory of change. As we saw with the Mozilla example, the optimal approach to fleshing out such a theory is to engage with relevant stakeholders. Since announcing its intention to develop a theory of change for trustworthy AI in 2019, the Mozilla Foundation first workshopped its ideas internally, then collaborated with hundreds of partners to define its terms and comment on an initial change framework.

By contrast, the GliaNet initiative is at the beginning stages of a fully developed theory of change. What is presented here as one person's proposal therefore should be considered provisional, subject to additional explorations. As we will discuss further in this part, a coalition of potential stakeholders, such as the newly-launched GliaNet Alliance, should come together to begin the process of assessing, validating, and improving upon the various elements of a provisional theory of change for GliaNet.

Our Outcome

For the GliaNet PToC, our overarching goal is adoption of the HAACS paradigm: human autonomy and agency achieved through computational systems. Our shorthand for these two components is the D>A governance principle and the e2a design principle. With this goal and these two overarching principles in mind, we can propose our long-term outcome for the 2032 time period:

> *In the market system, our primary target—willing sellers and buyers—have produced a viable, competitive marketplace for NetTMs and authentic PAI agents, operating consistently with the D>A and e2a principles.*

The Center for Theory of Change also recommends developing indicators to measure our outcomes to assess the performance of the initiative.[625] So, our GliaNet PToC also identifies our desired outcome in terms of two specific metrics.

By 2032:

- *at least 50 million Americans will be served by a Net fiduciary, data trust, or other NetTM, and*

- *at least 50 million Americans will be utilizing an authentic PAI agent.*

By that date, we should see a pronounced shift in the Web's governing principles—with a significant portion of the population moving away from entities that employ the SEAMs paradigm in favor of those that employ the HAACS paradigm. While the focus here is the United States (given my deeper understanding of its markets and public policy spaces), similar outcomes in other parts of the world are doable and obviously would be welcomed.

Now that we have our goals spelled out in more concrete terms, how do we get there from here?

Our Four Pathways

Crucially, change processes are not linear and one-dimensional but consist of overlapping complex systems and feedback loops.[626] Given the complexity of the Web ecosystem, we can follow Mozilla's expert lead and recognize four intertwined systems pathways that would collectively lead us to our desired markets-based outcome:

- Private governance systems
- Public governance systems
- Technology design systems
- Social fabric

For each of these four pathways, in the rest of this book we will meet the basic theory of change requirements by laying out the assumptions, the preconditions, and the interventions. The initial assumptions are fairly straightforward as you will see. The following chapters will discuss the necessary precondition of willing competitors and consumers, then our proposed change-making interventions.

Our Assumptions

Under the theory of change literature, an assumption is a necessary condition to achieving the preferred outcome. By definition, this condition already exists, and so is considered non-problematic. With our admittedly narrow gaze primarily (but not exclusively) on the United States, our four provisional assumptions focus on affirmative statements about opportunities for change:

- Private governance: Stakeholders such as for-profit companies have the ability to willingly become NetTMs and Net fiduciaries.

- Technology design: Software and hardware engineers have the ability to create new, interconnected edgetech technologies

- Public governance: Policymakers have the ability to use their powers to adopt a range of "hard law" (laws, regulations) and "soft law" (policies, inducements) that benefit the GliaNet initiative.

- Social fabric: All of us (as Web users, consumers, citizens, investors) have the ability to utilize more ethical companies and more human-empowering technologies.

Our Preconditions

With our GliaNet PToC, now we move from opportunities for change, to incentives for change. Seeing that the door is open for new human-centered systems to be born provides no guarantee that anyone will actually decide to walk through it. In the next chapter, we will take on perhaps the most crucial of our preconditions—that a number of willing entities agree to become NetTMs and Net fiduciaries. From there, our main task in the following four chapters will be to develop tailored interventions for our four pathways.

For now, here is a sketch of our PToC for GliaNet:

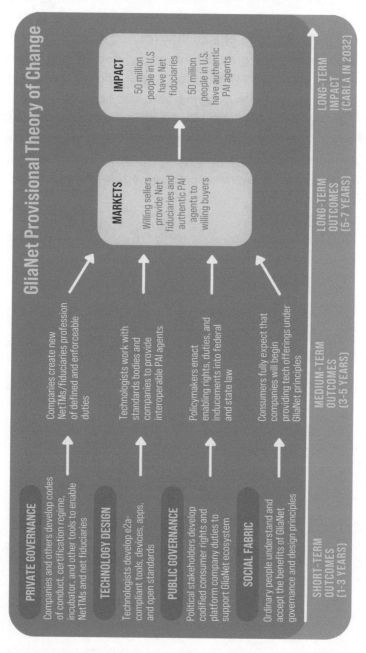

Finding the market players

As we have seen, any successful theory of change must be supported by necessary preconditions. In the case of GliaNet, our preferred outcome of a healthy marketplace of NetTMs and Net fiduciaries serving customers and clients hinges decidedly on market dynamics. An obvious precondition is that a suitable number of marketplace players (for-profit companies large and small, as well as non-profits) find it attractive to voluntarily take on the fiduciary duties of care and loyalty, embed them in useful tech service offerings, and offer them to willing consumers. In the next chapter, we will explore whether such a market can actually exist.

/C19/SATISFYING THE PRECONDITION OF WILLING COMPETITORS

"The interest of the producer ought to be attended to, only so far as it may be necessary for promoting that of the consumer."

– Adam Smith, The Wealth of Nations

The GliaNet PToC relies on the presence of NetTMs voluntarily engaging with customers under a general duty of care (no harms), and Net fiduciaries voluntarily engaging with clients under duties of fidelity (no conflicts of duty) and loyalty (promote the client's best interests). A key question presents itself: can we rely on markets to deliver us the benefits of GliaNet? This would entail bringing together willing sellers and willing buyers, based on new relationships of trust and ethical practice.

For-profit companies and other entities must be willing to take on the mantle of data steward, and ordinary people must be willing to utilize these services, probably for a fee. Can such an ecosystem not just survive but flourish in competition with the SEAMs-based Web of today?

This chapter seeks to answer that question, relying on the Carla in 2032 thought experiment. Imagine a world where there was an actual Net fiduciary providing advanced technologies to its clientele under duties of care and loyalty. What exactly would it look like, and what would be its motivations to exist in the first place? This chapter will unpack some of those challenges, including both specific inducements for companies to voluntarily accept the mantle of a Net fiduciary, and growing instabilities in the current Web market that provide competitive opportunities for GliaNet-inspired market entry.

Confronting a Mixed History

We should acknowledge an important historical fact: no technology company grounded in fiduciary duties is operating in the market today. Why is that? A first study from the dawn of the 21st century may provide some clues.

In their 1999 book *Net Worth*, John Hagel and Marc Singer first raised the concept of what they called an "information intermediary".[627] They posited that the coming years of the 21st century would see a flourishing new market in such "infomediaries," who would act as digital agents to manage the collection and sale of a consumer's information. The authors even worked out the math, showing how companies would make billions of dollars in revenue from serving customers, which in turn would receive $1,400 in 1999 dollars (approximately $2,650 in 2024 dollars) in annual benefits from such services. Yet, over the next 20 years, no such market emerged.

In 2019, Hagel revisited his book's original premise.[628] Acknowledging the paucity of infomediaries, he observed that two different waves of companies sought to target the infomediary opportunity: those focused on protecting the consumer's privacy, and those focused on providing revenue opportunities in exchange for the consumer's sale of their personal data. Hagel concluded that there was insufficient value in either the data privacy or the data monetization business models for consumers to be interested.[629]

Instead, Hagel realized that the true market value of the infomediary was in providing timely access to Web resources that truly matter to the consumer. This more expansive business model "assumed that the infomediary would be a trusted advisor who would be proactive in connecting us to relevant resources based on deep insight into our individual needs and aspirations."[630] While few such advisors had emerged by 2019, he saw signs of progress, stating "The key is to pick the right entry point and to build trust and scale as rapidly as possible."[631]

Obviously, Hagel's proposed trusted advisor role fits well with the fiduciary duties of fidelity and/or loyalty. Perhaps adding these duties as a company branding element, plus widening the scope of service offerings beyond just protecting privacy and selling data, will make for a more attractive consumer offering.

Less Attractive SEAMs-Based Commerce

There may be another reason why a market for information intermediaries has not yet developed. The assumption of most people today is that the SEAMs-based marketplace is all but impervious to outside competition, that the MOPS and DAMBs have developed an unassailable "secret sauce" yielding them exorbitant revenues and profits. If this assessment is true, it would deter most companies from even bothering to compete in the commercial Web space.

What, however, if that assumption is incorrect? What if the current Web regime is actually becoming less attractive for the MOPs and their ecosystem of DAMBs?

In reality, while the SEAMs paradigm seems to be firmly entrenched at the heart of the Web, the dubious online tracking and extraction approach that helps fuel it is slowly but surely shifting. There are five main causes:

- *User awareness:* As end users become more cognizant of the uneven tradeoffs in terms of eroded privacy and loss of control, their trust in ads-based platforms is ebbing. One remarkable figure is that over a third of Web users globally, and nearly half of Web users in the United States, have adopted browser applications that block much if not all online advertising. [632] Those numbers continue to rise every year, especially among younger people. Consequently, marketers are having difficulty tracking and measuring the actual successes of their advertising campaigns.[633] Sites such as YouTube, Spotify, and Pandora are implementing various anti-ad blocking technologies,[634] which is likely to further alienate users.

- *Advertiser skepticism:* Ironically, advertisers themselves are growing wary of the markets they have helped create.

As former Googler Tim Hwang explains, the industry is grappling with well-founded concerns about the opacity of measures for success, the decreasing value of ad inventory, widespread fraud, the persistence of data silos, and "subprime user attention."[635] In late 2021, noted tech guru Scott Galloway proclaimed the imminent collapse of the entire digital advertising market, in large part due to persistent and rising levels of online ad fraud—some $150B worth by 2025.[636]

- More recently, Jon Bradshaw of Brand Traction has queried how the online marketing tech sector is a $700 billion industry, "but the ads you see are still crap."[637] From his extensive research and "jaw-dropping insights," Bradshaw concludes that much of that ad spending is a "delusion" because the underlying user data is so poor—to the point that the expense of ads targeting actually outweighs the return.[638] Taken together, these concerns point to the potential for an outright digital advertising market implosion.

- *Regulatory compliance:* The continuing desire of Web-based companies to collect, store, and analyze personal data is running into the harsh reality of increased risks from regulatory compliance and accompanying brand erosion. The European Union's e-commerce directive requires that an end user give "informed consent" before a website can use cookie tracking. GDPR, in effect since 2018, goes further by branding cookie identifiers as personal data, which triggers a lengthy list of compliance mandates. More than two dozen states in the United States have enacted data protection laws, while the US Congress has been debating a federal data privacy statute. So long as online companies fail to take advantage of new technologies that reduce the need to collect, hold, and analyze third party data, these regulatory compliance and brand risks only grow more acute.

- *Eroding MOPs support:* Even the online platforms themselves are growing increasingly uneasy at the paradigm they have helped foster. Mozilla, Apple, and Microsoft were first to pull away from supporting third-party tracking. Even Google's on-again, off-again plans to deprecate third party cookies on its Chrome browser demonstrates its concerns about the continuing efficacy of that surveillance mechanism.[639] Concurrently, the MOPs and DAMBs have been exploring alternative ways of surreptitiously tracking users, including device fingerprinting. This creates an intriguing opening for other market-based models that do not rely on cookies-based surveillance and data extraction.

If true, even to some extent, these instabilities in current Web markets leave intriguing breathing space for new competitive challenge. What then are some of the positive incentives for market entry by a Net fiduciary?

Inducements for Competitive Entry

The GliaNet PToC posits that sufficient numbers of for-profit companies are willing and able to voluntarily take on the mantle of a NetTM, and provide the kinds of services that Carla enjoys in 2032. Here, we will unpack some of the net benefits that a for-profit company considering becoming a Net fiduciary might enjoy.

The virtuous feedback cycle

First and foremost, a loyalty-based commercial relationship opens up opportunities to provide trusted services and offerings that SEAMs-based companies cannot match. Today's SEAMs-based companies typically acquire their data and inferences surreptitiously from websites, apps, and environments that capture data points about us, hiding their true intentions in opaque policies behind tightly-controlled interfaces. The insights they glean tend to reflect our recent past (what we said or did today or yesterday) rather than the present and future (what we intend to do today, or tomorrow, or next week). As a result, while germane as a stitched-together snapshot, these assessments are incomplete and even inaccurate going forward as a portrait of a living, breathing, ever-evolving human being.

So, for example, the pair of blue travel pants that Carla purchases online in her 2032 era JOYCE cart appears to be a relevant data point to non-trustworthy companies seeking to sell her other clothing in the near future. However, the informational content of that single data point has its limits. Perhaps, as turns out to be the case, Carla likes travel pants but already has what she needs. Perhaps next week, she will want different pants, or a matching jacket, or shoes. Perhaps the data point itself is incorrect, as she bought the pants for someone else, or by mistake, or was prodded by persistent marketing and now regrets the purchase. These important indicators of true intention—actual knowledge, rather than isolated bits of information—will likely not come through in the surreptitious data inferences that the MOPs collect through SEAMs cycles.

A Net fiduciary could have trusted access to that real-time personal knowledge, and so would ensure that your present and future intentions are fully met. Its actions would be a more accurate reflection of who you are and how you want to be in the world. As these intentions are made real through those entities' actions, your satisfaction level rises. Your social trust deepens. As the entity both protects you from harm and actively finds tangible ways to enhance and promote your best interests over time, you become willing to volunteer more of yourself. In complex system terms, a virtuous feedback cycle of mutual benefit forms, then strengthens, and this spurs the addition of still more empowering service offerings.

This is also why those same travel pants already purchased by someone today, without the benefit of a Net fiduciary, will follow that person around in repeated ads, pointlessly, creepily, for days, weeks, even months. This reality is an obvious indicator that today's ads-based market has its problems, but also points the way to the obvious solution of right relationship. Carla in 2032 is an individual embedded in personal and social trust webs of her own creation. On her terms. In ways that the MOPs and DAMBs and their SEAMs paradigm cannot effectively reach.

This observation also links back to Hagel's research-based realization in 2019. He concluded that protecting a consumer's privacy and selling her data, while perhaps useful functions, are not sufficient in themselves to entice consumers to sign up with an "infomediary." By contrast, the GliaNet initiative offers agential and relational advantages not found in his study, and that certainly cannot be duplicated in SEAMs-based markets. In brief, the proposed value proposition is unique among would-be competitors. For consumers, no other market entity currently offers the unique combination of tangible benefits: the loyal support of a true fiduciary, the vigilant defense of a Web guardian, the mediating function of a "digital lifestreams" manager, and empowering cool edgetech.

Other tangible benefits of market entry

- *Offers companies the ability to define addressable market*: At the outset, Net fiduciaries likely would not look to directly supplant the many entities operating under the SEAMs paradigm or ask Web users to do the same. Doing so would only draw them into fruitless market battles with dominant players. Instead, in keeping with "blue ocean" strategies, the real advantage comes from playing a completely different commercial game, using authentic trust as a market differentiator. As such, Net fiduciaries seek to create new commercial opportunities focused not on replacing what exists now but introducing novel ways for users to interact with the current Web, and where individuals have newfound power to leverage more respectful commercial dialogue and connections. The addressable market is very real, but the Net fiduciary would have the flexibility to define it to match its own capabilities and aspirations.

- *Opens up opportunities for smaller players*: Entrepreneurial opportunities abound in such a nascent sector. Smaller entities, including start-ups, may perceive niche business-to-business (B2B) opportunities. This could include pursuing disruptive market options (such as the blockchain-based tokenization of data) and developing advanced edgetech tools (such as authentic PAI agents and personal data pods) that larger client-facing companies will want to employ. As part of a larger human-centered ecosystem, entities offering data monetization opportunities also can find a place. Examples of novel data-centric business models include "PIMs" (personal information managers) in the United Kingdom,[640] and Jaron Lanier's "MIDs" (mediators of individual data).[641] While none of these entities are NetTMs (operating under a duty of care) or Net fiduciaries (operating under duties of fidelity and loyalty), they have demonstrated the more limited viability of markets built for sharing a customer's personal data in exchange for compensation.

- *Provides new relevance to larger companies*: Potential market entrants could include larger companies seeking additional services to both retain existing customers and attract new ones. These companies could range from retailers of goods and services to news organizations, broadband providers, entertainment companies, and financial firms. Many such entities struggle to find relevance and revenue in a market dominated by the MOPs and their DAMB ecosystems. Digital offerings provided under a more ethical "race-to-the-top" business ethos could complement current service offerings and tap into the network effects of having an embedded customer base. Incumbents with existing customers or subscribers can use the NetTM model to create more "stickiness" in those relationships.

- *Invites exploration of different payment models:* For-profit Net fiduciaries can explore a variety of compensation mechanisms. This can include higher quality advertising, marketing, and branding arrangements, built on the client "intent-casting" their aspirations to the Web, rather than the other way around. Established commercial brands may welcome the opportunity to explore alternative mutually beneficial arrangements with their customers. Other funding models (from monthly subscriptions to per-transaction fees to blockchain utility tokens) are also possible. Another approach is where businesses utilize so-called "reverse meters," which compensate users with data/attention credits whenever they watch an ad or otherwise interact with specified content.[642]

- *Harnesses trust-as-a-service:* Enhancing trust with clients can foster its own attractive incentives. The corporate world is beginning to take notice of the financial value of generating "trust-as-a-service" when deploying digital services. Accenture's 2020 Vision report for global corporate leaders observes: "In the future, people don't just want more technology in our products and services; we want technology that is more human... Trust and accountability are the new litmus tests for businesses in a world where digital is everywhere."[643]

- *Creates a brand differentiator:* Companies who especially care about bolstering their branding may find the fiduciary mantle an attractive one. As we see for example in the financial advisors space,[644] adopting fiduciary duties could be one way for an entity to stand out in a crowded marketplace.

- *Avoids unnecessary legal liability:* Another set of incentives is a favorite of lawyers: risk mitigation. The Web involves an increasingly complicated and messy set of legal and regulatory compliance obligations, such as GDPR in Europe and state privacy laws in the United States. A fiduciary-based model that includes limited control over its client's data could provide a feasible way to minimize liability and compliance risks from data breaches, identity theft, and a host of other SEAMs-based ills. Such a model also could be a useful way to influence future legislative efforts.

- *Gets ahead of the herd:* Finally, there is the reality of bandwagon effects. Once a number of entities enter the Net fiduciaries market, others may feel compelled to do so—motivated by preventing competitors from seizing early market advantage. And, if nothing else, out of the fear of being left behind in the digital economy.

Progressing to the How

These two chapters have laid out GliaNet's provisional theory of change, leading us to a world populated by Net fiduciaries and authentic PAI agents, along with a brief analysis of the crucial precondition of a willing marketplace of such entities. The remaining chapters provide four "how" pathways, through private governance, technology design, public governance, and social fabric. As we will see, these pathways provide levers of change that each of us can pull, bringing us ever closer to the Carla of 2032.

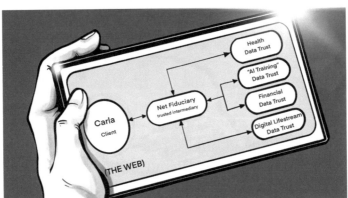

/C20/LEVERS OF CHANGE: A PRIVATE GOVERNANCE FRAMEWORK

As we saw in Part One, governance refers to the set of rules that establishes how a particular organization or institution operates. We also distinguished between two forms. Public (also called macro) governance encompasses the laws, regulations, and other binding policy instruments typically adopted by governmental bodies. These tend to mandate, preclude, or incentivize certain marketplace actions.

In the data protection context, examples include GDPR in Europe, California Consumer Privacy Act (CCPA)/California Privacy Rights Act (CPRA) in California, and sector-specific laws at the US federal level, such as Health Insurance Portability and Accountability Act (HIPAA) (health care data) and Children's Online Privacy Protection Act (COPPA) (children's data).

By contrast, private (also called micro) governance is the set of rules that an entity (often, a corporation) adopts to manage its own practices. In the data protection context, for example, a company would agree to embed certain elements of data governance into the user privacy policies that apply to its daily offerings and activities.

Importantly, while public governance policies tend to be imposed by government decree, private governance policies can be crafted and implemented unilaterally by entities, reflecting commercial priorities, societal mandates, and/or voluntary obligations. Indeed, one noteworthy advantage of the NetTMs and Net fiduciaries models is that they need not be adopted via prescriptive legislation and managed through challenging political processes. Instead, interested entities and individuals can use private governance tools to begin to establish these loyalty-based fiduciary relationships right now, as anchors to a more trustworthy and accountable Web ecosystem.

The GliaNet PToC proposed in this book relies on a marketplace of willing Net fiduciaries. The particular intervention or lever of change to be discussed in this chapter is that embedding trust-based governance inputs within voluntary online entities can jumpstart an ecosystem that revolves around ethically minded players. With these entities, the concepts of ethical data governance can become instantiated in commercial operations. How then do we get from here to there? To answer this, we will look at a few initial intervention ideas that revolve around a new "coalition of the willing" called the GliaNet Alliance.

Inviting Willing Collaborators

A productive first step is to assemble a coalition of companies interested in becoming a NetTM or Net fiduciary. We'll call it the GliaNet Alliance. Obviously, these entities will have resisted the SEAMs paradigm, instead seeing true market value in serving customers in relationships based on genuine trust, support, and mutual benefit. While these entities may have the perspective and incentives to provide ethically based service offerings, most probably lack the necessary expertise to translate such motives into principles, policies, and practices. By the same token, academics and experts who propose ethical data governance have developed a number of intriguing proposals but have been largely consigned to proverbial whiteboards and may lack the validation of real-world marketplace experience.

One crucial premise of the GliaNet PToC is that to be successful, the fiduciary duty of loyalty must be adopted voluntarily, by a willing entity, rather than turned into a legal mandate. As we saw in the last chapter, the Net fiduciaries model rests on a base of positive incentives and motivations due to its reliance on voluntary, opt-in relationships between willing parties. Otherwise, imposing a legal requirement of loyalty on existing SEAMs-based companies will likely for most turn it into an unwanted compliance program, with minimal buy-in. As Tamar Frankel and others have observed from historical precedent, forced loyalty is no loyalty at all. [645] This also raises the question of whether the MOPs themselves should be welcomed into the field of Net fiduciaries. Operating as they do today under the SEAMs paradigm, the answer surely is no. However, this does not mean they cannot renunciate that paradigm and take affirmative steps to become bona fide fiduciaries.

What follows are a few useful theory of change interventions that such an alliance could take on.

Casting a Wide Net

While the core work of the GliaNet Alliance is to determine whether and how new trust-based commercial markets can be formed, its membership should not be limited to traditional for-profit companies. For example, many social mission-driven entities may have their own motivations to become Net fiduciaries. In particular, the Certified B corp model requires companies to balance purpose and profit by considering the impact of their decisions on workers, customers, suppliers, community, and the environment.

Other potential Alliance members with more community-focused charters include credit unions, agricultural co-ops, membership organizations, and trade unions. Non-profit organizations seeking to become Net fiduciaries could be supported by foundations and charitable entities. In many countries, public libraries are chartered to provide the general public with knowledge and information and are managed by professional librarians who already act as quasi-fiduciaries towards their patrons.

In addition, those with an interest in the topic (such as academics, researchers, public interest entities, and the like) should participate in the Alliance as well. Indeed, the GliaNet PToC generally—and this intervention in particular—will mean little if not subject to validation by a wide variety of interested stakeholders. The provisional nature of our theory of change means that it should be seen as the beginning point for exploration, not the end.

Exploring Frameworks

As I have suggested, we can imagine two different tiers of NetTMs. The core level of NetTM would operate under a general tort-like duty of care, while an actual Net fiduciary would operate under heightened duties of fidelity and loyalty. Part of the new Alliance's role could be to confirm the viability of this layered approach, and in the process flesh out what it means in everyday contexts. After all, sheer loyalty in the absence of any sense of care does not necessarily guarantee the moral quality of the actions that are informed by it.[646]

As we will see, one version of this two-tiered framework could be carried over into the public governance space. While Net fiduciaries would continue to remain outside the realm of legal mandates, government bodies could decide that the duty of care should extend as a requirement to any entity who becomes involved with personal data and/or consequential AI decision engines. The "do no harm" and "act prudently" injunctions that accompany a broad duty of care seem well-suited for such a mandate. We will discuss this further in Chapter Twenty-Two.

Devising Uniform Policies and Practices

While each online company operates in its own way, most share certain common private governance instruments. Typically, these include a corporate mission statement, terms of service (ToS), code of conduct, data protection policy, and privacy policy, Authorized Use Policy (AUP), Application Programming Interface (API) policy, and others. To the extent that the Alliance membership believes these governance instruments should fully reflect what it means to be a NetTM or Net fiduciary in the world, it would make sense to work together to develop some uniformity in definition and nomenclature.

The book has also proposed the "PEP" model (protecting, enhancing, and promoting the individual) as a way to capture the core fiduciary duties and match them up against particular service offerings. The GliaNet Alliance could investigate whether this framing is useful and can be implemented as a template by the new ranks of NetTMs and Net fiduciaries.

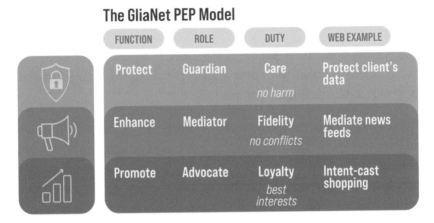

The GliaNet PEP Model

	FUNCTION	ROLE	DUTY	WEB EXAMPLE
	Protect	Guardian	Care *no harm*	Protect client's data
	Enhance	Mediator	Fidelity *no conflicts*	Mediate news feeds
	Promote	Advocate	Loyalty *best interests*	Intent-cast shopping

Defining Our Digital Rights

If GliaNet's *D>A* governance principle is to be upheld, it would be useful to understand how our rights as a digital citizen should be defined and applied. As one example, members of the Alliance could work with human rights lawyers and other experts to create a new *Human:Digital Code* that would help translate greater autonomy and agency into a viable set of online rights. For ordinary people, these could include the right to:

Delegation: The ability to delegate their *human:digital* rights to any designated third-party entities (natural or artificial persons), operating under a confirmed duty of fidelity and loyalty to them.

Clarity: The ability to understand the impact of Institutional AI systems on them and their *human:digital* rights.

<u>Query</u>: The ability to ask relevant questions about the consequential decisions and impacts of such computational systems.

<u>Negotiate</u>: The ability to engage in give-and-take over the terms and conditions of such decisions and impacts on them.

<u>Challenge</u>: The ability to oppose the consequential decisions and their impacts on them.

<u>Recourse</u>: The ability to seek and gain recourse for the impact of such decisions on them.

<u>Consent</u>: The ability to provide meaningful, voluntary, opt-in consent to decisions of consequence by any attempted computational system, via symmetrical interfaces of screens, scenes, and unseens.

Balancing Societal Interests

Under the HAACS paradigm, the individual can be considered as the center point of concentric rings that in turn include agential relationships with her NetTM, her authentic PAI agent, other technology developers/companies, and of course society at large. Nonetheless, a singular focus on an individual's digital rights, grounded in freedom of thought (autonomy) and action (agency), understates the complexity of the human being as a social creature. As we saw in Chapter One, constraints on our freedoms are both inevitable, and sometimes absolutely necessary.

As one example, in the face of bad acts and bad actors, the fiduciary duties of fidelity and loyalty have proven not to be absolute. Loyalty to an individual does not provide a shield against that person's ultimate responsibility for harmful or even illegal acts. The common law of fiduciaries has always recognized and incorporated these larger societal considerations. Physicians for example typically must identify to health authorities highly contagious patients—even against their wishes—as well as report to licensing authorities about negligent acts committed by fellow physicians. Under the "crime-fraud" exception, attorneys must report to law enforcement about clients about to commit serious crimes. A similar balancing of interests must be established for the new sector of NetTMs and Net fiduciaries, and applied as guardrails to the authentic PAI agents that represent the individual in the world.

Building a New Profession

An option worth exploring is turning the concept of a Net fiduciary into an actual profession. Much as society today has bona fide professionals who manage our health (physicians), our legal status (attorneys), and our money (certain financial advisors), we should consider having a new set of professionals who help manage important aspects of our digital selves.

By way of example, Jerry Kang and others have suggested that what they call "personal data guardians" play an intermediary role in the information ecosystem, complete with "a professional identity of expertise and service."[647] The core of this new profession would be acting as a client's trustworthy confidante, zealous advocate, and wise counsellor.[648]

One avenue to explore is the creation of a novel type of corporation: the "D Corp." This for-profit company would provide data-based digital services to clients. But importantly, these digital corporations would be chartered to operate under express fiduciary duties of care and loyalty. Operating much like a partnership firm of attorneys or doctors, the D Corp could be set up in the United States at the State level and potentially become the vehicle for a new profession of Net fiduciaries.

Crafting an Enforceable Certification Regime

Any viable profession includes an acknowledged accountability requirement, typically promoted through the official granting of a license or certification to provide services. Experts in fiduciary law note that the existence of such accountability and compliance mechanisms can enhance trust, and greatly reduce entrustors' risks.[649] Such a certification requirement could include awarding entities a so-called "trust mark" for meeting certain requirements to become a NetTM or Net fiduciary.

These indicia of trust provide a transparent basis for consumers to rely on the fact that the entity is operating as it claims to be. Such trust is vital if this new class of professionals is to find footing in the market. As with other professions, enforcing any certification or license can be handled by a self-regulating industry group, or via a governmental body.

Advising Policymakers

Given their potential involvement in many facets of establishing trust-based mechanisms for the Web, members of the GliaNet Alliance will over time develop relevant expertise. As policymakers in the US Congress and in other law-making bodies consider legislative approaches to regulating Web activities, the Alliance can serve as an educational resource. One example is defining with some particularity the duties of care, fidelity, and loyalty, as they apply to the complexities of Web-based interactions. More on these topics will be discussed in Chapter Twenty-Two.

/C21/LEVERS OF CHANGE: OPPORTUNITIES FOR TECHNOLOGISTS

Much as the Internet has served as a generalized platform supporting the Web, so can it serve a similar role for future platforms such as GliaNet. In particular, as we saw earlier, forward-thinking tech standards bodies like the IEEE have staked out important claims about how advanced AI tools should be used to further, and not dampen, human autonomy and agency. We will need many committed technologists on board with that vision.

At the individual human level, the picture that emerges from more edgetech design principles, such as e2a, is one of personal autonomy and control. Depending on which initiatives are pursued, people will be able to enjoy for the first time individual network connectivity, personalized cloudlets, localized lifestreams, fully owned personal devices, intelligent personal agents—all tied to a trusted NetTM. The hope is that these technology tools can enable human flourishing for each individual, on their own terms. At the same time, ethical protocols built into the technologies and their standards can help ensure that the people being represented are not themselves the source of bad acts against others.

The larger collective benefits should also be noted. Deliberately pushing more intelligence and control to the edge of the network—consistent with the Net's end-to-end principle—opens up new vistas for experimentation, self-organizing, and self-governing, all based on mutual trust. The potential impact on society, markets, and politics (how we work and live, who we interact with and vote for, and what we create, modify, and preserve) cannot be overestimated.

Role for AI Interoperability: The Virtual Glue

As explained earlier, interoperability (interop) refers to the ability for different computer networks to interact, and to exchange data. A related function, data portability, refers to end users' ability to use interoperable systems to move their data from one online platform to another. Together, these two technical requirements can open up existing online services to greater end user choice and facilitate new forms of competition. This chapter will focus on AI interop as perhaps the most important technical requirement to enable the related edgetech levers of change for our GliaNet PToC. There is also important overlap with the governance practices of industry standards bodies like IEEE and IETF.

With regard to two different computational systems, AI interop refers to the ways they connect and interact with each other at physical and virtual levels. As an example, for one PAI to "talk" directly with an Institutional AI, there must be an accepted means of two-way communication, and an agreement to act upon it.

The basic interop fabric is already there to support robust binary interfaces. After all, the Internet is a splendid example of an interconnected "network of networks." Symmetrical interfaces using the e2a design principle can mirror that same peer-to-peer architecture, so my system would speak on equal terms with your system in a reciprocal manner. What would change is the Web's current overlay of unidirectional interfaces leading to tightly controlled platforms.

In the context of AI systems, experts have recognized two basic forms of interop: vertical, where an AI agent can connect to multiple AI platforms, and horizontal, where AI platforms and agents can connect with each other.

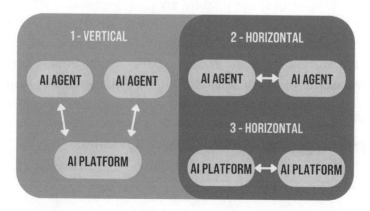

Mozilla Corporation has been a leading advocate for interop. In 2019, they released a working paper arguing that in any pro-competition policy adopted by governments, "standards and interoperability [must] be at the center."[650] Chris Riley, former head of US policy for Mozilla, wrote a follow-up paper explaining the core role of interop in fostering competition in networked platforms such as the Internet.[651]

Other influential voices agree. In March 2020, New America Foundation published a detailed research report describing interoperability as having "a unique ability to promote and incentivize competition—especially competition between platforms," as well as offering end users "greater privacy and better control over their personal data generally."[652]

Most recently, Cory Doctorow penned an essay lauding interop and in particular a form he calls "competitive compatibility" where smaller startups can build innovative new products on top of preexisting ones. He prefers such competition-bolstering measures as a way to "fix the Internet, not the tech giants."[653]

Even the larger MOPs themselves have recognized the utility of network interop and data portability. Beginning in 2007, a small group of engineers at Google created a project in their spare time called the Data Liberation Front (DLF). This project became a collection of tools to help end users download their data from Google.[654] DLF eventually led to a product called Google Takeout. More recently, groups of engineers from various companies created the Data Transfer Project (DTP), which aims to build an open-source platform to bridge the technical hurdles involved in moving data between various platforms. Despite its name, DTP is intended to address both data portability and platform-to-platform interop. As the DTP sponsors put it:

"[We] believe portability and interoperability are central to innovation. Making it easier for individuals to choose among services facilitates competition, empowers individuals to try new services and enables them to choose the offering that best suits their needs."[655]

A variety of independent organizations, companies, and individuals who recognize the need for this kind of "interop" infrastructure are beginning to build solutions. Of course, giving ordinary end users the ability to direct and control their own interop and data porting decisions (sometimes known as "open interop") would be a step towards recapturing the original ethos of the Internet as the ultimate interconnection platform.

In health care and IoT systems, early work has produced a leading technical framework for open AI interop: the Levels of Conceptual Interoperability Model (LCIM).[656] Here is a modified version of that model, placed at the center of the interaction between an individual and Institutional AIs:

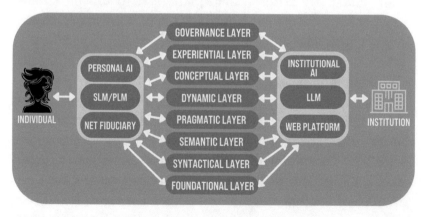

One of the challenges with interop is how it is actually defined, accepted, and implemented in the marketplace. In most cases, industry standards are entirely voluntary in nature. This means that, for example, a MOP may decide on its own not to implement a new interop technical standard for its AI platform. Alternatively, the MOP could point to its open APIs as a sufficient interface for creating AI-to-AI interop. But is this truly the case?

Open APIs: a sufficient starting point?

Open APIs are software interfaces that allow third parties to connect with a particular platform's resources. Over the past several decades, they have been utilized with much success across a wide swath of the digital economy[657] and rightly lauded as being potentially powerful drivers of innovation.[658] Where these APIs can approach the functionality of interop, they should at least be useful stop-gap options. In the context of AI systems, however, that similarity in functionality is unclear.

Web APIs exist for the purpose of gaining access to a platform's specified resources to build something new. However, they do not exist for the purpose of conveying a client's intentions in order to gain specified actions. As cloudtech, they are more a means for the third party to pull in some platform functionalities, rather than pushing out its intentionalities. So, if a Web company employs a typical API to allow access to its Institutional AI system, a third party might be able to connect its PAI agent and use certain computational resources. But that agent would be constrained in its "edge-push" ability to fully represent its client with a full panoply of queries, negotiations, and challenges. Further, in the absence of vertical interop, that PAI would be tied inextricably to that one platform, and that platform's particular specifications. This asymmetric arrangement for the Web lets the API owner dictate the terms to those who seek to utilize it, and those terms can change unilaterally. Would a future of "AI APIs" look and act any differently?

An important consideration is the unilateral nature of these interfaces, rendered by entities with evolving motivations. As

New America points out, vertically integrated platforms have incentives to build their API design solely for their own needs, tailored to their own specific apps, features, and competitive strategy.[659] They note:

"By setting API design and policy, [online platforms] have the ability to control who has access to critical aspects of the vast datasets and user bases they've built—things like a user's social graph that enables a hopeful competitor to grow its own user base and establish itself. Once a platform is sufficiently scaled, and especially if it is dominant, it no longer has the incentives to grant access to its APIs to facilitate a healthy downstream ecosystem. The more vertically integrated a platform is, too, the higher the risk that it may not offer APIs with sufficient data and functionality for other companies. Whereas our current antitrust framework may not sufficiently ensure platform competition, platform interop offers a solution to promote a more competitive ecosystem."[660]

In sum, open APIs may be a stepping stone to broaden access to a platform's AI systems. But vertical AI interop would provide the necessary tools for a robust market of independent PAIs.

Open standards for digital agents

To date, there are no open standards or protocols to support vertical AI interop. One promising development is Kwaai.ai, an open-source platform for PAIs.[661] Unlike for-profit, proprietary AI platforms that hid their core operating code and utilize constraining user interfaces, Kwaai is a non-profit, volunteer based AI research and development lab focused on "democratizing artificial intelligence."[662] Kwaai is building a Personal AI Operating System, intended to empower individuals to "retain and own their personal data and knowledge model, enhancing their digital abilities and competitiveness in the modern economy."[663] In keeping with the proposed e2a design principle, PAI Owners are able to keep their data secured locally, and utilize intent-casting (edge-pushing) when interacting with Institutional AIs.

Another route to achieving open standards is through an existing standards organization. As noted, IEEE's Global Initiative on Ethics of Autonomous and Intelligent Systems has created some important intellectual groundwork for authentic digital agents that fully represent the autonomous human being.[664] Work had been underway at the IEEE to build out an open software standard for Personal AIs, via the P7006 working group.[665] That standard "describes the technical elements required to create and grant access to a personalized AI that will comprise inputs, learning, ethics, rules and values controlled by individuals."[666] As of 2024, that project unfortunately remains suspended due to expiration of the Working Group's original mandate.[667] Moreover, their work related to the standards governing operation of these agents, rather than the interoperability connecting them to third parties. A related IEEE P7012 working group is developing an open standard for machines to read and agree to personal privacy terms.[668]

At the IETF, a new initiative is underway that may be picking up where the IEEE's P7006 working group has left off. The "Personal Digital Assistant Protocol" (PDAP) is based on the Universal Human Right of Freedom of Association and Assembly, which the initiative translates as an individual's choice of hosting and support communities for one's digital agent.[669] Its overarching purpose is to enable a shift from proprietary platforms to personal AI agents. These agents would be interoperable by vendors and service providers, avoid lock-in to hosts, give individuals a choice of community to replace forced platform association, and allow the agent's policies to be portable across host communities.[670] Even if that IETF-sponsored work is successful and related efforts are launched, more networking and interfaces standards development will be necessary to move us to a world of robust AI interop.

Voluntary interop?

Some for-profit Web platforms may perceive that voluntarily supporting and adopting vertical AI interop could open up vast new markets they can serve, while also forestalling calls for more direct government regulation of their business practices. As some commenters note:

"First and foremost, it is part of the entrepreneurial freedom of firms to decide themselves on the extent of the interoperability of their products and services. Selling products that are interoperable with other products, or offering an open platform that allows for sharing products and services with other platforms, can increase the value for customers and therefore increase profits. In the same way, the use of standardized components in a production value chain can reduce production costs and therefore allow for lower prices."[671]

The Data Transfer Initiative could be one industry forum for leading such activities.[672]

One set of commenters has contributed an important concept worth fleshing out in the context of pro-interop corporate policies. A Design for Interoperability, or "DfIOp," would build in digital interop as a core component of future product design.[673] This would include an outer interop between the system's boundaries and its environment of third-party agents and applications.

As we have seen, having the appropriate technical requirements in place is key to support a GliaNet ecosystem of edgetech capabilities. In the next chapter on public governance, we will query whether it is necessary in some cases to turn to governments to assist.

/C22/LEVERS OF CHANGE: OPPORTUNITIES FOR PUBLIC POLICYMAKERS

Another lever of change we can pull is the classic implementation of politics. Whether as a policymaker, a citizen and voter, or a technology lobbyist, we can help shape the public governance interventions that will translate GliaNet from concepts into reality.

So, how exactly do we bring into real life elements of the proposed GliaNet initiative – including its *Human:Digital Code* and two fiduciary-informed policy tiers? In this chapter, you will see a few such examples as addressed in proposed legislation in the United States.

Obviously, this book cannot foresee all the permutations in the United States of national, state, and local politics, let alone the political systems in other nations and at the global level. Nonetheless, there are some commonalities that are useful to discuss at this juncture.

Sketching a Policy Design Space

When it comes to mapping out possible changes, political scientists talk about defining a "policy design space." This space articulates all the components necessary to achieve public policy ends in a dynamic market environment. Because the policymaking function in a modern nation state is its own complex system, each component constitutes a separate set of decisions to be made, which in turn feeds back on the other decisions in dynamic and sometimes unpredictable ways. The optimal approach is to combine the policy goals and objectives, various organizations and institutions, competing frames and tools, and proposed projects—all contributing to the overall non-linear process. One can see that a policy design space has much in common with a theory of change framework.

The pioneering work of political scientist John Kingdon can be a helpful guide here.[674] Kingdon identifies three separate process "streams" that flow through a typical political system: problems, policies, and politics. The "problems" stream includes certain societal conditions that are defined by some as problems in need of a policy solution. The "policies" stream includes a wide variety of ideas for solutions floating around in a "policy primeval soup," waiting for the opportunity to be heard. Finally, the "politics" stream is the players working inside and outside the formal administrative and legislative processes. Each process stream is independent of the others, yet can be brought together at certain "policy windows" in an interactive "coupling." Such a coupling enhances the prospects for competing policy solutions to be recognized and added to the political agenda for final action.

In crafting a policy design space, we first need to distinguish between the different elements. The components I suggest here include the why (purpose, goals, and objectives), the how/who (institutions and organizations), the which/when/where (tools), and the what (projects). The goals are the largest, longest-term elements to be accomplished, much like the proposed GliaNet PToC outcomes.

As it turns out, the why component is the largely normative task of formulating issues to be addressed, which correlates roughly to Kingdon's problems stream. The how and who components match up well to Kingdon's politics stream, while the what component is similar to his policy stream. Policymakers often overlook the rich variety of players, processes, and tools available to help achieve their ultimate policy agenda.

In the context of advocating positions before the government, it is also useful to delineate which kinds of policy tools to utilize. Most would assume, for example, that the end game is having the government adopt a piece of legislation into law, which is then implemented via regulatory proceedings and enforced over time. However, this so-called "power of the pen" is only one way that governments can use their ability to shape market outcomes. A second is the "power of the purse," which can be triggered through procurement mandates, monetary grants, tax breaks, and other fiscal exercises. A third is the "power of the pulpit," where political leaders make public statements supporting or opposing certain market outcomes. Collectively, these three governmental powers provide significant windows of opportunity for policy entrepreneurs to pursue successfully.

So how should we be thinking about bringing public policymakers into the conversation about enabling the scenario of Carla in 2032?

Adopting a Two-Tiered GliaNet Framework

As noted in the private governance chapter, one proposed framework that the GliaNet Alliance could investigate is a two-tiered approach, which combines a general duty of care that covers many Web entities, and a fiduciary duty of loyalty that applies to Net fiduciaries. We could imagine taking that construct a step further by turning the duty of care into an actual legal requirement for specified entities.

Getzler observes that fiduciary law can serve as a protective, relatively stringent "penalty default rule," with parties able to negotiate downward from a particular duty.[675] The suggestion here would go the other way—to adopt the "default rule" of a broad duty of care (no harm, and prudent conduct), then allow parties to negotiate upward to higher duties of fidelity and loyalty. This would accommodate the legal and political obstacles of gaining adoption of a loyalty mandate, as well as recognize the imprudence of compelling loyalty from otherwise unwilling entities.

The structural pluralism school of political science provides some useful guidance here. Ideally, law should protect our core interests while at the same time allowing latitude for people to engage in autonomous behaviors. According to Dagan and Hannes:

"People should be able to choose from these institutions in line with their own conceptions of the good and the means necessary for its realization given their particular needs and circumstances... This fundamental commitment to self-authorship ... accommodate[s] heterogeneity... [T]o the extent possible, private law should attempt to overcome problems of information asymmetry and cognitive biases by prescribing sticky defaults rather than by curtailing choice through mandatory rules."[676]

This observation suggests that a two-tiered fiduciary approach is a doable way to protect us from the downside risks posed by SEAMs-based companies, while enabling the upside mutual benefits of Net fiduciaries. A protective floor and a promotional ceiling. In fact, each duty can reinforce the other, for example, by building forms of online human agency on top of basic institutional accountability. While an imposed duty of care facilitates higher degrees of accountability for the MOPs, a voluntary duty of loyalty gives individuals new agency as empowered clients of Net fiduciaries.

Such a legally mandated duty of care could apply to two-types of SEAMS-based entities: those involved in collecting and processing our personal data, and those engaging in algorithmic decision-making about our fundamental rights and interests. Various financial and other incentives for entities to voluntarily opt into Net privity-based relationships of fidelity and loyalty could be adopted as well. Among other advantages, establishing two separate policy tiers would provide a basis for parties to explore and adopt a graduated set of obligations.

PRIVATE GOVERNANCE

Voluntary duties of fidelity and loyalty

PUBLIC GOVERNANCE

Mandatory duty of care

When MOPs Refuse to Play

Some MOPs and others may resist having Net fiduciaries enter the Web marketplace. Such resistance could become manifest by refusing to engage in meaningful commercial transactions, or to provide functional access to necessary platform inputs. In those instances, some public policy assistance may be required, which could include a mix of tailored market inputs and incentives.

Governments can use a variety of mechanisms to incentivize new digital ecosystems founded on fiduciary obligations. Utilizing the power of the public purse, for example, agencies could attach fiduciary-style conditions to their procurement activities. To avoid creation of a new class of "digital left-behinds," governments also could create targeted subsidies—such as consumer payment vouchers funded by levies on SEAMs-based advertising—to benefit economically disadvantaged citizens.

Policymakers also can require that the MOPs supply discrete market inputs to spur new forms of competition and innovation. This could include, for example, giving Net fiduciaries rights to interoperate with the MOPs, port client data away, and act under express delegation on behalf of their clients. We'll discuss below a few of those codified rights.

Codifying duties of care and loyalty

In the United States, Federal legislation appears to be a leading implementation option for creating a fiduciaries-based policy model. A notable example came in 2018 with Senate Bill 3744, the "Data Care Act of 2018."[677] Section 3 of the bill lays out the specific duties of what it calls online service providers (OSPs)—more or less equivalent to MOPs—with regard to personal data. Three sets of obligations are laid out for these entities:

- *Duty of care*: Reasonably secure a user's data from unauthorized access and provide a prompt notice of any data breach.

- *Duty of loyalty*: Not use data in any way that would benefit the OSP to the detriment of the user, would result in reasonably foreseeable and material physical or financial harm, or would be unexpected and highly offensive to the user.

- *Duty of confidentiality*: Not disclose or sell individual identifying data except as consistent with the duties of care and loyalty.

The proposed Data Care Act seeks to apply various fiduciary-based duties to the MOPs. To that end, it is a laudable contribution to the conversation. As discussed earlier, however, a two-tiered model with a mandatory duty of care and a voluntary duty of loyalty would strike a better balance.

More recently, the US Senate in August 2024 overwhelmingly passed the Kids Online Safety and Privacy Act (KOSPA).[678] If signed into law, the bill would impose a new "duty of care" on covered platform companies, requiring them to "exercise reasonable care in the creation and implementation of any design feature to protect and mitigate" a range of harms to minors.[679] Those harms include mental health disorders, addiction-like behaviors, violence and bullying, sexual exploitation and abuse, providing narcotic drugs, and "predatory, unfair, or deceptive marketing practices, or other financial harms." While some have raised First Amendment concerns about the potential for censoring certain topics of online conversation, the bill is notable for its embrace of a mandatory duty of care to protect children against harmful MOPs practices.

Codifying AI interop rights

Voluntary agreement on the operative protocols and standards for AI interop would be an optimal outcome. However, relying solely on the self-regulatory model under private governance can be a shaky basis for establishing digital rights and duties. As such, there may well be a role for governments to play in creating market-based incentives for such agreement. Importantly, as Kerber and Schweitzer state:

> "[I]nteroperability is not—or should not be—an end in itself; it is a means to a broader set of goals: to address market fragmentation, to avoid market tipping towards monopoly, to open downstream markets for competition where the upstream market is monopolized, to increase follow-on innovation irrespective of market power, or to address a perceived societal need for general interconnectedness and communication across competing networks. In each case, before taking action, a clear and strong market failure or public service rationale should be identified."[680]

In other words, a government's direct involvement requires sufficient evidence that interop as a public good will not occur otherwise.

In Europe, interop has become a key component of the legal landscape.[681] Competition law has incorporated interop to address supposed abuses of dominance under Article 102 of the Treaty on the Functioning of the European Union (TFEU).[682] More recently, the EU's Digital Markets Act (DMA) of 2020 introduces new obligations for core platform providers, or "gatekeepers." Article 6 makes it clear that interop is one way to address concerns about various self-preferencing behaviors by attaching it to operating systems with third-party software applications or stores, and to ancillary services. Article 6 also specifies real-time data portability and gives business users the right to access their own end user data.[683]

Chris Riley proposed an intriguing option when he was with Mozilla Corporation. Section 230 of the U.S. Communications Decency Act provides immunity to online companies that host user-generated content. In recent years, that provision has come under political attack by those who believe the larger social media companies and other online entities have done an insufficient job of moderating that content. Riley's proposal would continue immunity under Section 230 only for those large online intermediaries who provide "an open, raw feed for independent downstream presentation."[684]

Riley's thesis is that centralizing and siloing one's Internet experience has produced "a lack of meaningful user agency." He states that "[t]here are fundamental limits on users' ability to customize, or replace, the recommendation algorithm that mediates the lion's share of their interaction with the social networks and the user-generated content that it hosts."[685] Interop here would allow end users to customize their online experiences and experiment with substituting new types of presentation algorithms or other "middleware" options. In return, Riley's proposal would allow platforms to adopt reasonable security and privacy access controls for their APIs or other interop interfaces.[686]

In the United States, relevant bipartisan legislation for interop was introduced in October 2019 and reintroduced in 2021. Senate Bill 26581, the ACCESS ("Augmenting Compatibility and Competition by Enabling Service Switching") Act, was brought forward by a bipartisan group of US Senators.[687] The bill combines several functional openness provisions and recognizes "custodial" third parties operating on behalf of users under specified care-like duties. The bill's sponsors recognized that empowering such "intermediaries" with "interoperability, portability, and delegatability will enhance user choices and put consumers in the driver's seat."[688]

If adopted into law, the ACCESS Act legislation would codify the end user's right to interoperate with online platforms and the related right to transfer their data to other destinations.[689] As co-sponsoring Senator Mark Warner remarked in October 2019:

> "By making it easier for social media users to easily move their data or to continue to communicate with their friends after switching platforms, startups will be able to compete on equal terms with the biggest social media companies."[690]

This same logic applies to the present context of two AI systems that lack an ability to connect and communicate.

Nonetheless, no explicit interop right exists today for AI systems. Given this gap and the potential significant benefits from such a right, policymakers may need to be prepared to step in. One approach here is to utilize various "soft power" inducements to stimulate the adoption of vertical interop to stimulate new AI markets. These inducements could include procurement preferences, tax breaks, and government grants. Without AI interop, and perhaps without some form codified into Federal law, a truly robust market for authentic PAI agents cannot exist.

Codifying a right to trustworthy delegation

An often-overlooked new frontier in data rights is the opportunity to empower people to delegate their data rights, including portability and interop, to a trusted third party. While data portability and related rights are important, they will mean little if not provided in a way that ordinary people can actually utilize. There are real-world implications of this. For example, we have seen how the GDPR with good intentions gave European citizens more choice in protecting their data, yet many people found the expanded agency overwhelming.[691]

This is where introducing an express legal right to trustworthy delegation becomes crucial. Allowing a trusted company or non-profit to help its patrons exercise their interop and portability rights (and the numerous follow-on decisions) can make those rights far more impactful. Adding a duty of loyalty would make that pledge even more meaningful and enforceable. Such a right of delegation also gives MOPs and others greater assurance that the entity in fact is operating under the individual's express designation, and has in place appropriate checks and balances to safeguard against improper actions. Conversely, the lack of an express right of delegation may make it all but impossible for NetTMs and Net fiduciaries to interact with other online entities to support their clients.

Importantly, Section 5 of the ACCESS Act bill recognizes these important facts. This provision allows users to "delegate trusted custodial services, which are required to act in a user's best interests through a strong duty of care, with the task of managing their account settings, content, and online interactions." Senator Warner's 2019 observation on this crucial provision still rings true:

"Empowering trusted custodial companies to step in on behalf of users to better manage their accounts across different platforms will help balance the playing field between consumers and companies. In other words – by enabling portability, interoperability, and delegatability, this bill will help put consumers in the driver's seat when it comes to how and where they use social media."[692]

As Nobel prize winning economist Paul Romer observed in his statement supporting the original 2019 version of the ACCESS Act bill, "By giving consumers the ability to delegate decisions to organizations working on their behalf, the ACCESS Act gives consumers some hope that they can understand what they are giving up and getting in the opaque world that the tech firms have created."[693] Without express delegation rights, Professor Romer is right that end users will largely be left stranded and vulnerable to the worst practices of predatory entities on the Web.

Codifying a right to query

Having the ability to delegate our agency to another entity—be it an individual, a company, a non-profit, a government agency, or even an authentic PAI agent—provides little value unless that entity can actually speak on our behalf. Even if we are able to build and deploy authentic PAI agents, their utility would be largely wasted if they lacked the ability to not just interpret what an Institutional AI is doing, but query and even challenge its decision-making approach and outcomes. Without such a right, we may find ourselves marooned in the near future with Theodore Twombly, powerless to intercede as our PAI responds only to its own programming and the company that developed it.

Policymakers can change this near-term bleak future by codifying a fundamental right to query. When and if any Institutional AI system makes a consequential decision about you—your employment, your health, your legal status—you should be able to employ similar computational firepower to fully represent your own interests, in your own way.

The most recent lost opportunity can be found in Europe, where the EU's Artificial Intelligence Act was adopted in early 2024.[694] The Act is designed to provide "harmonized rules for AI" in the European Union, aimed at the sale and use of AI systems. At its heart is a categorization system based on the levels of risk that various use cases pose to the "health, safety, and fundamental rights" of "natural persons."[695] And yet, these actual humans are barely found in the text. The "natural persons" who are the supposed subjects of the legislation ironically play no active role of their own. Instead, they are treated as passive recipients of actions defined and granted to them by others. Without recognizing some of the separate rights discussed in this chapter (including the rights of AI interop, delegation, and query), an individual has no realistic recourse against the powerful Institutional AIs that operate here. If the riskiest use cases constitute the floor of accountability, the management of personal contours via rights of delegation, query, and challenge should also be established as the attainable ceiling.

Similar proposals across the globe—from the White House 2023 Executive Order on AI[696], to the G7 declaration on AI[697], to the Bletchley Park principles[698]—fail to include such rights to query. Indeed, they lack any of the *human:digital* rights outlined earlier. These oversights are missed opportunities to place humans on an equal footing with our AI technologies, with potentially dire consequences.

/C23/LEVERS OF CHANGE: ALL OF US

"Don't be the pinball. Be the machine."

– Doc Searls

The fourth and final intervention prescribed in GliaNet's PToC is in many ways the most powerful: the role played by each of us in society. Using our collective voices, we can influence the outcomes in each of the other pathways—public and private governance, technologies, and of course the markets. This energy for change is mobilized by firmly establishing a discrepancy between what people want and where they are. The future has yet to be defined by the present.

Speaking Truth to Power

In our earlier analysis of human power, we saw how often those with control use hidden means to retain and expand their power base. This aspect of the GliaNet PToC proposes to make what is invisible visible, and thus susceptible to a much broader audience of people, acting as consumers, citizens, and more.

Lukes highlights for us how power is exercised in society under three "faces" or dimensions: decision-making power, non-decision-making power, and ideological power. The latter two allow those with power to set the agenda in public debates and even influence people's wishes and thoughts to want or do things contrary to their own self-interest. The less direct-seeming forms of power—agenda and influence—are key to the persistence of the current Web paradigm and MOPs policies and practices. In particular, SEAMs-based activities gain much of their effectiveness due to one-sided company policies, constraining user interfaces, and even manipulation of peoples' behaviors—often without the individual's full awareness and consent. Challenging this power asymmetry would be fruitless without shining a brighter public light on such practices.

Mann's "organizational outflanking" concept also shows what is necessary to organize efficient resistance against power. Those who exist outside current networks of power tend to lack adequate organizational resources. A key obstacle is overcoming their lack of knowledge, which often stems from a missing knowledge base, isolation, and/or division. Hence, organizing and educating the vast community of Web users is a key counter-power tool.

As described earlier, a powerful metaphorical image to present to people is that of personal contours emanating from the individual, subject to constant change from within and from without. In turn, we are increasingly immersed in digital lifestreams comprised of a plethora of relevant data points representing us as fully fledged human beings. Power in the Web space is with those who control access to those personal boundaries and define the substance of those lifestreams. Context and content. Shifting greater autonomy (freedom of thought) and agency (freedom of action) to the individual amounts to claiming greater control over the personal contours and digital lifestreams of the self. Creating and elevating that analogical vision with wider audiences means sowing seeds for change that can be supported by a broad base of people.

Here, we will consider a few suggestions for how the societal power of engaged individuals can bring about lasting change to the Net. Many more remain to be explored. Sometimes, simply knowing what to insist upon is more than half the battle.

Stakeholders with Many Hats

A key framing device is to convince people from all walks of life that they are stakeholders in the Net's future. And we should all have an abiding and vested interest in that future, for a variety of reasons. Of course, our stakes depend on the particular roles we play—the metaphorical hats that we wear:

- *As a consumer*, we have a stake in the goods and services we use every day. Economists refer to this as our "purchasing power." Some also believe it is the only way we can have a voice in a capitalist society. It is true that we help shape the marketplace every time we choose one product or service over another. Seeking for example to purchase products only from companies that abide by robust privacy policies, per Mozilla Foundation's "Privacy Not Included" campaign.[699] But this is just one voice of many that we can raise.

- *As a parent*, we have a stake in how our children are raised and educated. With so few meaningful limitations on the kinds of software and hardware devices that are brought into our educational systems, we can demand that our children are exposed only to those capabilities that foster their human development. The Internet Safety Labs, which develops open standards and conducts audits to assess the data protection practices behind our connected technologies, is an excellent resource for assessing the many privacy failings of "edtech" applications in America's schools.[700]

- *As a friend*, we have a stake in meaningful relationships. We know that social media platforms can serve our interests better, fostering bonds rather than wedges. We can insist at minimum that their algorithms reflect who we are and strengthen relationships of mutual trust and caring.

- *As a neighbor*, we have a stake in the health and safety of the local community. Smart technologies can improve our sense of security, so long as we know exactly how it is being used. We can attend local city and town meetings to debate the policies that govern these devices and applications. As part of those efforts, we can support the adoption of standards such as DTPR (described in Chapter Fourteen) that provide meaningful interfaces for us to engage directly with smart city networks and devices.[701]

- *As an employee*, we have a stake in our work environment. Post COVID-19, company and government online systems that connect employees can also increasingly surveil them, whether in the office or remotely, and often without legitimate reason or recourse. We can ask that any such technologies be deployed with full transparency and consistently with a "do no harm" duty of care standard.

- *As a voter*, we have a stake in the nation where we live. As citizens, we are supposed to hold the ultimate power in a democracy. We should use it, demanding that our elected officials and candidates utilize their own levers of change to promote our digital rights and incentivize new markets based on legitimate trust.

- *As an investor*, we have a stake in how our money is used by business entrepreneurs. For those of us fortunate enough to be able to invest in markets, we should insist that the for-profit tech companies in our portfolio aspire to become NetTMs and Net fiduciaries.

- *As an early adopter*, we have a stake in being the first to use "cool" tech. We should ask hard questions about who is actually operating behind the screens and only use technologies that adhere to agency-enhancing standards like e2a.

The point is a simple one. Wearing many hats, we have far more power for meaningful change than we realize. We should use that power.

CONCLUSION

WEAVING WEBS OF ONE'S OWN

"Control of data and ownership of the [AI] models learned from it is what many of the twenty-first century's battles will be about—between governments, corporations, unions, and individuals."

– Pedro Domingos, *The Master Algorithm*

Hopefully, the last chapter provided inspiration, a call to action, or even a battle cry to grasp the levers of meaningful change that reside with each of us. And for this proposed future to become a reality, complacency must give way to determination.

The coming technology frontier looms before us. It will include millions of times more processing power using quantum computing, billions of connected IoT devices, trillions of AR experiences, and countless impactful interactions between human beings and AI-trained algorithmic systems. The potential benefits are immense, as are the likely pitfalls.

With the SEAMs paradigm, humans will increasingly be considered valuable only as digital entities to be mined and manipulated, a virtually endless supply of 1s and 0s to faceless data brokers and influencers. In this context, how do we address legitimate social concerns about power, trust, consent, and accountability? At the end of the day, can the autonomous human being still be enabled to interact, decide, and choose, on their own terms? These questions remain unanswered for now.

Unless we join the fight, however, those battles for our future will never materialize. We should not cede victory to the most powerful companies and governments on the planet, simply by declining to challenge their foundational paradigms. For those of us who demand more from our digital existences, we can proactively build ecosystems that serve our best interests. The crucial link is an ethos that cultivates human autonomy and agency, and informs the countless decisions that trustworthy entities will make on our behalf.

This book has laid out a variety of "levers of change" we can pull, to help us accomplish the promising Carla scenario of 2032. These key interventions include:

- In the private governance system of corporate practices, companies and others create a profession of NetTMs and Net fiduciaries, complete with codes of conduct, trust marks certification, and enforcement regimes.

- In technological design, software and hardware engineers produce a viable assortment of interoperable tech tools, such as authentic PAI agents, operating consistent with the *e2a* design principle.

- In the public governance system of politics, policymakers codify a codified range of individual rights and company duties that together enable a viable, successful ecosystem of competing NetTMs.

- In the larger social fabric, ordinary people gain a widespread understanding and acceptance of the basic elements of the GliaNet ecosystem, an appreciation of its benefits, and growing expectations of new human-centric norms.

Perhaps the single greatest challenge and opportunity for the GliaNet vision is human choice. We cannot compel an individual to gain a deeper appreciation for the realities of the Web, ask tough questions about SEAMs, seek out agential alternatives in the marketplace, and alter their daily routines to accommodate these alternatives. Put this way, the steep climb toward digital agency seems ever more daunting. But we can paint a picture with enough clarity that all of us become the most powerful levers of solutions.

This book has shown that our digital lives can be reclaimed in viable and sustainable ways. If individuals, communities, and organizations work together, the SEAMs paradigm can give way to a better tomorrow. Where all of us, ordinary people, can use computational systems to enhance our freedom to think, interact, and pursue our dreams.

In the future that is always approaching, simply turning over our autonomy and agency to the MOPs and DAMBs need not be the status quo. The SEAMs paradigm can be challenged, and even in time overcome. By laying bare the countless ways we are being influenced by external sources, we can take steps to hold the underlying systems accountable for the harms against us. As empowered stakeholders, we can grasp a bold new vision of enhancing human power and control in the computational era.

Together, we can ensure the availability of social, relational, and virtual infrastructures to support robust autonomy and agency for all human beings. A near future where we are weaving empowering webs of our own creation.

GLOSSARY OF TERMS

Agentiality – Dimension one of true agency (relationship).

Agenticity – Dimension two of true agency (capability).

Authentic PAI agent – A PAI that actually acts on behalf of the individual, typically by being provided and managed on her behalf by a NetTM or Net fiduciary.

client – Person who is the subject of a commercial relationship with a Net fiduciary.

cloudtech – Technologies that tend to consolidate control at the core of incumbent Web networks.

Code – In governance, this refers to the underlying content.

Computational systems – A mix of data (information), algorithms (AI), and interfaces (devices).

customer – Person who is the subject of a commercial relationship with a NetTM.

DAMBs – Data-based advertisers, marketers, and brokers. The DAMB ecosystem feeds upon the MOPs and their SEAMs feedback cycles.

Data trust – A collective form of NetTM, which incorporates equity-based duties of care, fidelity, and loyalty into its operations.

Digital lifestreams – Translating human lifestreams into the 1s and 0s of the digital world.

Digital life support system – An individualized mix of PEP model protection/enhancement/promotion service offerings that the client can assemble.

Duty of care – Fiduciary and equities law-based obligation for an entity to engage in reasonably prudent conduct, and not to cause harm to others.

Duty of fidelity – Fiduciary law-based obligation for an entity to have no conflicts of duties or interests with its client or customer, vis-à-vis other parties. Also called the "thin" form of loyalty.

Duty of loyalty – Fiduciary law-based obligation for an entity to promote the best interests of its client. Also called the "thick" form of loyalty.

D > A – The proposed governance principle of GliaNet, which stands for "digital is greater than analog." This refers to the desirability of new technologies that enhance and extend our human rights from the analog world, rather than constrain them.

D < A – The prevailing governance principle of the Web, which stands for "digital is less than analog." This refers to the spread of new technologies that constrain the human rights we derive from the everyday, offline world.

edge-pull – Technology configurations that support importing information from the Web, typically with outside-in interface actions.

edge-push – Technology configurations that support exporting influence into the Web, typically with inside-out interface actions.

edgetech – Technologies that tend to consolidate control at the edges of incumbent Web networks.

e2a – "edge-to-any," the proposed GliaNet technology design principle.

GliaNet – The proposed ecosystem initiative for creating a new overlay to the Internet, consisting of fiduciaries-based human governance (D > A) and empowering technology design principles (e2a).

HAACS – The proposed paradigm of GliaNet, which stands for "human autonomy/agency via computational systems."

Institutional AI – Established corporate or governmental entities that own or operate AI systems that are generally pervasive, consequential, inscrutable, and (in)fallible.

lifestreams – The experiential flow of space and time, including thoughts and emotions, that is core to being a human being.

MOPs – Multisided online platforms. This refers to the larger incumbent providers of cloud-based applications and services to their end users, who typically employ the SEAMs paradigm.

Net fiduciary – A type of NetTM that incorporates fiduciary law-based duties of fidelity and loyalty into its business model.

Net trustmediary (NetTM) – An entity that incorporates ethical duty of care practices into its business models, above and beyond compliance with the dictates of law.

PEP model – Denotes an alignment of the three phases of NetTM duties and services, from protection (guardian, duty of care) to enhancement (mediator, duty of fidelity), to promotion (advocate, duty of loyalty).

Personal AI – A digital assistant that purports to act on behalf of the end user.

Personal contours – The psychologically maintained boundaries of the human self, imagined as an enclosing bubble with semi-permeable barriers that contract and expand with each experience of the world.

Players – In governance, this refers to the organizations.

PToC – a provisional theory of change, subject to further testing and refinement.

Rules – In governance, this refers to the institutions.

SEAMs – The prevailing economic paradigm of the Web: surveillances, extractions, analyses, and manipulations.

Screens, scenes, and unseens – The primary digital interfaces for our online screens, environmental scenes, and bureaucratic unseens.

Trustmediaries (TM) – Individuals or entities in our daily lives in which we hold a basic level of trust to help us and not to harm us, based on past dealings, reputation, or other indicia of trustworthiness.

user – Definition applied by MOPs and others to describe those individuals who utilize their service offerings and ostensibly consent to their terms. Aside from applicable consumer protection laws or regulations, users have no inherent rights on the Web beyond what the MOPs and others grant unilaterally.

ACKNOWLEDGEMENTS

No book is ever written alone. Over my many years in the technology policy space, I have gained so much from a plethora of amazing individuals and organizations. While there are way too many people to acknowledge to name them all, I will offer here an abbreviated list:

Vint Cerf, my mentor and friend, whose lifework on the Internet helped inspire this work (even if he may not always concur with all of my conclusions).

Doc Searls, whose vigorous assertions about human agency and the Web remain profound and prescient.

Mark Surman and Mozilla Foundation, whose generous support and encouragement helped gestate many of these proposals.

Sushant Kumar and Omidyar Network, whose funding helped enable the Carla series of articles, which resonates at the heart of this book.

The Rockefeller Foundation, whose 2019 fellowship program at Lake Bellagio brought me together with some truly remarkable people and ideas.

Maura Corbett and Glen Echo Group, who were instrumental in the early days of marketing GliaNet to the public policy world.

Milton Pedraza and John Dewees, two ethics-minded investors and GliaNet enthusiasts.

NetsEdge Consulting clients and advised companies, including DataLucent, FID, emortal, Reliabl, DataGrade, and Sybal.

Martha Sperry, talented illustrator for the Carla narrative of 2020 and 2032.

Ameesha Green, Niall Burgess, Gabriel Both, Kyle Albuquerque, and all the other fine folks at The Book Shelf for helping bring my words to life.

A special thanks to Todd Kelsey, whose long-standing contributions to the GliaNet initiative have helped make it what it is today. Since early 2019, as my conception of this project was still in its infancy, Todd has offered to the cause his sage advice, substantive ideas, and lots of productive brainstorming. Some of his standalone concepts, on topics such as data archaeology and data fluency, also found their way into a number of pieces co-written for Medium, and of course our original illustrated "Carla and Her Data" booklet. Along the way, Todd has also become an indispensable ally as we tested out various ways of bringing GliaNet to life.

And Kathrin O'Sullivan (of course, and always).

ENDNOTES

1   Isenberg, David. "Stupid Network: Why the Intelligent Network Was Once a Good Idea, but Isn't Anymore. One Telephone Company Nerd's Odd Perspective on the Changing Value Proposition." Computer Telephony 16–26 (August 1997). https://www.hyperorg.com/misc/stupidnet.html.

2   Searls, Doc. "The Giant Zero." DOC SEARLS WEBLOG (blog), February 1997. Accessed August 3, 2016. https://www.hyperorg.com/misc/stupidnet.html.

3   If we need to pick a date, use April 30, 1995. That was the day that NSFNet—the only Internet "backbone" that had forbade commercial activity—was decommissioned. This made the Internet a commercial free-for-all.

4   Taleb, Nassim Nicholas Nicholas. The Black Swan: The Impact of the Highly Improbable. 2nd ed. London, United Kingdom of Great Britain and Northern Ireland: Random House Publishing Group, 1994. Accessed August 3, 2016. (on describing highly improbable but sizable threats).

5   Wucker, Michele. The Gray Rhino: How to Recognize and Act on the Obvious Dangers We Ignore. Smp, 2017. (On describing highly obvious but ignored threats).

6   Zuckerman, Ethan. "Why Filming Police Violence Has Done Nothing to Stop It." MIT Technology Review (blog). https://www.technologyreview.com/2020/06/03/1002587/sousveillance-george-floyd-police-body-cams/, June 3, 2020.

7   Stroh, David Peter. Systems Thinking for Social Change: A Practical Guide to Solving Complex Problems, Avoiding Unintended Consequences, and Achieving Lasting Results. 36–37. Vermont, United States of America: Chelsea Green Publishing Co, 2015.

8   Zuboff, Shoshana. The Age of Surveillance Capitalism: The Fight for a Human Future at the New Frontier of Power. 97. London, United Kingdom of Great Britain and Northern Ireland: Profile Books, 2019.

9   O'Reilly, Tom. WTF: What's the Future and Why It's Up to Us. 249. London, United Kingdom of Great Britain and Northern Ireland: Harper Business, 2017.

10   Giridharadas, Anand. Winners Take All: The Elite Charade of Changing the World. 11. London, United Kingdom of Great Britain and Northern Ireland: Penguin, 2006.

11   Renieris, Elizabeth M. Beyond Data: Reclaiming Human Rights at the Dawn of the Metaverse. Massachusetts, Cambridge, United States of America: MIT Press, 2023.

12   Varoufakis, Yanis. Technofeudalism: What Killed Capitalism. London, United Kingdom of Great Britain and Northern Ireland: Bodley Head, 2023.

13   Stroh, David Peter. Systems Thinking for Social Change: A Practical Guide to Solving Complex Problems, Avoiding Unintended Consequences, and Achieving Lasting Results. 60–61. Vermont, United States of America: Chelsea Green Publishing Co;, 2015.

14 D'Ignazio, Catherine, and Lauren F. Klein. *Data Feminism*. 12. Massachusetts, Cambridge, United States of America: MIT Press, 2023.

15 Moore, Jason W. *Capitalism in the Web of Life: Ecology and the Accumulation of Capital*. 2. New York, United States of America: Verso Books, 2015.

16 Moore, Jason W. *Capitalism in the Web of Life: Ecology and the Accumulation of Capital*. 7. New York, United States of America: Verso Books, 2015.

17 Meadows, Donella. *Thinking in Systems: A Primer. Edited by Diana Wright*. 145. Vermont, United States of America: Chelsea Green Publishing Co, 2017.

18 Ibid, 153–159.

19 Ibid, 162.

20 Ibid, 163–64.

21 Stroh, *Systems Thinking for Social Change*, at 73–74.

22 Taylor, Mark C. *The Moment of Complexity: Emerging Network Culture*. 224. Illinois, United States of America: University of Chicago Press, 2002.

23 Stroh, *Systems Thinking for Social Change*, at 167.

24 Solnit, Rebecca. *A Paradise Built in Hell: The Extraordinary Communities That Arise in Disaster*. 313. London, United Kingdom of Great Britain and Northern Ireland: Granta Books, 2025.

25 Cummins, Fred. "Agency is Distinct from Autonomy." Avant., 2 (2014): 98–112. https://doi.org/10.26913/50202014.0109.0005.

26 Ibid, 107–108.

27 Ibid, 103.

28 See also Ganeri, Jonardon. The Self: Naturalism, Consciousness, and the First-Person Stance. 252–255. Oxford, United Kingdom of Great Britain and Northern Ireland: Oxford University Press, 2015., ("[Autonomy] is the decision, a state of the self, that supervenes on a happening, a state of the body..."); Luck, M. "A Formal Framework for Agency and Autonomy: Proceedings of the First International Conference on Multi-Agent Systems." Edited by Victor Lesser. 252–255. Massachusetts, Cambridge, United Kingdom of Great Britain and Northern Ireland: MIT Press, 1996. (autonomy motivates agency).

29 Frischmann, Brett, and Evan Selinger. Re-Engineering Humanity. Vol. 225–302. Cambridge, United Kingdom of Great Britain and Northern Ireland: Cambridge University Press, 2019. (Free will defined as the "capability to engage in reflective self-determination about [one's] will," and autonomy as an intentional aspect of free will, serving as a "bridge between will and action." Practical agency then is the freedom to exercise one's will.)

30 See generally Fromm, Erich. *Escape From Freedom*. Cambridge, United Kingdom of Great Britain and Northern Ireland: Cambridge University Press, 1974.

31 Ibid.

32 See Ryan, R. M, and E. L. Deci. "Self-determination Theory and the Facilitation of Intrinsic Motivation, Social Development, and Well-being." *American Psychologist*. 68–78 (2000): 75–77.

33 Kompa, Joana Stella. "Defining Human Autonomy: Towards an Interdependent Model of Human Agency." *Digital Educ. & Social Change Blog*, June 18, 2016, 75–77. https://joanakompa.com/2016/06/18/

defining-human-autonomy-in-search-of-richer-psychological-frameworks/ https://perma.cc/4YSH-T26F.

34   Camus, Albert. The Rebel: An Essay on Man in Revolt. Manhattan, United States of America: Random House USA, 1992. 287-288.

35   Unger, Roberto. The Religion of the Future. Massachusetts, Cambridge, United States of America: Harvard University Press, 1997. 320. (deep freedom is "the dialectic between the conception of a free society, and the cumulative institutional innovations that will make this conception real").

36   Taylor, Mark. "The Moment of Complexity" Emerging Network Culture. 224 (2001). See also Richard Whitt & Stephen Schultze, "The New 'Emergence Economics' of Innovation and Growth, and What it Means for Communications Policy," 7 J. On Telecomm. & High Tech. L. 217, 309 (2009).

37   Couldry, Nick, and Andreas Hepp. The Mediated Construction of Reality: Society, Culture, Mediatization. Cambridge, United Kingdom of Great Britain and Northern Ireland: Polity, 2016. 157.

38   Chirkov, Valery I., Richard Ryan, and Kennon M. Sheldon. "Human Autonomy in Cross-Cultural Context: Perspectives on the Psychology of Agency, Freedom, and Well-Being" Cross-Cultural Advancements in Positive Psychology, 1. New York, United States of America: Springer, 2010. https://doi.org/10.1007/978-90-481-9667-8. 19-20.

39   Whitt, Richard S. "Through A Glass, Darkly: Technical, Policy, and Financial Actions to Avert the Coming Digital Dark Ages." Santa Clara High Tech, no. 33 (2017): 117–48. https://digitalcommons.law.scu.edu/chtlj/vol33/iss2/1.

40   Whitt, Through A Glass Darkly.

41   Kuang, Cliff, and Robert Fabricante. User Friendly: How The Hidden Rules of Design Are Changing the Way We Live, Work & Play. London, United Kingdom of Great Britain and Northern Ireland: Virgin Digital, 2019.

42   Ibid, 33-34.

43   Floridi, Luciano. Information: A Very Short Introduction (Very Short Introductions). Oxford, United Kingdom of Great Britain and Northern Ireland: OUP Oxford, 2010.

44   Whitt, Through A Glass Darkly, 145–147.

45   Altman, Irwin. "A Personal Perspective on the Environment and Behavior Field." In Visions of Aesthetics, the Environment & Development, 1st ed., 26. United Kingdom of Great Britain and Northern Ireland: Psychology Press, 1991.

46   Petronio, Sandra. Boundaries of Privacy: Dialectics of Disclosure (Suny Series in Communication Studies). Visions of Aesthetics, the Environment & Development. New York, United States of America: State University of New York Press;, 2002.

47   "Hiding in the Open: How Tech Network Policies Can Inform Openness by Design (and Vice Versa)." Georgetown Law Technology Review 3, no. 28 (2004). https://georgetownlawtechreview.org/hiding-in-the-open-how-tech-network-policies-can-inform-openness-by-design-and-vice-versa/GLTR-01-2019/.

48   Unger, The Religion of the Future, 441.

49   Unger, Roberto Mangabeira. Self Awakened: Pragmatism Unbound. New York, United States of America: Harvard University Press, 2009. 166.

50   Ibid, 343.

51   Ibid, 180.

52   Ryan and Deci. *Self-determination Theory and the Facilitation of Intrinsic Motivation, Social Development, and Well-being*, 51–79, 383–392. (describes the development of one's personal identities through both the self-as-process and the self-as-object prisms).

53   Cummins, *Agency is Distinct from Autonomy*. 98.

54   Panksepp, Jaak, and Lucy Biven. *The Archaeology of Mind: Neuroevolutionary Origins of Human Emotions* (Norton Series on Interpersonal). London, United Kingdom of Great Britain and Northern Ireland: W. W. Norton & Co, 2012.

55   Chrikov, Valery I. Human Autonomy in Cross-Cultural Context: Perspectives on the Psychology of Agency, Freedom, and Well-Being (Cross-Cultural Advancements in Positive Psychology Book 1). Edited by Richard Ryan and Kennon M. Sheldon. London, United Kingdom of Great Britain and Northern Ireland: Springer, 2004.

56   See generally Gallagher, S. "Phenomenology and Embodied Cognition." In *Routledge Handbook of Embodied Cognition*, 9–17:9–17. London, United Kingdom of Great Britain and Northern Ireland: Routledge, 2014. https://www.taylorfrancis.com/chapters/edit/10.4324/97810033225 11-3/phenomenology-embodied-cognition-shaun-gallagher.

57   Couldry, Nick. The Costs of Connection: How Data Is Colonizing Human Life and Appropriating It for Capitalism (Culture and Economic Life). Edited by Ulises A. Mejias. California, United States of America: Stanford University Press, 2019.

58   Ibid, 156.

59   Brincker, Maria, *Privacy in public and the contextual conditions of agency*, in Privacy in Public Space: Regulatory and Legal Challenges, 84, 85 (Edited by Tjerk Timan, Bryce Clayton Newell, Bert-Jaap Koops, Cheltenham: Edward Elgar Publishing, 2017.

60   Newen, Albert, Leon De Bruin, and Shaun Gallagher. *The Oxford Handbook of 4E Cognition: How Data Is Colonizing Human Life and Appropriating It for Capitalism* (Culture and Economic Life). Oxford, United Kingdom of Great Britain and Northern Ireland: Oxford University Press, 2018. https://doi.org/10.1093/oxfordhb/9780198735410.001.0001.

61   Devine, Nesta, and Ruth Irwin. "Autonomy, Agency and Education: He Tangata, He Tangata, He Tangata." *Educational Philosophy and Theory 37*, no. 3 (2005): 317–31. https://doi.org/10.1093/oxfordhb/978019873 5410.001.0001. (the Enlightenment era edifice crumbles of the fully rational and autonomous self).

62   Kompa, Joana Stella, *Defining Human Autonomy: Towards an Interdependent Model of Human Agency*, 4.

63   Thucydides. *The History of the Peloponnesian War*. Edited by M. I. Finley and Rex Warner. London, United Kingdom of Great Britain and Northern Ireland: Penguin Books, 1961.

64   Kauffman, Stuart A. *Investigations*. Oxford, United Kingdom of Great Britain and Northern Ireland: Oxford University Press Inc, 2000.

65   Lukes, Steven. *Power: A Radical View* (2nd edition). New York. Palgrave Macmillan.

66   Ibid.

67   Gaventa, John. "Finding the Space for Change: A Power Analysis." *IDS Bulleton*, Vol. 37, No. 6 (November, 2006). 23, 25.

68   Allen, John. "Topological Twists: Power's Shifting Geographies." *Dialogues in Human Geography 1*, no. 3 (November 11, 2011): 3. https://doi.org/10.1177/2043820611421546.

69   Edenberg, Elizabeth, and Meg Leta Jones. "Analyzing the Legal Roots and Moral Core of Digital Consent." *New Media & Society 21*, no. 8 (November 11, 2011): 20. https://doi.org/10.1177/146144481983132.

70   Edenberg and Jones, *Analyzing the Legal Roots and Moral Core of Digital Consent*, 2.

71   Herzog. *Happy Slaves*. Chicago, United States of America: University of Chicago Press, 1974. 229.

72   Covey, Stephen R. "'Trust is the glue of life. It is the most essential ingredient in effective communication. It's the foundational principle that holds all relationships.' - Stephen R. Covey." X. Chicago, United States of America: University of Chicago Press, March 18, 2020. Accessed August 23, 2024. https://x.com/stephenrcovey/status/1240277058082811904?lang=en.

73   Botsman, Rachel. Who Can You Trust?: How Technology Brought Us Together – and Why It Could Drive Us Apart. 7-9. London, United Kingdom of Great Britain and Northern Ireland: Portfolio Penguin, 2017. (2017).

74   Ibid, 28.

75   Ibid, 28.

76   Ibid, 40–41.

77   Ibid, 50–51, 257–260.

78   Ibid, 50–51.

79   Ibid, 262–263.

80   Ibid, 148.

81   See, e.g., Uslaner, Eric M. The Oxford Handbook of Social and Political Trust. Maryland, United States of America: Academic, 2010. (On writing that levels of trust in other people and institutions seems lower today than in the past); Uslaner, Eric M. "The 2020 Edelman Trust Barometer." Maryland, United States of America: Edelman Trust Barometer, January 19, 2020. Accessed August 23, 2024. https://www.edelman.com/trustbarometer?te=1&nl=the-interpreter&emc=edit_int_20200228&campaign_id=30&instance_id=16345&segment_id=21717&user_id=809a67bf3380d4e9e018934dc88fe3ac®i_id=8282764120200228 https://perma.cc/MJW9-2KPV. (Showing that none of the four societal institutions of government, business, NGOs, and media is well trusted).

82   Botsman, *Who Can You Trust?* 8-9, 259-260.

83   Woermann, Minka. "The Ethics of Complexity and the Complexity of Ethics." South African Journal of Philosophy, no. 31 (January 19, 2020): 134-35. 447–63. https://doi.org/10.1080/02580136.2012.10751787

84   Woermann, *The Ethics of Complexity and the Complexity of Ethics*, 142-43.

85   Woermann, *The Ethics of Complexity and the Complexity of Ethics*, 134-35.

86   Spivey, Michael J., and Stephanie Huette. "The Embodiment of Attention

in the Perception-Action Loop." *The Routledge Handbook of Embodied Cognition*, January 19, 2014, 306–14.

87   Werbach, Kevin. "The Federal Computer Commission." *The Routledge Handbook of Embodied Cognition 13*, no. 84 (January 19, 2014). Accessed August 23, 2024. https://scholarship.law.unc.edu/nclr/vol84/iss1/3.

88   For further discussion of these following points, see Richard S. Whitt, HIDING IN THE OPEN, 28.

89   Hanamura, Wendy. "Decentralized Web FAQ." *Internet Archive Blogs* (blog). Oxford, United Kingdom of Great Britain and Northern Ireland: Oxford University Press Inc, July 21, 2018. https://blog.archive.org/2018/07/21/decentralized-web-faq/.

90   Russell, Andrew L. Open Standards and the Digital Age: History, Ideology, and Networks (Cambridge Studies in the Emergence of Global Enterprise). Cambridge, United Kingdom of Great Britain and Northern Ireland: Cambridge University Press, 2014. 279.

91   Clark, David D. "The Design Philosophy of the DARPA Internet Protocols." *Laboratory for Computer Science 4* (August 1998). http://ccr.sigcomm.org/archive/1995/jan95/ccr-9501-clark.pdf.

92   The Importance of Voluntary Technical Standards for the Internet and Its Users, Center for Democracy & Tech. 3 (Aug. 29, 2012), https://www.cdt.org/files/pdfs/Importance%20of%20Voluntary%20Technical%20Standards.pdf.

93   Laboratory for Computer Science. "The Arpanet: Forerunner of Today's Internet." Cambridge, United Kingdom of Great Britain and Northern Ireland: BBN, 2024. Accessed August 27, 2024. http://www.bbn.com/about/timeline/arpanet.

94   Ibid.

95   Leiner, Barry M., Vinton G. Cerf, David D. Clark, Robert E. Kahn, Leonard Kleinrock, Daniel C. Lynch, Jon Postel, Larry G. Roberts, and Stephen Wolff. "A Brief History of the Internet." *ACM SIGCOMM Computer Communication Review 39*, no. 5 (October 7, 2009): 22–31. https://doi.org/10.1145/1629607.1629613.

96   Vinton G. Cerf & Robert E. Kahn, *A Protocol for Packet Network Intercommunication*, 22 IEEE Transactions on Comm. 637 (1974). In essence, TCP creates and organizes data packets, while IP wraps a header with routing instructions around each packet. UDP was another host-to-host protocol developed in this same timeframe.

97   Ronda Hauben, *From the ARPANET to the Internet*, Columbia University, http://www.columbia.edu/~rh120/other/tcpdigest_paper.txt.

98   Clark, The Design Philosophy of the DARPA Internet Protocols, 106.

99   Internet Architecture Board. "History." Accessed September 4, 2024. https://www.iab.org/about/history/.

100   Yale Information Society Project Working Paper Series, and Laura DeNardis. "The Emerging Field of Internet Governance." *Yale Law School*, 2010. https://typeset.io/pdf/the-emerging-field-of-internet-governance-3xpefhvteo.pdf.

101   Alvestrand, H. "A Mission Statement for the IETF." Best Current Practice, Network Working Group, 2004. https://datatracker.ietf.org/doc/html/rfc3935.

102 Ibid. 231.

103 Ibid.

104 Laboratory for Computer Science. "THE IMPORTANCE OF VOLUNTARY TECHNICAL STANDARDS FOR THE INTERNET AND ITS USERS." Cambridge, United Kingdom of Great Britain and Northern Ireland: Centre for Democracy & Technology, 2012. Accessed August 27, 2024. https://www.cdt.org/wp-content/uploads/pdfs/Importance%20of%20 Voluntary%20Technical%20Standards.pdf.

105 See Richard S. Whitt, "A Horizontal Leap Forward: Formulating a New Communications Public Policy Framework Based on the Network Layers Model," *FED. COM. L.J.* 56: 587, 601-02, http://www.fclj.org/wp-content/uploads/2013/01/Whitt-Final-2.pdf.

106 Richard S. Whitt, "Evolving Broadband Policy: Taking Adaptive Stances to Foster Optimal Internet Platforms," *COMMLAW CONSPECTUS* 17: 418 (2009), 507-533, https://scholarship.law.edu/cgi/viewcontent.cgi? article=1411&context=commlaw.

107 Justyna Hofmok, "The Internet commons: towards an eclectic theoretical framework," *International Journal of the Commons*, 4:1, 226, 230, https://www.jstor.org/stable/pdf/26523021.pdf?refreqid=fastly-defa ult%3A11c83192bf5637a32b76499604a0a296&ab_segments=&origin =&initiator=&acceptTC=1.

108 JPostel, J. "Domain Name System Structure and Delegation." Laboratory for Computer Science, March 3, 1994, 4–5. Accessed August 27, 2024. http://www.ietf.org/rfc/rfc1591.txt.

109 Bernbom, Gerald. "Analyzing the Internet as a Common Pool Resource: The Problem of Network Congestion." Pre-Conference Draft 13 (2000). Accessed August 27, 2024. http://citeseerx.ist.psu.edu/viewdoc/ summary?doi=10.1.1.119.9942.

110 Waz, Joe, and Phil Weiser. "Internet Governance: The Role of Multistakeholder Organizations." Telecomm 10 (2041): 322–31. Accessed August 27, 2024. https://scholar.law.colorado.edu/faculty-articles/149.

111 Solum, Lawrence B., and Minn Chung. "The Layers Principle: Internet Architecture and the Law." *Notre Dame Law Review* 79, no. 3 (January 4, 2004). https://scholarship.law.nd.edu/cgi/viewcontent. cgi?article=1432&context=ndlr.

112 Searls, Doc, and David Weinberger. "World of Ends." *What the Internet Is and How to Stop Mistaking It for Something Else* (blog), January 29, 2008. (Accessed September 4, 2024). https://worldofends.com.

113 Ibid, 6.

114 "A Mission Statement for the IETF: RFC 3935." *Cisco Systems*, October 2004. Accessed August 27, 2024. https://datatracker.ietf.org/doc/html/ rfc3935.

115 "Architectural Principles of the Internet: 1958." *Cisco Systems*, June 1996. Accessed August 27, 2024. https://www.rfc-editor.org/rfc/rfc1958.

116 Whitt, *Emergence Economics*.

117 Whitt, *Emergence Economics*. 256.

118 Architectural Principles of the Internet: 1958., 4. On the other hand, some forms of layering (or vertical integration) can be harmful if the complete separation of functions makes the network operate less efficiently. See R.

Bush & D. Meyer, Some Internet Architectural Guidelines and Philosophy 7–8, *Network Working Group*, Request for Comment No. 3439 (Dec. 2002), http://www.ietf.org/rfc/rfc3439.txt [hereinafter RFC 3439].

119 Whitt, *Emergence Economics*, at 257–58.

120 Architectural Principles of the Internet: 1958., 2, 4.

121 Isenberg, David S. Networker: The Craft of Network Computing (blog). 1998. Accessed August 27, 2024. https://www.isen.com/papers/Dawnstupid.html.

122 Van Schewick, Barbara. *Internet Architecture and Innovation*. Massachusetts, United States of America: MIT Press, 2010: 107. https://www.amazon.co.uk/Internet-Architecture-Innovation-MIT-Press/dp/0262013975. Barbara van Schewick, Internet Architecture and Innovation (2010), at 107.

123 Whitt, *Emergence Economics*, at 258.

124 Frischmann, Brett M. Infrastructure: The Social Value of Shared Resources. Oxford, United Kingdom of Great Britain and Northern Ireland: OXFORD UNIV PR, 322. 2012.

125 Architectural Principles of the Internet: 1958, 2.

126 Architectural Principles of the Internet: 1958, 2.

127 Whitt, *Broadband Policy,* 504.

128 Palfrey, John, and Urs Gasser. *Interop: The Promise and Perils of Highly Interconnected Systems*. New York City, United States of America: Basic Books, 22, 2012.

129 Ibid, 23.

130 Ibid, 108.

131 Ibid, 121. Standard processes play a particularly important role in getting to interoperability. At least 250 technical interoperability standards are involved in the manufacture of the average laptop computer produced today. Ibid, 163.

132 *Architectural Principles of the Internet*, 2.

133 Palfrey and Gasser, Interop: The Promise and Perils of Highly Interconnected Systems, 108.

134 Doria, Avri. "Policy Implications of Future Network Architectures and Technology." *1st Berlin Symposium on Internet and Society*, 2011. https://www.hiig.de/wp-content/uploads/2012/04/Future-Network-Architecture-Draft-Paper.pdf.

135 Ibid, 137.

136 Whitt, *A Deference to Protocol: Fashioning a Three-Dimensional Public Policy Framework for the Internet Age*, Cardozo Arts and Entertainment Law Journal, 31:3, 707. 2013.

137 Doria, 7.

138 *Architectural Principles of the Internet*, 2, 3. The layer principle is related to, but separate from, the broad version of the end-to-end principle. See van Schewick, at 104–06.

139 Doria, 7.

140 Whitt, *Emergence Economics*, 300–01.

141 Searls and Weinberger, *World of Ends.*

142 Whitt, Richard. "A Deference to Protocol: Fashioning a Three-Dimensional Public Policy Framework for the Internet Age" *Cardozo Arts and Entertainment Law Journal*, 31:3, 689 (2013), 717-729.

143 Gunderson, J., I. Jacobs, and E. Hansen. "Architecture of the World Wide Web: Volume One." Edited by Ian Jacobs. W3C Recommendation, December 15, 2004. Accessed August 27, 2024. http://www.w3.org/TR/webarch/.

144 Geeks for Geeks. "World Wide Web (WWW), Often Called the Web, Is a System of Interconnected Webpages and Information That You Can Access Using the Internet.", June 26, 2024. Accessed August 27, 2024. https://www.geeksforgeeks.org/world-wide-web-www/.

145 Web Foundation. "History of the Web.", 2022. Accessed August 27, 2024. https://webfoundation.org/about/vision/history-of-the-web/.

146 Searls, Doc. "Beyond the Web." Doc Searls Weblog (blog)., August 15, 2021. Accessed August 27, 2024. https://doc.searls.com/2021/08/15/beyond-the-web/.

147 Whitt, *Hiding in the Open*, 66-70.

148 Searls, Doc. "How the cookie poisoned the Web." Doc Searls Weblog (blog). -, May 14, 2021. Accessed August 27, 2024. https://doc.searls.com/2021/05/14/poison/.

149 Whitt, *Hiding in the Open*, 66-70.

150 Whitt, *Hiding in the Open*, 66.

151 Ibid.

152 Ibid.

153 "Chapter 4 Computational Systems: Computational Systems." *Weapons and Systems Engineering Department United States Naval Academy*, 1999. Accessed August 27, 2024. https://man.fas.org/dod-101/navy/docs/fun/part04.htm.

154 Whitt, *Hiding in the Open*, 103.

155 Whitt, *Hiding in the Open*, 69.

156 Whitt, *Hiding in the Open*, 103. See generally Amy Webb, *The Big Nine: How the Tech Titans and Their Thinking Machines Could Warp Humanity*. 2019. (Webb includes the three Chinese companies in her pantheon of "tech titans" built on the Web platforms ecosystem model).

157 Whitt, *Hiding in the Open*, at 74; *see also* Adam Thierer, The Internet of Things and Wearable Technology: Addressing Privacy and Security Concerns Without Derailing Innovation, 21 *Rich. J.L. & Tech.* 6, 12 (2015).

158 Srnicek, Nick. *Platform Capitalism: Theory Redux*. Cambridge, United Kingdom of Great Britain and Northern Ireland: Polity Press, 40. 2017.

159 Whitt, *Through A Glass Darkly*, 130.

160 Whitt, *A Deference to Protocol*, 133.

161 Nick Srnicek, *Platform Capitalism*, 40.

162 Pedro Domingos, *The Master Algorithm: How the Quest for the Ultimate Learning Machine Will Remake Our World* 1, London, United Kingdom of Great Britain and Northern Ireland: Allen Lane. 2015.

163 Ibid, 13-16.

164 Ibid, 13-16.

165 For a more in-depth analysis, *see* Whitt, Richard. *A Web That Weaves Itself: Foundational Dimensions of the New Machine Intelligence Era.* 63-75 (unpublished manuscript) (on file with Author).

166 Ibid.

167 Ibid.

168 Whitt, *A Web That Weaves Itself.*

169 Ibid.

170 Ibid.

171 See Frischmann and Selinger, *Re-Engineering Humanity*, 184-208.

172 Ibid.

173 Galloway, Alexander. *The Interface Effect.* Cambridge, United Kingdom of Great Britain and Northern Ireland: Polity Press, 10. 2012.

174 Galloway, *The Interface Effect*, 32. See also Galloway, Alexander. *The Exploit: A Theory of Networks (Electronic Mediations).* Cambridge, United Kingdom of Great Britain and Northern Ireland: Polity Press, 2007.

175 Galloway, *The Interface*, 18.

176 Bratton, Benjamin H., *The Stack: On Software and Sovereignty*, Cambridge, United Kingdom of Great Britain and Northern Ireland: Polity Press, 2016.

177 Ibid, 228.

178 Whitt, Richard. "Democratize AI: (Part 1)." Richard Whitt (blog). June 3, 2019. Accessed August 27, 2024. https://medium.com/swlh/democratize-ai-part-i-ade3cc7f727d.

179 Ibid.

180 Whitt, *Democratize AI.*

181 Ibid.

182 Ibid.

183 Ibid.

184 Ibid.

185 Weiser, Mark. "The Computer for the 21st Century." *Scientific American* 94 (September 1991). Accessed August 27, 2024. https://www.scientificamerican.com/article/the-computer-for-the-21st-century/.

186 Couldry, Nick., and Andreas Hepp, *The Mediated Construction of Reality: Society, Culture, Mediatization*, Cambridge, United Kingdom of Great Britain and Northern Ireland: Polity Press, 223, 2016.

187 Lidwell, William., Kritina Holden., and Jill Butler, *Universal Principles of Design: Updated and Expanded Third Edition: 200 Ways to Increase Appeal, Enhance Usability, Influence Perception, and Make Better Design Decisions* (1) (Rockport Universal), Massachusetts, United States of America: Rockport Publishers, 92-93., 2003; Meadows, supra note 3, 153-156.

188 Schumpeter. "So Long iPhone. Generative AI Needs a New Device: Is This the Twilight of the Screen Age?" *The Economist*, October 5, 2023. Accessed August 27, 2024. https://www.economist.com/business/2023/10/05/so-long-iphone-generative-ai-needs-a-new-device.

189 Berners-Lee, Tim. "The World Wide Web Turns 30 Today: Here's How Its Inventor Thinks We Can Fix It." Time, March 12, 2019. Accessed August 27, 2024. https://time.com/5549635/tim-berners-lee-interview-web/.

190 Whitt, *Old School Goes Online*; Whitt, *Hiding in the Open*.

191 Greenfield, Adam. *Radical Technologies: The Design of Everyday Life*. London, United Kingdom of Great Britain and Northern Ireland: Verso, 308. 2017.

192 See Zuboff, Shoshana., *The Age of Surveillance Capitalism: The Fight for a Human Future at the New Frontier of Power*, London, United Kingdom of Great Britain and Northern Ireland: Profile Books, 2019.; see also Tim O'Reilly, *WTF, What's the Future and Why It's Up to Us.*, London, United Kingdom of Great Britain and Northern Ireland: Cornerstone Digital. 2017.; Roger McNamee, Zucked: *Waking up to the Facebook Catastrophe.*, London, United Kingdom of Great Britain and Northern Ireland: HarperCollins. 2019.

193 Whitt, *Hiding in the Open*, 68.

194 Ibid.

195 Ibid, 66-70.

196 Whitt, *Old School Goes Online*, 102-105.

197 Ibid.

198 Zuboff, *The Age of Surveillance Capitalism*, 293-297.

199 Whitt, *Hiding in the Open*, 69-70.

200 Ibid, 68.

201 Evgeny Morozov, *The True Threat of Artificial Intelligence*, The New York Times, June 30, 2023.

202 Hetzner, Christiaan. "Former Google CEO Eric Schmidt Tells Government to Leave A.I. Regulation to Big Tech." *Yahoo Finance*. May 15, 2023. Accessed August 27, 2024. https://finance.yahoo.com/news/former-google-ceo-eric-schmidt-155901279.html.

203 Cantu, Javier Livas., *What Is Cybernetics*, Stafford Beer, Honoris Causa at Universidad de Valladolid, YouTube, Jun. 3, 2013., Accessed August 27, 2024. https://www.youtube.com/watch?v=uOj3Brkd_DE https://perma.cc/Q4W3-VF4C.

204 See Nissenbaum, Helen. *Privacy in Context: Technology, Policy, and the Integrity of Social Life*. California, United States of America: Stanford Law Books, 2009. (In 2010, Helen Nissenbaum preferred to surveillance the phrase "monitoring and tracking." She explained that the term surveillance suggests that those in power are monitoring people for purposes of modifying and controlling their behaviors. Some ten years later, the connotation actually fits rather well).

205 Zuboff, *The Age of Surveillance Capitalism*, 64; Whitt, *Old School Goes Online*, 103. (This particular nomenclature draws from Hal Varian, Chief Economist at Google, who has used the phrase "data extraction and analysis" to describe some of what Web platforms do.)

206 Whitt, *Old School Goes Online*, 103.

207 Nissenbaum, *Privacy in Context*, 22

208 "MANIPULATE: Definition in the Cambridge English Dictionary." In Cambridge University Press & Assessment. California, United States of America: Stanford Law Books, 2024. Accessed August 28, 2024. https://dictionary.cambridge.org/us/dictionary/english/manipulate.

209 Benkler, Yochai, Robert Faris, and Hal Roberts. *Network Propaganda: Manipulation, Disinformation, and Radicalization in American Politics.* Oxford, United Kingdom of Great Britain and Northern Ireland: Oxford University Press, 2009.

210 Ibid.

211 Floridi, Luciano. "Marketing as Control of Human Interfaces and Its Political Exploitation." *Philosophy & Technology* 32 (August 10, 2019): 379–88. https://link.springer.com/article/10.1007/s13347-019-00374-7.

212 Zuboff, *The Age of Surveillance Capitalism*, 18, 186-187.

213 Ibid, 386.

214 Jaiswal, Arushi. "Dark Patterns in UX: How Designers Should Be Responsible for Their Actions,." Medium, April 15, 2018. https://uxdesign.cc/dark-patterns-in-ux-design-7009a83b233c. (Jaiswal lists some eleven different misleading/deceptive UI/UX interfaces).

215 Floridi, *Marketing as Control of Human Interfaces and Its Political Exploitation*, 383

216 Zuboff, *The Age of Surveillance Capitalism*, 293.

217 Zuboff, *The Age of Surveillance Capitalism*.

218 Ibid. 294-297.

219 Ibid. 294.

220 Ibid. 295.

221 Ibid. 295-296.

222 Ibid. 293.

223 Ibid. 507-512.

224 Ibid. 16.; Furman, Jason, and Tim Simcoe. "The Economics of Big Data and Differential Pricing." The White House, February 6, 2015. https://obamawhitehouse.archives.gov/blog/2015/02/06/economics-big-data-and-differential-pricing.

225 Zuboff, *The Age of Surveillance Capitalism*, 307.

226 Frischmann and Selinger, *Re-engineering Humanity*, 270.

227 Žižek, Slavoj. Like a Thief in Broad Daylight: Power in the Era of Post-Humanity. London, United Kingdom of Great Britain and Northern Ireland: Penguin, 42. 2019.

228 Brin, Sergey., and Lawrence Page, *The Anatomy of a Large-Scale Hypertextual Web Search Engine*. Stanford, The United States of America, Computer Science Department, 1997.

229 https://abc.xyz/investor/founders-letters/ipo-letter/.

230 Ibid.

231 Brin, Sergey, and Lawrence Page. "The Anatomy of a Large-Scale Hypertextual Web Search Engine." *WWW7* 30 (1998): 107–17: Appendix A. https://snap.stanford.edu/class/cs224w-readings/Brin98Anatomy.pdf.

232 Plehegar. "WG closed." GitHub. London, United Kingdom of Great Britain and Northern Ireland: Penguin, 2019. Accessed August 28, 2024. https://github.com/w3c/dnt/commit/5d85d6c3d116b5eb29fddc6935 2a77d87dfd2310.

233 Suzor, Nicolas. "Digital Constitutionalism: Using the Rule of Law to Evaluate the Legitimacy of Governance by Platforms." Social Media + Society, July 17, 2013, 1–3. https://doi.org/10.1177/20563051187878.

234 Ibid. 5.

235 Ibid.

236 Whitt, *Old School Goes Online*, 115.

237 Ibid. 116-117.

238 Ibid. 117.

239 Ibid. 117, 203.

240 Whitt, *Hiding in the Open*, *supra* note 12, 65.

241 Ibid.

242 Whitt, Richard S. "A Deference to Protocol: Fashioning a Three-Dimensional Public Policy Framework for the Internet Age." Cardozo Arts & Entertainment Law Journal, July 12, 2013, 689–747. https://papers.ssrn.com/sol3/papers.cfm?abstract_id=2031186.; Whitt, *Hiding in the Open*, 65; Whitt, *Old School Goes Online*, 116.

243 See Whitt, *Old School Goes Online*, 116.

244 D'Ignazio, Catherine, and Lauren F. Klein. *Data Feminism*. Massachusetts, United States of America: MIT Press, 60. 2020.

245 See, e.g., Kiran Bhageshipur, *Data is the New Oil—And That's A Good Thing*, Forbes: Tech. Council (Nov. 15, 2019, 8:15 AM), https://www.forbes.com/sites/forbestechcouncil/2019/11/15/data-is-the-new-oil-and-thats-a-good-thing/#13627bb73045 https://perma.cc/3PCP-VKPE (data is "the new oil" has become a common refrain).

246 Suzor, *Digital Constitutionalism*, 5.

247 Suzor, *Digital Constitutionalism*.

248 Suzor, *Digital Constitutionalism*, 6, 8.

249 Sharwood, Simon, and Scott McNealy. "Your Data is Safer With Marketers Than Governments." *The Register*, March 14, 2017. https://www.theregister.com/2017/03/14/scott_mcnealy_on_privacy/.

250 Esguerra, Richard, "Google CEO Eric Schmidt Dismisses the Importance of Privacy." Electronic Frontier Found. Dec. 10, 2009. https://www.eff.org/deeplinks/2009/12/google-ceo-eric-schmidt-dismisses-privacy https://perma.cc/GA2V-R7G9.

251 Zuboff, supra note 18, 293-297.

252 Ibid.

253 Ibid.

254 Tisne, Martin,. "The Data Delusion: Protecting Individual Data Isn't Enough When the Harm is Collective." Stan. Cyber Pol'y Ctr. 1, 2-4. 2020. https://cyber.fsi.stanford.edu/publication/data-delusion https://perma.cc/U7VS-2GYU.

255 Ibid. 5-6.

256 Molitorisz, Sacha. *Net Privacy: How We Can Be Free in an Age of Surveillance*. Montreal, Canada: McGill-Queen's University Press, 2020.

257 Molitorisz, *Net Privacy*, 239-40.

258 Molitorisz, *Net Privacy*, 137.

259 Renieris, Elizabeth. "Rebuilding Respectful Relationships in the Digital Realm." *MIT Computational Law Report*, 2021. https://law.mit.edu/pub/rebuildingrespectfulrelationships/release/4.

260 Renieris, Elizabeth. "Rebuilding Respectful Relationships in the Digital Realm." *MIT Computational Law Report*, May 14, 2021: 23. https://law.mit.edu/pub/rebuildingrespectfulrelationships.

261 LeVasseur, Lisa, and Eve Maler. "Beyond Consent: A Right-to-Use License for Mutual Agency." *MIT Computational Law Report* 3, no. 4 (December 31, 2019): 52–59. https://doi.org/10.1109/MCOMSTD.001.1900031.

262 Kim, Nancy S. *Consentability*. Cambridge, United Kingdom of Great Britain and Northern Ireland: Cambridge University Press, 2019. https://doi.org/10.1017/9781316691311.

263 Richards, Neil. "The Pathologies of Digital Consent." *Washington University Law Review* 96 (2019). https://openscholarship.wustl.edu/cgi/viewcontent.cgi?article=6460&context=law_lawreview.

264 Meadows, supra note 3, 145-166 (discusses ways people can intervene to restructure the systems we live in, Identifying leverage points for change).

265 Whitt, Richard. "Human Agency in the Digital Era." January 8, 2020. Accessed August 29, 2024. https://notsimple.libsyn.com/richard-whitt-human-agency-in-the-digital-era.; Whitt, Richard. "What if the Internet Was Safe?: SU Global Summit." 2019. Accessed August 29, 2024. https://www.youtube.com/watch?v=NyQFbu5SUYo%20https://perma.cc/FYD4-4JZ4.; Whitt, Richard. "To Fix the Web, Give It Back to the Users." Fast Company, January 22, 2019. Accessed August 22, 2024. https://www.fastcompany.com/90293980/to-fix-the-web-give-it-back-to-the-users.

266 See, e.g., Rozzi, Ricardo. "Earth Stewardship: Linking Ecology and Ethics in Theory and Practice." Springer 2 (2015): 10–13. Accessed August 22, 2024. https://link.springer.com/book/10.1007/978-3-319-12133-8. (integrating ecology and ethics forms the foundation for earth stewardship action); Chapin, F. Stuart, Gary P. Kofinas, and Carl Folke. Principles of Ecosystem Stewardship: Resilience-Based Natural Resource Management in a Changing World. New York City, United States of America: Springer, 2014.

267 See Berry, R. J. *Environmental Stewardship: Critical Perspectives, Past and Present*. London, United Kingdom of Great Britain and Northern Ireland: Bloomsbury, 2006. (Judeo-Christian religious doctrine includes care and stewardship of creation). Some suggest that Buddhism includes "ecodharma," which includes collective responsibility and action to protect the natural world. David R. Loy, Ecodharma: Buddhist Teachings for the Ecological Crisis. Somerville, United States of America: Wisdom Publications, 2019.

268 Kimberly K. Smith, *Exploring Environmental Ethics: An Introduction*. Springer, United States of America: New York City, 2019.

269 Stuart et al. Principles of Ecosystem Stewardship. (Goals of stewardship include encouraging the ecosystem's resilience, sustainability, and diversity, and recognizing and managing the uncertainty from multiple feedback loops and tipping points).

270 "EQUITY: Equity Definition & Meaning." In Merriam-Webster. 2024. Accessed August 22, 2024. https://www.merriam-webster.com/

dictionary/equity.

271 D'Ignazio and Klein, *Data Feminism*, 60.

272 D'Ignazio and Klein, *Data Feminism*, 62.

273 D'Ignazio and Klein, *Data Feminism*, 216.

274 D'Ignazio and Klein, *Data Feminism*, 61–65.

275 Szabo, Nick. "Recovering Privity." *First Monday. In View of Formalizing and Securing Relationships on Public Networks*. 1997. https://firstmonday.org/ojs/index.php/fm/article/view/548/469/.

276 Szabo, *Recovering Privity*.

277 Apologies to some traditionalists for employing here the plural rather than the singular form (datum).

278 Rosenberg, Daniel. "Infastructure: 'Raw Data' Is an Oxymoron." **First Monday**. MIT Press 15, no. 9 (September 1, 1997): 36–37. https://doi.org/10.7551/mitpress/9302.001.0001. See also D'Ignazio and Klein, Data Feminism, t 10 (the word "data" was introduced in the mid-seventeenth century to supplement pre-existing terms such as "evidence" and "fact.").

279 Louikissas, Yanni Alexander. "All Data Are Local: Thinking Critically in a Data-Driven Society." First Monday. MIT Press, 2002. https://doi.org/10.7551/mitpress/11543.001.0001.

280 Whitt, *Hiding in the Open*, 66–70.

281 Whitt, *Through a Glass Darkly*.

282 Ibid, 188–192 (information lifecycles and systems layers models can support long-term digital preservation proposals).

283 Whitt, *Old School Goes Online*, 103–105.

284 Dyson, Freeman. "IS LIFE ANALOG OR DIGITAL? | Edge.org," *Edge*. https://www.edge.org/conversation/freeman_dyson-is-life-analog-or-digital.

285 Ibid.

286 Koops, Bert-Jaap, Bryce Clayton Newell, Tjerk Timan, Ivan Škorvánek, Tomislav Chokrevski, and Maša Galič. "A Typology of Privacy." *Penn Carey Law* 38 (2017). https://scholarship.law.upenn.edu/jil/vol38/iss2/4/. (describing eight types of personal privacy that align with different data types).

287 D'Ignazio & Klein, *Data Feminism*, 10.

288 Whitt, *Through a Glass Darkly, supra* note 105, at 145-147 (providing an overview of the long-debated data-information-knowledge-wisdom ("DIKW") hierarchy).

289 Hand, David J. *Dark Data: Why What You Don't Know Matters*. Princeton, United States of America: Princeton University Press, 2020. ("[E]xamples of this second kind, in which we don't know that something is missing, are ubiquitous... As you will see, dark data have many forms. Unless we are aware that data might be incomplete,... we could get a very misleading impression of what's going on.").

290 Couldry and Hepp, *The Mediated Construction of Reality*, 124-25.

291 D'Ignazio & Klein, *Data Feminism*, 12.

292 Couldry and Hepp, *The Mediated Construction of Reality*, 124-25.

293 Brincker, *Privacy in public and the contextual conditions of agency*, 65.

294 Zuboff, *The Age of Surveillance Capitalism*, 93–97, 293–297.

295 Thales. "Biometrics: definition, use cases, latest news: What Is Biometrics?" 2023. Accessed August 29, 2024. https://www.thalesgroup.com/ en/markets/digital-identity-and-security/government/inspired/bio metrics#:~:text=Biometrics%3A%20trends&text=Biometrics%20can%20 be%20defined%20as,falling%20prices%20of%20sensors%2C%20I.P.

296 IBIA. "Behavioural Biometrics.", 2020. Accessed August 29, 2024. https:// www.ibia.org/download/datasets/3839/Behavioral%20Biometrics%20 white%20paper.pdf.

297 Koops et al., 560–62.

298 Bolle, C. J. M. "Empathy 2.0: What it means to be empathetic in a diverse and digital world." Ethics & Philosophy of Technology, 2024. Accessed August 29, 2024. https://doi.org/10.4233/uuid:5c1d9753-ab5b-4812-ab29-b66a6d0d772d.

299 Ibid.

300 Wakabayashi, Daisuke, and Alistair Barr. "Apple and Google Know What You Want Before You Do." WSJ, August 3, 2015. Accessed August 29, 2024. https://doi.org/10.4233/uuid:5c1d9753-ab5b-4812-ab29-b66a6d 0d772d.

301 Stephen T. Asma & Rami Gabriel, *The Emotional Mind: The Affective Roots of Culture and Cognition*. Harvard, United States of America: Belknap Press. 25-27. 2019.

302 Louikissas, Yanni Alexander. *All Data Are Local: Thinking Critically in a Data-Driven Society*.

303 "Lifestreaming" was coined in the mid-2000s to describe the process of documenting and sharing outputs of one's social experiences. "Live-streaming: WikiVisually." Har, United States of America: Wiki Visually, 2024. Accessed August 29, 2024. https://wikivisually.com/wiki/ Lifestreaming. Steve Rubel, an early enthusiast, likened lifestreaming to the digital equivalent of Leonardo da Vinci's notebooks—his recorded notes, drawings, questions, and more. Id. In HAACS parlance, these products are indicia of one's agency in the world. A more intriguing angle is to utilize digital technology to tap into the raw material of the autonomous self.

304 D'Ignazio and Klein, *Data Feminism*, 5.

305 See *infra* Chapter 3.

306 Brincker, *Privacy in public and the Contextual Conditions of Agency*, 85.

307 *Rethinking Data*, Ada Lovelace Inst. (2020), https://www.adalovelace institute.org/wp-content/uploads/2020/01/Rethinking-Data-Prospectus-Print-Ada-Lovelace-Institute-2019.pdf https://perma.cc/ AH3K-PUSA.

308 Aryan, Aashish. "Explained: What is non-personal data?" *The Indian Express*, July 27, 2020. Accessed August 29, 2024. https://indianexpress. com/article/explained/non-personal-data-explained-6506613/#.

309 Nick Srnicek, *Platform Capitalism*, 40.

310 Ibid.

311 Using the phraseology of the SEAM cycle also is an attempt to capture

that connotation of a dirty resource—in this case, "seams" of coal.

312   Gilman, Nils., and Indira Ganesh, Maya,. "Making Sense of the Unknown" *AI +1: Shaping Our Integrated Future* 74, 77. 2024. Accessed August 29, 2024. https://www.rockefellerfoundation.org/insights/perspective/making-sense-of-the-unknown/.

313   Rouse, Margaret. "Data Exhaust" *techopedia*, 2014. Accessed August 29, 2024. https://www.techopedia.com/definition/30319/data-exhaust#:~:text=Data%20exhaust%20refers%20to%20the,all%20digital%20or%20online%20activities.

314   Lanier, Jarod, *Who Owns the Future*. Simon & Schuster, United Kingdom & Northern Ireland: London. 2013. (On stating that users should be paid for their data).

315   Benson, Jeff. "Harvard's Elizabeth Renieris: Privacy Is an Inalienable Right." *Digital Privacy News*, 2020. Accessed August 29, 2024. https://digitalprivacy.news/2020/03/31/harvards-elizabeth-renieris-privacy-is-an-inalienable-right/.

316   Searls, Doc., "We Can Do Better Than Selling Our Data", Doc *Searls Weblog* (Sept. 18, 2018),Accessed August 29, 2024. https://blogs.harvard.edu/doc/2018/09/18/data/ https://perma.cc/59LY-AERK; Elizabeth Renieris et al., "You Really Don't Want to Sell Your Data", Slate. April 7, 2020. Accessed August 29, 2024. https://slate.com/technology/2020/04/sell-your-own-data-bad-idea.html https://perma.cc/4XFX-JMRX.

317   The Economist, " Are Data More Like Oil or Sunlight?" Economist. Feb. 20 2020, https://www.economist.com/special-report/2020/02/20/are-data-more-like-oil-or-sunlight https://perma.cc/ZET2-GNTA.

318   See *supra*.

319   See *supra*.

320   See *supra*.

321   "12E.1.2 Factors of Production: The Economic Lowdown Podcast series, Episode 2." *Digital Privacy News*. Har, United States of America: Teaching California, 2020. Accessed August 29, 2024. https://www.teachingcalifornia.org/resource/12e-1-2-factors-of-production-the-economic-lowdown-podcast-series-episode-2/.

322   Kim, Eugene K. "Data as Labor: Retrofitting Labor Law for the Platform Economy." *Minnesota Journal of Law*, Science & Technology Minnesota Journal of Law, Science & Technology 23, no. 1 (August 23, 2022): 38. Accessed August 29, 2024. https://scholarship.law.umn.edu/mjlst/vol23/iss1/4. (Data as labor offers a radical opportunity to shape new digital markets).

323   Frischmann, Brett M., *Infrastructure: The Social Value of Shared Resources*. New York, United States of America: Oxford University Press, U.S.A. 24-30 (2012).

324   Ibid, at 25.

325   Ibid, at 27.

326   *Data's Identity in Today's Economy*, MIT Tech. Rev. (Apr. 7, 2016), https://www.technologyreview.com/2016/04/07/108767/datas-identity-in-todays-economy/ https://perma.cc/YX4J-ZEG8.

327   Ibid.

328   Frischmann, *Infrastructure: The Social Value of Shared Resources*, 25.

329   Ibid.

330   Ibid, 39.

331   Ibid, 32.

332   Ibid, 38.

333   Whitt, Richard., "Adaptive Policymaking: Evolving and Applying Emergent Solutions for U.S." *Communications Policy*, 61 Fed. Comm. L. J. 483, 512-26., 2009. https://www.repository.law.indiana.edu/fclj/vol61/iss3/2/.

334   Frischmann, *Infrastructure: The Social Value of Shared Resources*, 26-33.

335   Whitt, *Adaptive Policymaking*, at 522-23.

336   Frischmann, *Infrastructure: The Social Value of Shared Resources*, 30-34.

337   Panfi, Yuliyal., and Hagopian, Andrew., "A Commons Approach to Data Governance," *New Am.* Sept. 5, 2019, https://www.newamerica.org/weekly/edition-260/commons-approach-to-data-governance/ https://perma.cc/F7QR-ZSEY.

338   Frischmann, *Infrastructure: The Social Value of Shared Resources*, 8.

339   Whitt, *A Deference to Protocol*, 747-48.

340   Ibid, 747.

341   Frischmann, *Infrastructure: The Social Value of Shared Resources*, 253-314. Closely related to the concept of "data" is "ideas." New growth economist Paul Romer found ideas to be both non-rivalrous (readily shared for re-use) and at least partially excludable (sharing can be limited). See Richard Whitt & Stephen Schultze, "The New 'Emergence Economic' of Innovation and Growth, and What It Means for Communications Policy," Telecomm & High Tech. 217, 264-67. 2009. https://www.repository.law.indiana.edu/fclj/vol61/iss3/2/.

342   Frischmann, *Infrastructure: The Social Value of Shared Resources*, 253.

343   Ibid, 254.

344   Charlotte Hess, "The Unfolding of the Knowledge Commons," *St. Anthony's Int'l R.* 13, 20-21. 2012. https://surface.syr.edu/cgi/viewcontent.cgi?article=1113&context=sul.

345   Linebaugh, Peter,. "Enclosures from the Bottom Up, in The Wealth of the Commons: A World Beyond Market & State", *The Commons Strategies Group.* 114-124. 2012. (Explores opposition to various market enclosures of shared resources, and the generative power of the commons).

346   Zuboff, *The Age of Surveillance Capitalism*.

347   Nicholas Taleb, Nassim,. *Skin in the Game: Hidden Asymmetries in Daily Life.* London: United Kingdom and Ireland: Allen Lane. 154. 2018.

348   For a deeper exploration of fiduciary law in the context of the digital world, *Old School Goes Online*.

349   Ibid, 86.

350   Frankel, Tamar,. *Fiduciary Law.* London: United Kingdom and Ireland: Allen Lane. 79. 2010.

351   Criddle, Evan J. *The Oxford Handbook of Fiduciary Duties.* London: United Kingdom and Ireland: Academic. 2019.

352   Ibid, 471-663.

353 Whitt, *Old School Goes Online*, 86.

354 Frankel, *Fiduciary Law*, 6.

355 Whitt, *Old School Goes Online*, 87.

356 Ibid, 88.

357 Ibid, 89.

358 Ibid, 88.

359 Ibid, 86.

360 Ibid, 88.

361 Ibid.

362 Ibid, 91.

363 Whitt, *Old School Goes Online*.

364 Ibid. Other fiduciary duties include good faith and confidentiality. Fiduciary Duties, Black's Law Dictionary (11th ed. 2019) (defining other fiduciary duties as " ...good faith, trust, special confidence, and candor...").

365 Whitt, *Old School Goes Online,* 89.

366 Ibid.

367 Ibid.

368 Ibid.

369 Ibid, 87.

370 Ibid, 129.

371 Whitt, *Old School Goes Online*, 87-88.

372 Renieris, Elizabeth Renieris and Greenwood, Dazza,. "Do we really want to 'sell' ourselves? The risks of a property law paradigm for personal data ownership", Medium. Sept. 23, 2018., https://medium.com/@hackylawyER/do-we-really-want-to-sell-ourselves-the-risks-of-a-property-law-paradigm-for-data-ownership-b217e42edffa https://perma.cc/Y6FX-3J4R (arguing for inclusion of constitutional or human rights laws in the framing for our identity-related data).

373 See *supra*.

374 "The Advocates for Human Rights." United States of America: The Advocates for Human Rights, August 23, 2023. Accessed August 30, 2024. https://www.theadvocatesforhumanrights.org/human_rights_and_the_united_states.

375 Criddle, Evan J., and Evan Fox-Decent, eds. *Fiduciary Government*. Cambridge, United Kingdom of Great Britain and Northern Ireland: Cambridge University Press, 2019.

376 Whitt, *Hiding in the Open*, 86; Fiduciary Government.

377 Criddle, *Fiduciary Government*.

378 Lawson, Gary S., and Guy I. Seidman. "A Great Power of Attorney: Understanding the Fiduciary Constitution." *Scholarly Commons at Boston University School of Law* 29 (2017). https://scholarship.law.bu.edu/books/29/.; see also Common Law Liberty: Rethinking American Constitutionalism. Kansas, United States of America: University Press of Kansas, 2003. (making the case for the US Constitution's grounding in the common law).

379 Lawson and Seidman, *A Great Power of Attorney: Understanding the Fiduciary Constitution*, 172.

380 Criddle, Evan J., and Evan Fox-Decent. "The Internal Morality of International Law." *McGill Law Journal* 54, no. 2 (June 1, 2017). https://lawjournal.mcgill.ca/wp-content/uploads/2018/06/ARTICLE-10-Fox-Decent-and-Criddle-EMBEDDED-FONTS.pdf. (writing that leading theories struggle to offer persuasive support for the basis, content, and scope of human rights).

381 Whitt, *Old School Goes Online*, 86.

382 Criddle & Fox, *The Internal Morality of International Law*, 94.

383 Criddle & Fox, *The Internal Morality of International Law*.

384 Whitt, *Old School Goes Online*, 128-130, for a discussion on common law doctrine that may be worth investigating as well, as part of fashioning a broad-based "digital common law" for the 21st Century. Examples include the law of "information torts," misappropriation, and bailment.

385 Flanagan, Anne Josephine, and Sheila Warren. "Advancing Digital Agency: The Power of Data Intermediaries." *Insight Report*, February 22, 2022, 14–15. https://www3.weforum.org/docs/WEF_Advancing_towards_Digital_Agency_2022.pdf.

386 Flanagan, *Advancing Digital Agency: The Power of Data Intermediaries*, 262.

387 Flanagan, *Advancing Digital Agency: The Power of Data Intermediaries*, 50-51.

388 Botsman, *Who Can You Trust?*, 8-9, 259-260.

389 *See generally* Whitt, *A Human-Centered Paradigm for the Web* (discusses the online paradigm of SEAM cycles, and advances a counter-paradigm of enhancing human autonomy; suggests creating effective leverage points that include more human-centric infrastructures).

390 Norman, Don. "Words Matter. Talk About People: Not Customers, Not Consumers, Not Users," *jnd.org*. February 16, 2023. https://jnd.org/words-matter-talk-about-people-not-customers-not-consumers-not-users/.

391 https://jacks.tumblr.com/post/33785796042/lets-reconsider-our-users.

392 Norman, *Words Matter*.

393 Searls, Doc. "How Adtech, Not Ad Blocking, Breaks the Social Contract," *Doc Searls Weblog*. September 23, 2015. https://doc.searls.com/2015/09/23/how-adtech-not-ad-blocking-breaks-the-social-contract/.

394 https://www.fastcompany.com/90310803/here-are-the-data-brokers-quietly-buying-and-selling-your-personal-information.

395 https://blogs.harvard.edu/doc/2018/10/12/naked/.

396 Taleb, *supra* note 213.

397 Botsman, 108.

398 Botsman.

399 Whitt, *Digital Stewardship*, 13-16.

400 Meadows, *Thinking in Systems*, 157.

401 Searls, Doc. "Privacy = Personal Agency + Respect by Others for Personal Dignity – ProjectVRM," July 10, 2018, https://blogs.harvard.edu/vrm/2018/07/10/privacy/.

402 D'Ignazio and Klein, *Data Feminism*, 8-26 (describing the structural privilege and oppression inherent in power, and different domains of domination).

403 Whitt, Richard. "A Human-Centered Paradigm for the Web - Richard Whitt - Medium," Medium, December 15, 2021, https://whitt.medium.com/a-human-centered-paradigm-for-the-web-e7ceaee8fb0e.

404 Whitt, *Old School Goes Online*, 107.

405 Ibid.

406 Ibid.

407 Ibid.

408 Ibid.

409 Ibid.

410 Ibid.

411 Ibid.

412 Ibid.

413 Ibid.

414 Whitt, Richard. "A Human-Centered Paradigm for the Web - Richard Whitt - Medium," Medium, December 16, 2021, https://whitt.medium.com/a-human-centered-paradigm-for-the-web-27ae40159778?sk=00552857950f20678d5cdc1f103145e3.

415 Kapoor, A, *Practising Data Stewardship in India* (2020) Ada Lovelace Institute. Available at https://www.adalovelaceinstitute.org/practising-data-stewardship-in-india/

416 Garrett, *Betrayal of Trust: The Collapse of Global Public Health*, 591.

417 *See* Whitt, *Hacking the SEAMs*.

418 Whitt, *Old School Goes Online*, at 102-109

419 Delacroix, Sylvie. and Neil D. Lawrence, "Bottom-Up Data Trusts: Disturbing the 'One Size Fits All'" *Approach to Data Governance*, 9 Int'l Data Privacy L. 236 (2019), https://academic.oup.com/idpl/article/9/4/236/5579842 https://perma.cc/4EN3-6WEM.

420 *See* Whitt, *Old School Goes Online*, 126; *See* ibid.

421 Whitt, Richard. "A Human-Centered Paradigm for the Web - Richard Whitt - Medium," Medium, December 16, 2021, https://whitt.medium.com/a-human-centered-paradigm-for-the-web-27ae40159778.

422 Whitt, Richard. *From Thurii to Quayside: Creating Inclusive Blended Spaces in Digital Communities*, posted October 4, 2020. https://papers.ssrn.com/sol3/papers.cfm?abstract_id=3709111.

423 Richardson, Benjamin Ward. The Life of John Snow, M.D. 1858.

424 Ibid.

425 Ibid.

426 Ibid.

427 Steven Johnson, *The Ghost Map*, 153.

428 Ibid.

429 Steven Johnson, *The Ghost Map*, 147.

430 Centers for Disease Control and Prevention (CDC). *Contact Tracing*. Public Health, 2021. https://www.cdc.gov/museum/pdf/cdcm-pha-stem-lesson-contact-tracing-lesson.pdf.

431 Kolata, Gina. "On Native American Land, Contact Tracing Is Saving Lives," *New York Times*. August 13, 2020. https://www.nytimes.com/2020/08/13/health/coronavirus-contact-tracing-apaches.html.

432 https://uploads.strikinglycdn.com/files/64aa4010-6c11-4d6f-8463-efaed964d7d9/Understanding%20Data%20Stewardship%20-%20Aapti%20Institute.pdf

433 Apple. "Privacy-Preserving Contact Tracing - Apple and Google," n.d. https://covid19.apple.com/contacttracing.

434 As just one example, the Epione proposal promises "lightweight contact tracing with strong privacy" measures; the project utilizes a blockchain data tokenization process intended to "blind" the token to the underlying medical data.

435 Whitt, Richard. *Old School Goes Online*, 115-117.

436 Bennet, Steve."For Effective Contact Tracing, Epidemiologists Must Embrace Advanced Analytics," *HealthyIT Outcomes*. July 27, 2020. https://www.healthitoutcomes.com/doc/for-effective-contact-tracing-epidemiologists-must-embrace-advanced-analytics-0001.

437 Garrett, *Betrayal of Trust: The Collapse of Global Public Health*, 591.

438 Penner, *The Law of Trusts*, 21.

439 In New Zealand, for example, the Maori people have come to consider data as "taonga," meaning (roughly) a type of "treasured possession." Aimee Whitcroft, *data trusts+*, March 3, 2020. https://medium.com/proceeding-by-inquiry/data-trusts-ee494010082.

440 Ruhaak, Anouk. "Data Trusts: Why, What and How - Anouk Ruhaak - Medium," *Medium*, December 12, 2021, https://medium.com/@anoukruhaak/data-trusts-why-what-and-how-a8b53b53d34. .

441 Delacroix, Sylvie. and Neil Lawrence, "Disturbing the 'One Size Fits All', Feudal Ap-proach to Data Governance: Bottom-Up Data Trusts," *SSRN Electronic Journal*, January 1, 2018, https://doi.org/10.2139/ssrn.3265315.

442 O'Hara, Kieron. "Data Trusts: Ethics, Architecture and Governance for Trustworthy Data Stewardship" Web Science Institute White Paper. February 2019, (doi:10.5258/SOTON/WSI-WP001).

443 Malik Ghallab et al., *Data Trusts*, 2018, https://hello.elementai.com/rs/024-OAQ-547/images/Data_Trusts_EN_201914.pdf. .

444 Soni, Shivam. "Fostering Participatory Data Stewardship | Aapti Institute." *Aapti Institute*, June 7, 2023. https://aapti.in/fostering-participatory-data-stewardship/

445 Mozilla Foundation. "Data Futures Lab." *Mozilla*. Accessed September 5, 2024. https://foundation.mozilla.org/en/data-futures-lab/.

446 Pentland, Alex, Alexander Lipton, and Thomas Hardjono. *Building the New Economy: Data as Capital*. MIT Press, 2021.

447   Sylvie Delacroix and Neil D Lawrence, "Bottom-up Data Trusts: Disturbing the 'One Size Fits All' Approach to Data Governance," *International Data Privacy Law*, October 1, 2019: 248-249. https://doi.org/10.1093/idpl/ipz014. [first citation at n. 416]

448   Ghallab, Malik, Rob Van Kranenburg, Sylvie Delacroix, Jonnie Penn, UNI Global Union, Edward Santow, John Howell, et al. *Data Trusts*, 2018. https://hello.elementai.com/rs/024-OAQ-547/images/Data_Trusts_EN_201914.pdf.

449   Steven Johnson, *The Ghost Map*, 149.

450   Steven Johnson, *The Ghost Map*, 155.

451   Steven Johnson, *The Ghost Map*, 197-198.

452   Public health workers commonly ask themselves "where is the handle to this pump?" as they seek solutions to thorny epidemiological problems. Hempel, San-dra. *The Medical Detective: John Snow, Cholera and the Mystery of the Broad Street Pump*, 279. 2007.

453   Lofting, Hugh. *The Story of Doctor Dolittle*. Open Road Media, 2017.

454   Bob Kahn and Vinton Cerf, "An Open Architecture for a Digital Library System and a Plan for its Development" (March 1988), https://www.cnri.reston.va.us/kahn-cerf-88.pdf.

455   Ibid, 17.

456   "Agent." In Merriam-Webster Dictionary, September 6, 2024. https://www.merriam-webster.com/dictionary/agent.;. LII / Legal Information Institute. "Agency," n.d. https://www.law.cornell.edu/wex/agency.

457   Shavit, Yonadav, Sandhini Agarwal, Miles Brundage, Steven Adler, OpenAI, Rosie Campbell, Teddy Lee, et al. "Practices for Governing Agentic AI Systems," 2023. Accessed September 10, 2024. https://cdn.openai.com/papers/practices-for-governing-agentic-ai-systems.pdf.

458   OpenAI Agenticity White Paper, 4

459   Ibid, 7-15.

460   Ibid, 5.

461   Ibid, 9-10.

462   Ibid, 10.

463   Ibid, 2, 4.

464   Google DeepMind. "The Ethics of Advanced AI Assistants," September 5, 2024.

465   Google DeepMind, *Ethics Paper*, 34.

466   Whitt, Richard. "Unleashing the Potential of Cryptodata - Oasis Foundation - Medium," *Medium*, March 18, 2022, https://medium.com/oasis-protocol-project/unleashing-the-potential-of-cryptodata-4707c86ada39.

467   Whitt, *A Deference to Protocol*, 717-729.

468   *Schollmeier, Rudiger. A Definition of Peer-to-Peer Networking for the Classification of Peer-to-Peer Architectures and Applications* (Sep. 2001): https://www.it.lut.fi/wiki/lib/exe/fetch.php/courses/ct30a6900/p2p_definitions.pdf https://perma.cc/5PDL-78FP (providing a clear definition of peer-to-peer networking).

469   Whitt, *Hacking the SEAMs*, 153-163.

470 FortifID, "FortifID: A Privacy-First Onboarding & Identity Verification Solution," January 26, 2024, https://fortifid.com/.

471 Doc Searls, "ProjectVRM," n.d., http://blogs.harvard.edu/vrm/.

472 "Mit-opal," n.d. https://mit-opal.mit.edu/.

473 FortifID, *A Privacy-First Onboarding & Identity Verification Solution*.

474 "About – ProjectVRM," n.d. http://blogs.harvard.edu/vrm/about/.

475 New America. "A Commons Approach to Data Governance," n.d. https://blogs.harvard.edu/vrm/2018/06/23/matters/.

476 Lidwell, William, Kritina Holden, and Jill Butler. Universal Principles of Design, Re-vised and Updated: 125 Ways to Enhance Usability, Influence Perception, Increase Appeal, Make Better Design Decisions, and Teach Through Design. Rockport Pub, 2010.

477 Ibid, 717-729.

478 *See supra.* Whitt, *Hiding in the Open*, 68-70; Whitt, *Old School Goes Online*, 102-105.

479 *See Whitt, Hiding in the Open,* 68-70.

480 Google DeepMind. *AI Ethics Paper*, 35-36.

481 Google DeepMind. *AI Ethics Paper*, 35, 36.

482 Ibid, 36.

483 Ibid.

484 Ibid, 36, 4.

485 Ibid.

486 Of course, potentially melding the Human and the AI raises profound questions. The "Becoming Human" community has an intriguing site to address some such questions. Medium: Becoming Human, https://becominghuman.ai/ https://perma.cc/4VX7-GXH8 (last visited Oct. 18, 2020).

487 "Bruce Schneier, "AI and Trust - Google Search," n.d. https://www.google.com/search?client=safari&rls=en&q=Bruce+Schneier%2C+%E2%80%9CAI+and+Trust&ie=UTF-8&oe=UTF-8.

488 The IEEE Global Initiative on Ethics of Autonomous and Intelligent Systems. *ETHICALLY ALIGNED DESIGN. ETHICALLY ALIGNED DESIGN.* First Edition., 2019. https://standards.ieee.org/wp-content/uploads/import/documents/other/ead1e.pdf?utm_medium=undefined&utm_source=undefined&utm_campaign=undefined&utm_content=undefined&utm_term=undefined.

489 Ibid, 114-115.

490 Ibid, 113-114.

491 Ibid, 113.

492 Google DeepMind. *AI Ethics Paper*, 108-110.

493 Ibid.

494 Ibid, 114 (emphasis in original).

495 Ibid, 116.

496 Ibid. (emphasis in original).

497 Ibid.

498 Whitt, *Old School Goes Online*, 121.

499 Fleming, David. "The Streets of Thurii: Discourse, Democracy, and Design in the Classical Polis." *Rhetoric Society Quarterly*, vol. 32, no. 3, 2002, pp. 5–32. *JSTOR*, www.jstor.org/stable/3886007. Accessed 10 Sept. 2020.

500 Fleming, *Streets of Thurii*, 6.

501 Fleming, *Streets of Thurii*, 27.

502 Fleming, *Streets of Thurii*, 12.

503 Brioschi S.A., Marino S.D. (2018) "Hypothesis of Reconstruction of Ancient Cities Through 3D Printing: The Case-Study of Thurii." *In: Amoruso G.* (eds) Putting Tradition into Practice: Heritage, Place and Design. INTBAU 2017. Lecture Notes in Civil Engineering, vol 3. Springer, Cham. https://doi.org/10.1007/978-3-319-57937-5_68.

504 Kirkpatrick, Aidan. *The Image of the City in Antiquity: Tracing the Origins of Urban Planning*, Hippodamian Theory, and the Orthogonal Grid in Classical Greece, 2015.

505 Kirkpatrick, *The Image of the City in Antiquity: Tracing the Origins of Urban Planning*.

506 Fleming, *Streets of Thurii*, 18.

507 Rutter, N. K. "Diodorus and the Foundation of Thurii." *Historia: Zeitschrift Für Alte Geschichte*, vol. 22, no. 2, Franz Steiner Verlag, 1973, pp. 155–76, http://www.jstor.org/stable/4435327.

508 Wikipedia contributors, "Planned Community - Wikipedia," September 5, 2024, https://en.wikipedia.org/wiki/Planned_community.

509 Digi.City. "Smart City Definitions," n.d. https://www.digi.city/smart-city-definitions.

510 Barcelona Digital City | Barcelona City Council. "Barcelona Digital City | Barcelona City Council," n.d. https://ajuntament.barcelona.cat/digital/en.

511 Amsterdam Smart City, "Home - Amsterdam Smart City," Amsterdam Smart City, n.d., https://amsterdamsmartcity.com/.

512 CIOI'[Nsights. "CIOInsights - Insights From Technology Leaders," n.d. https://cioinsights.com/blog/the-future-of-smart-cities.

513 PRS Legislative Research. "Committee Reports," n.d. https://prsindia.org/policy/report-summaries/non-personal-data-governance-framework.

514 httpGoogle Earth. "Build Sustainably With Google Earth – Google Earth," n.d. https://www.sidewalklabs.com/.

515 Google Earth. "Build Sustainably With Google Earth – Google Earth," n.d. https://www.sidewalklabs.com/.

516 Doctoroff, Daniel L. "Why We're No Longer Pursuing the Quayside Project — and What's Next for Sidewalk Labs." Medium, December 14, 2021. https://medium.com/sidewalk-talk/why-were-no-longer-pursuing-the-quayside-project-and-what-s-next-for-sidewalk-labs-9a61de3fee3a.

517 Whitt, *Hacking the SEAMs*, 158-161.

518 Alexander Galloway, *The Interface Effect*, 31.

519 Whitt, *Hacking the SEAMs*, 195.

520 Kuang and Fabricant, User Friendly, 32.

521 Kuang and Fabricant, User Friendly, 34.

522 Ibid. Frischmann and Selinger, Re-Engineering Humanity, 134-142. (discusses consid-erations of where and how intelligence and control technologies are deployed within infrastructure systems).

523 Galloway, *The Interface Effect*, 90-94.

524 Kuang and Fabricant, *User Friendly*, 145.

525 Whitt, *Hacking the SEAMs*, 195.

526 Frischmann and Selinger, *Re-Engineering Humanity*, 142-146 (design features of smart media limit direct human mediations).

527 Frischmann and Selinger, *Re-Engineering Humanity*, 124-136.

528 Floridi, Luciano. *The Fourth Revolution: How the Infosphere Is Reshaping Human Reality*, 2014, http://ci.nii.ac.jp/ncid/BB16630552.

529 Whitt, *Hacking the SEAMs*, 161-63.

530 Pettis, Ben. "The Costs of Connection: How Data Is Colonizing Human Life and Ap-propriating It for Capitalism." *Critical Studies in Media Communication* 37, no. 2 (February 2, 2020): 204–6. https://doi.org/10.1 080/15295036.2020.1718835.

531 Couldry and Mejias, *The Costs of Connection*, 156.

532 Maria Brincker, *Privacy in public and the contextual conditions of agency*, in Tjerk Timan, Bryce Clayton Newell, and Bert-Jaap Koops, eds. Privacy in Public Space (2017) 84, 85.

533 The Oxford Handbook of 4E Cognition. Oxford University Press eBooks, 2018. https://doi.org/10.1093/oxfordhb/9780198735410.001.0001; Michael J Spivery and Stephanie Huette, The Embodiment of Attention in the Perception- Action Loop, 306, in Lawrence Shapiro ed., The Routledge Handbook of Embodied Cognition (2014).

534 Frischmann and Selinger, *Re-Engineering Humanity*, 81-101 (describes the porous connections between mind, body, and world, through extended mind theory in the context of human bodies, cognition, and technology).

535 Whitt, *Hacking the SEAMs,* 162-63.

536 Behind the cityscapes, architect Stavros Stavrides challenges us to perceive of space-as-commons, expressing and exemplifying novel forms of social relations. Stavros Stavrides, Common Space: The City as Commons (2020).

537 "Biometrics: Definition, Use Cases, Latest News," Thales Group, June 12, 2023, https://www.thalesgroup.com/en/markets/digital-identity-and-security/government/inspired/biometrics. (last updated June 2, 2021).

538 Christofi, Athena and Verdoodt, Valerie, *Exploring the Essence of the Right to Data Protection and Smart Cities* (August 20, 2019), at: https://papers.ssrn.com/sol3/papers.cfm?abstract_id=3483616.

539 Stavrides, *Common Space*, 160.

540 Fleming, David. City of Rhetoric: Revitalizing the Public Sphere in Metropolitan America, 2008. https://www.amazon.com/City-Rhetoric-Revitalizing-Metropolitan-America/dp/0791476502.

541 Kirkpatrick, *The image of the city in antiquity: tracing the origins of urban planning, Hippodamian Theory, and the orthogonal grid in Classical Greece.*

542 Mcdonald, Sean. "The Civic Trust - Sean McDonald - Medium," Medium,

April 13, 2018, https://medium.com/@digitalpublic/the-civic-trust-e674f9aeab43.

543 "MaRS," n.d., https://marsdd.gitbook.io/datatrust/trusts/global-examples.

544 McDonald, Sean. "Toronto, Civic Data, and Trust - Sean McDonald - Medium." *Medium*, October 17, 2018. https://medium.com/@digitalpublic /toronto-civic-data-and-trust-ee7ab928fb68.

545 Dawson, Alyssa Harvey. "An Update on Data Governance for Sidewalk Toronto - Sidewalk Talk - Medium," *Medium*, October 17, 2018, https:// medium.com/sidewalk-talk/an-update-on-data-governance-for-sidewalk-toronto-d810245f10f7.

546 Dawson, Alyssa Harvey. "An Update on Data Governance for Sidewalk Toronto - Sidewalk Talk - Medium." *Medium*, October 17, 2018. https:// medium.com/sidewalk-talk/an-update-on-data-governance-for-sidewalk-toronto-d810245f10f7.

547 CBC. "Ontario Privacy Commissioner Raises Concerns Over Sidewalk Labs Data Proposals," September 27, 2019. https://www.cbc.ca/news/ canada/toronto/sidewalk-labs-privacy-comissioner-1.5299192.

548 McDonald, Sean. "Toronto, Civic Data, and Trust - Sean McDonald - Medium," *Medium*, October 17, 2018, https://medium.com/@ digitalpublic/toronto-civic-data-and-trust-ee7ab928fb68.

549 Ellen P. Goodman and Julia Powles, "Urbanism Under Google: Lessons from Sidewalk" *Toronto, 88 Fordham Law Review* 457 (2019).

550 Constance Carr and Markus Hesse, "When Alphabet Inc. Plans Toronto's Waterfront: New Post Political Modes of Urban Governance," Cogitatio, Urban Planning, Vol. 5 Issue 1 at 69 (2020).

551 Frischmann, *Governing Knowledge Commons*.

552 Stavrides, *Common Space*.

553 "The Commons | CLES," n.d. https://cles.org.uk/what-is-community -wealth-building/the-principles-of-community-wealth-building/ socially-just-use-of-land-and-property/the-commons/#:~:text=This %20can%20be%20understood%20through,direct%20control%20of%20 common%20assets.

554 Frischmann, *Infrastructure*, 253-314. Closely related to the concept of "data" is "ideas." New growth economist Paul Romer found ideas to be both non-rivalrous (readily shared for re-use) and at least partially excludable (sharing can be limited). *See* Richard Whitt and Stephen Schultze, "The New 'Emergence Economics' of Innovation and Growth, and What It Means for Communications Policy," *Journal on Telecommunications and High Technology Law*, Vol. 7, No. 2 (2007), 217, 264-267.

555 Frischmann, *Infrastructure*, 253.

556 Hess, Charlotte, and Elinor Ostrom. *Understanding Knowledge as a Commons: From Theory to Practice*. National Geographic Books, 2011.

557 The history of the commons, and subsequent enclosures by political and commercial interests, may provide a suitable framing for ongoing debates about treating as private property (or "enclosing") data. *See, e.g.,* David Bollier and Silke Helfrich, eds., The Wealth of the Commons: A World Beyond Market and State (2012) (explores opposition to various market enclosures of shared resources, and the generative power of the

commons). To some, data may represent the ultimate – last? – global enclosure opportunity, beyond the land and labor resources of the past.

558 Frischmann, Brett M., Michael J. Madison, and Madelyn Rose Sanfilippo. Governing Smart Cities as Knowledge Commons. Cambridge University Press, 2023.

559 Ibid.

560 Scassa, Teresa. "Designing Data Governance for Data Sharing: Lessons From Sidewalk Toronto," September 30, 2020, https://papers.ssrn.com/sol3/papers.cfm?abstract_id=3722204.

561 Scassa, Designing Data Governance, 56.

562 Scassa, Designing Data Governance, 56.

563 This platform is being implemented and prototyped by the GLIA Foundation.

564 "First-of-Its-Kind Blueprint for Data Policy Adopted by City of Helsinki," World Economic Forum Press Release, dated September 7, 2021, found at: https://www.weforum.org/press/2021/09/first-of-its-kind-blueprint-for-data-policy-adopted-by-city-of-helsinki/.

565 World Economic Forum. "Empowered Data Societies: A Human-Centric Approach to Data Relationships," October 9, 2023. https://www.weforum.org/publications/empowered-data-societies-a-human-centric-approach-to-data-relationships/.

566 Ibid, 15.

567 "Agora." Wikipedia, April 14, 2024. https://en.wikipedia.org/wiki/Agora.

568 Whipps, Heather. "How The Greek Agora Changed the World." Livescience.Com, March 17, 2008. https://www.livescience.com/4861-greek-agora-changed-world.html.

569 Google Earth. "Build Sustainably With Google Earth – Google Earth," n.d. https://www.sidewalklabs.com/dtpr/.

570 Medium. "Medium," n.d. https://medium.com/sidewalk-talk/how-can-we-make-urban-tech-transparent-these-icons-are-a-first-step-f03f237f8ff0.

571 Artyushina, Is Civic Data Governance the Key to Democratic Smart Cities?, 29.

572 Lu, Jacqueline. "How can we bring transparency to urban tech? These icons are a first step.," Medium, December 9, 2021, https://medium.com/sidewalk-talk/how-can-we-make-urban-tech-transparent-these-icons-are-a-first-step-f03f237f8ff0.

573 Renée. "Charrette #3 — DTPR." DTPR, May 21, 2020. https://web.archive.org/web/20200618143439/https://process.dtpr.dev/blog/third-and-last-charrette.

574 sidewalklabs. "Dtpr/Dtpr_Chatbot at Master · Sidewalklabs/Dtpr." GitHub, n.d. https://github.com/sidewalklabs/dtpr/tree/master/dtpr_chatbot.

575 "Charrette #3 — DTPR." DTPR, May 21, 2020. https://web.archive.org/web/20200618143439/https://process.dtpr.dev/blog/third-and-last-charrette.

576 "Research Session 3: Exploring the Potential of Trusted Digital

Assistants — DTPR." DTPR, May 21, 2020. https://web.archive.org/web/20201021034335/https://process.dtpr.dev/blog/research-session-3-exploring-the-potential-of-trusted-digital-assistants.

577 https://whitt.medium.com/a-human-centered-paradigm-for-the-web-e7ceaee8fb0e.

578 Fleming, City of Rhetoric, 32.

579 Solid, "https://solid.inrupt.com/" 2024. Accessed August 30, 2024. https://solid.inrupt.com/.

580 Holochain, "https://holochain.org/" 2024. Accessed August 30, 2024. https://holochain.org/.

581 digi.me, "https://digi.me/ 2024." Accessed August 30, 2024. https://digi.me/ 2024.

582 DuckDuckGo, "https://duckduckgo.com/" 2024. Accessed August 30, 2024. https://duckduckgo.com/.

583 Mozilla, "https://www.mozilla.org/en-US/firefox/" 2024. Accessed August 30, 2024. https://www.mozilla.org/en-US/firefox/; Brave, "https://brave.com/" 2024. Accessed August 30, 2024. https://brave.com.

584 Signal, "https://signal.org/" 2024. Accessed August 30, 2024. https://signal.org/.

585 Mycroft AI, "https://mycroft.ai/" 2024. Accessed August 30, 2024. https://mycroft.ai/.

586 "https://www.personal.ai/." 2024. Accessed August 30, 2024. https://www.personal.ai/.

587 "https://www.kwaai.ai/." 2024. Accessed August 30, 2024. https://www.kwaai.ai/.

588 Solid. "Solid." Solid: Your Data, Your Choice. Accessed August 30, 2024. https://solidproject.org

589 Perzanowski, Aaron., and Jason Schultz, The End of Ownership: Personal Property in the Digital Economy (MIT Press, 2018). https://doi.org/10.7551/mitpress/9780262035019.001.0001.

590 Topics | European Parliament. "Conflict Minerals: The Bloody Truth Behind Your Smartphone | Topics | European Parliament," n.d. https://www.europarl.europa.eu/topics/en/article/20170314STO66681/conflict-minerals-the-bloody-truth-behind-your-smartphone.

591 Moto Mod & Indiegogo. "Transform the Smartphone Challenge - Moto Mod; Indiegogo," April 12, 2018. https://enterprise.indiegogo.com/motomod/.

592 "DWeb," n.d. https://getdweb.net/.

593 Ibid.

594 Brunton, Finn, and Helen Nissenbaum. Obfuscation: A User's Guide for Privacy and Protest. MIT Press, 2016.

595 Tekisalp, Emre. "Understanding Web 3: A User Controlled Internet." Coinbase. August 29, 2018. https://www.coinbase.com/en-gb/blog/understanding-web-3-a-user-controlled-internet.

596 Werbach, Kevin. The Blockchain and the New Architecture of Trust. MIT Press, 3, 2023.

597 https://blog.coinbase.com/understanding-web-3-a-user-controlled-

internet-a39c21cf83f3.

598 Voshmgir, *Token Economy*, 29-30.

599 *See generally* Werbach, The Blockchain and the New Architecture of Trust.

600 Shermin Voshmgir, Token Economy (2d edition) (2020), at 20.

601 Voshmgir, *Token Economy*, 168-170.

602 *See generally* Voshmgir, Token Economy.

603 Whitt, *Hiding in the Open*, 66-70.

604 "IBM Blockchain - Enterprise Blockchain Solutions and Services," n.d. https://www.ibm.com/blockchain/for-good.

605 "Blockchain for Social Good," n.d. https://www.accenture.com/us-en/services/blockchain/blockchainforgood-index.

606 Kewell, Beth, Richard Adams, and Glenn Charles Parry. "Blockchain for Good?" Strategic Change Forthcoming 5 (September 2006). https://doi.org/10.1002/jsc.2143.

607 https://irishtechnews.ie/the-post-corona-business-model-machine-learning-with-tokenized-big-data.

608 See, e.g., Bluefin, "The Global Race to Secure Payment and Consumer Data by Merchants." Bluefin. June 20, 2020. https://www.bluefin.com/p/data-security-white-paper/. (Details use of encryptin and tokenization to address consumer data security challenges).

609 Tokenex, "Tokenizing the Insurance Industry." Whitepaper. 2019. https://www.tokenex.com/wp-content/uploads/2022/10/Whitepaper-Cyber-Insurance-d08-BW.pdf. (using data tokenization to secure and desensitize client insurance information).

610 Gupta, Dileep. "A Complete Guide to Healthcare Compliances." *Appinventiv* (blog), June 20, 2024. https://appinventiv.com/blog/healthcare-compliances-guide/.

611 Tomas Hardjono, Anne Kim, and Alex Pentland, "Health IT: Algorithms, Privacy, and Data" *Works in Progress: Building the New Economy* (April 2020), https://wip.mitpress.mit.edu/pub/a56wpt24/release/1.

612 Hardjono, Kim, and Pentland, "Health IT: Algorithms, Privacy, and Data," MIT Press. 9-10. 2020. https://doi.org/10.21428/ba67f642.0499afe0.

613 WEALTHCARE. "WEALTHCARE," n.d. https://www.blockhealth.us/

614 Brittan Heller and Avi Bar-Zeev, "The Problems with Immersive Advertising: In AR/VR, Nobody Knows You Are an Ad," Stanford Internet Observatory, 1. Journal of Trust and Safety, October 2021. https://www.researchgate.net/publication/355762066_The_Problems_with_Immersive_Advertising_In_ARVR_Nobody_Knows_You_Are_an_Ad.

615 Ibid, 1-2.

616 Named for Joyce Searls, who—at the dawn of the commercial Web in 1995—first came up with the request for "a shopping cart of my own I can take from site to site."

617 Theory of Change Community. "What Is Theory of Change? - Theory of Change Community," July 19, 2023. https://www.theoryofchange.org/what-is-theory-of-change/.

618 Ibid.

619 Muthle, Champion. Theory of Change: A Practical Guide to Social Impact. 108. Independently published, 2021.

620 Mozilla. "Introduction to the Theory of Change," 2023. Accessed August 30, 2024. https://foundation.mozilla.org/en/insights/trustworthy-ai-white paper/path-forward/shifting-industry-norms/

621 Ibid.

622 Mozilla. Introduction to the Theory of Change.

623 Mozilla Foundation, Accelerating Progress Toward Trustworthy AI, Version 0.9 – For Public Input, February 2024. https://foundation.mozilla.org/en/research/library/accelerating-progress-toward-trustworthy-ai/whitepaper/.

624 Ibid, 8.

625 Theory of Change Community. "What Is Theory of Change? - Theory of Change Community," July 19, 2023. https://www.theoryofchange.org/what-is-theory-of-change/.

626 Ibid.

627 Hagel, John., and Singer, Marc., Net Worth: Shaping Markets When Customers Make the Rules. New York, United States of America: Harvard Business Review Press, 1999.

628 Hagel, John,. "The Return of the Infomediary," The Marketing Journal, May 11, 2019. https://www.marketingjournal.org/the-return-of-the-infomediary-john-hagel/.

629 Ibid.

630 Ibid.

631 Ibid.

632 Wohr, James,. "Ad blocking: What it is, and why it matters to marketers and advertisers," EMarketer. October 11, 2023. https://www.emarketer.com/insights/ad-blocking/.

633 Ibid.

634 Ibid.

635 Hwang, Tim,. Subprime Attention Crisis: Advertising and the Time Bomb at the Heart of the Internet (FSG Originals x Logic). New York, United States of America: Farrar, Straus and Giroux, 2020.

636 Galloway, Scott,. "The Imminent Collapse of Digital Advertising," Medium. October 2021, https://marker.medium.com/the-imminent-collapse-of-digital-advertising-3ab4272be67c.

637 Bradshaw, Jon,. "$700bn delusion: Does using data to target specific audiences make advertising more effective? Latest studies suggest not," Mi3. June 26, 2024. https://www.mi-3.com.au/26-06-2024/data-delusion-does-using-data-target-specific-audiences-advertising-actually-make.

638 Ibid.

639 "Update on the Plan for Phase-out of Third-party Cookies on Chrome." Privacy and Sandbox, March 21, 2023. Accessed August 30, 2024. https://privacysandbox.com/intl/en_us/news/update-on-the-plan-for-phase-out-of-third-party-cookies-on-chrome/.

640 Loayza, Allen. "IAPP." Personal Information Management Systems: A New

Era for Individual Privacy? March 21, 2019. https://iapp.org/news/a/personal-information-management-systems-a-new-era-for-individual-privacy.

641 Lanier, Jaron. and Weyl, Glen, "A Blueprint for a Better Digital Society," *Harvard Business Review*, Sept. 26, 2018. https://hbr.org/2018/09/a-blueprint-for-a-better-digital-society.

642 Reisman, Richard. "Reverse the Biz Model!—Undo the Faustian Bargain for Ads and Data," December 3, 2018. https://www.linkedin.com/pulse/reverse-biz-model-undo-faustian-bargain-ads-data-richard-reisman/. See also Reisman, Richard, and Marco Bertini. "A Novel Architecture to Monetize Digital Offerings." Journal of Revenue and Pricing Management 17, no. 6 (February 26, 2018): 453–58. https://doi.org/10.1057/s41272-018-0143-3.

643 Accenture, "We the Post Digital People," *Technology Vision* 2020, https://www.accenture.com/us-en/insights/technology/technology-trends-2020.

644 "What Is a Fiduciary? | Personal Wealth Management | Fisher Investments," n.d. https://www.fisherinvestments.com/en-us/personal-wealth-management/how-we-are-different/fiduciary.

645 The Harvard Law School Forum on Corporate Governance. "The Rise of Fiduciary Law," September 10, 2018: 3. https://corpgov.law.harvard.edu/2018/09/10/the-rise-of-fiduciary-law/. ("[f]iduciary services are best rendered voluntarily.").

646 Samet, Irit. "Fiduciary Loyalty as Kantian Virtue." *Philosophical Foundations of Fiduciary Law*, August 2014, 125–40. https://doi.org/10.1093/acprof:oso/9780198701729.003.0006.

647 Kang, Jerry, Katie Shilton, Deborah Estrin, Jeff Burke, and Mark Hansen. "Self-Surveillance Privacy." SSRN 97 (December 14, 2014): 809, 828. https://papers.ssrn.com/sol3/papers.cfm?abstract_id=1729332.

648 Godwin, Mike. *The Splinters of Our Discontent: How to Fix Social Media and Democracy Without Breaking Them*. Zenger Press, 2019: 34-35.

649 Frankel, Fiduciary Law, 31.

650 Riley, Chris. "A Framework for Forward-looking Tech Competition Policy." 2003 Fall Simulation Interoperability Workshop. Mozilla Working Paper, April 12, 2023. https://blog.mozilla.org/netpolicy/files/2019/09/Mozilla-Competition-Working-Paper.pdf.

651 Chris Riley (2020) "Unpacking Interoperability in Competition," Journal of Cyber Policy, 5.1, 94–106, 10.1080/23738871.2020.1740754. https://www.tandfonline.com/doi/full/10.1080/23738871.2020.1740754.

652 Chao, Becky., and Schulman, Ross Schulman,. "Promoting Platform Interoperability," *New America Foundation*, March 13, 2020. https://www.newamerica.org/oti/reports/promoting-platform-interoperability/.

653 Arnao, Zander. "Cory Doctorow on Why Interoperability Would Boost Digital Competition." Chicago Policy Review, April 12, 2023. https://chicagopolicyreview.org/2023/04/12/cory-doctorow-on-why-interoperability-would-boost-digital-competition/.

654 "Google Data Liberation Front." Wikipedia, June 13, 2024. https://en.wikipedia.org/wiki/Google_Data_Liberation_Front.

655 Data Transfer Initiative. "Data Transfer Initiative," n.d. https://dtinit.org/.

656 Tolk, Andreas, and James A. Muguira. "The Levels of Conceptual Interoperability Model." *2003 Fall Simulation Interoperability Workshop, Old Dominion University*, 2022. https://www.mscoe.org/content/uploads /2017/12/Tolk-Muguira-The-Levels-of-Conceptual-Interoperability-Models.pdf.

657 OpenAPI Initiative. "The OpenAPI Initiative (OAI)." OpenAPI Initiative. 2022. Accessed August 30, 2024. https://www.openapis.org/about.

658 Palfrey and Gasser, *Interop: The Promise and Perils of Highly Interconnected Systems*, 116.

659 Schulman, Chao. "Promoting Platform Interoperability." OPEN TECHNOLOGY INSTITUTE. New Jersey, United States of America: Pearson, May 13, 2020. Accessed August 30, 2024. https://www.newamerica.org/ oti/reports/promoting-platform-interoperability/. 15.

660 Schulman, *Promoting Platform Interoperability*, 12.

661 "Kwaai," n.d. https://www.kwaai.ai/.

662 Ibid.

663 Ibid.

664 IEEE SA Standards Association. "Ethically Aligned Design: Personal Data and Individual Agency," *IEEE SA*, December 1, 2024. Accessed August 30, 2024. https://standards.ieee.org/content/dam/ieee-standards/ standards/web/documents/other/ead1e_personal_data.pdf https:// perma.cc/RH35-ZEKM.

665 "Standards Repository | StandICT.eu 2026," n.d. https://www.standict. eu/standards-repository/ieee-p7006-standard-personal-data-artificial -intelligence-ai-agent.

666 StandICT2023 Logo. "Landscape and Gap Analysis Reports." *ICT Standardisation Observatory and Support Facility in Europe*. Accessed September 5, 2024. https://www.standict.eu/sites/default/files/2021 -01/P7006.pdf.

667 Ben Salem, Malek, IEEE P7006 Working Group, Juxtopia, DataEthics. eu, Southwest Research Institute, University of West of Scotland, UK, ChannelScience, and IEEE Standards Association. "IEEE P7006 Working Group Meeting Draft Minutes," January 25, 2021. https://sagroups. ieee.org/7006/wp-content/uploads/sites/213/2021/07/Meeting-Minutes-Jan-25-2021.pdf.

668 IEEE SA Standards Association. "Standard for Machine Readable Personal Privacy Terms: P7012." IEEE SA, December 1, 2024. Accessed August 30, 2024. https://standards.ieee.org/ieee/7012/7192/.

669 Ibid.

670 Ibid.

671 Wolfgang Kerber and Heike Schweitzer, "Interoperability in the digital economy," Joint Discussion Paper. 12-20. January 31, 2017.

672 Riley, Chris. "The Future of Generative AI Is Personal – and Portable?" *Data Transfer Initiative* (blog), November 21, 2023. https://dtinit.org/ blog/2023/11/21/future-AI-portable.

673 Sjarov, Martin, Dominik Kißkalt, Tobias Lechler, Andreas Selmaier, and Jörg Franke Franke. "Towards 'Design for Interoperability' in the Context of Systems Engineering." Elsevier, December 1, 2010. https://doi. org/10.1016/j.procir.2021.01.067.

674 Kingdon, John. *Agendas, Alternatives, and Public Policies*, Update Edition, With an Epilogue on Health Care (Longman Classics in Political Science). New Jersey, United States of America: Pearson, 2010.

675 Getzler, Joshua. "An Interdisciplinary View of Fiduciary Law 'as if.' Accountability and Counterfactual Trust." *ResearchGate*, May 1, 2011: 988-989. https://www.researchgate.net/publication/289850556_An_interdisciplinary_view_of_fiduciary_law_as_if_Accountability_and_counterfactual_trust.

676 Gold, Andrew S., and Paul B. Miller. Philosophical Foundations of Fiduciary Law. Oxford University Press eBooks, 2014. https://doi.org/10.1093/acprof:oso/9780198701729.001.0001.

677 Chatz, Mr. S, Ms. Hassan, Mr. Bennet, Ms. Duckworth, Ms. Klobuchar, Mrs. Murray, Mr. Booker, et al. "Data Care Act of 2018," n.d. https://www.schatz.senate.gov/imo/media/doc/Data%20Care%20Act%20of%202018.pdf.

678 "S.2073: Kids Online Safety and Privacy Act." Centre on Regulation in Europe, July 30, 2007. Accessed August 30, 2024. https://cerre.eu/wp-content/uploads/2022/03/220321_CERRE_Report_Interoperability-in-Digital-Markets_FINAL.pdf.

679 Ibid, 102(a).

680 Kerber and Schweitzer, *Interoperability in the digital economy*, 30.

681 Bourreau, Marc, Jan Krämer, Miriam Buiten, and Centre on Regulation in Europe (CERRE). "Interoperability in Digital Markets," March 2022: 36-42. https://cerre.eu/wp-content/uploads/2022/03/220321_CERRE_Report_Interoperability-in-Digital-Markets_FINAL.pdf.

682 OPOCE. "EUR-Lex - 12008E102 - EN," n.d. https://eur-lex.europa.eu/legal-content/EN/TXT/HTML/?uri=CELEX%3A12008E102.

683 Bourrea, Marc, Jan Krämer, and Miriam Buiten. "INTEROPERABILITY IN DIGITAL MARKETS." Centre on Regulation in Europe, 27-29. March 2022. Accessed August 30, 2024. https://cerre.eu/wp-content/uploads/2022/03/220321_CERRE_Report_Interoperability-in-Digital-Markets_FINAL.pdf.

684 Riley, Chris. "Section 230 and Interoperability." Medium, September 10, 2020. Accessed August 30, 2024. https://mchrisriley.medium.com/section-230-and-interoperability-2d63e225088d.

685 Ibid.

686 Ibid.

687 S. 2658. Federal government of the United States: 11th Congress, *S.2658 - ACCESS Act of 2019*, Sen. Mark R. Warner. Publication/Report Number, Washington: United States Congress, 2019. https://www.congress.gov/bill/116th-congress/senate-bill/2658 (Accessed 5 Sep 2024). [note that the bill number in the manuscript is incorrect – should read "2658."]

688 Mark R. Warner. "Senators Introduce Bipartisan Bill to Encourage Competition in Social Media," n.d. https://www.warner.senate.gov/public/index.cfm/2019/10/senators-introduce-bipartisan-bill-to-encourage-competition-in-social-media.

689 "GOE19968: In The Senate of the United States." United States Code, 2024. Accessed August 30, 2024. https://www.scribd.com/document/431507473/GOE19968.

690 Warner, Senators Introduce Bipartisan Bill to Encourage Competition in Social Media.

691 Fazzini, Kate. "Europe's Sweeping Privacy Rule Was Supposed to Change the Internet, but so Far It's Mostly Created Frustration for Users, Companies, and Regulators." CNBC, May 5, 2019. https://www.cnbc.com/2019/05/04/gdpr-has-frustrated-users-and-regulators.html.

692 Mark R. Warner. "Warner, Colleagues Reintroduce Bipartisan Legislation to Encourage Competition in Social Media," n.d. https://www.warner.senate.gov/public/index.cfm/2023/7/warner-colleagues-reintroduce-bipartisan-legislation-to-encourage-competition-in-social-media#:~:text=Warner%20(D%2DVA)%2C,social%20media%20platforms%20by%20requiring.

693 Ibid.

694 Future of Life Institute. "The Act Texts." *EU Artificial Intelligence Act.*, 2024. Accessed August 30, 2024. https://artificialintelligenceact.eu/the-act/.

695 Ibid.

696 "Executive Order on the Safe, Secure, and Trustworthy Development and Use of Artificial Intelligence." *The White House*, October 30, 2023. https://www.whitehouse.gov/briefing-room/presidential-actions/2023/10/30/executive-order-on-the-safe-secure-and-trustworthy-development-and-use-of-artificial-intelligence/.

697 "G7: Ministerial Declaration on Industry, Technology, and Digital," March 15, 2024. https://innovazione.gov.it/notizie/articoli/en/g7-ministerial-declaration-on-industry-technology-and-digital/.

698 Department for Science, Innovation & Technology, Foreign, Commonwealth & Development Office, The Bletchley Declaration by Countries Attending the AI Safety Summit, 1-2 November 2023, November 2023, https://www.gov.uk/government/publications/ai-safety-summit-2023-the-bletchley-declaration/the-bletchley-declaration-by-countries-attending-the-ai-safety-summit-1-2-november-2023.

699 Mozilla. "Privacy Not Include: Shop Smart and Safe." Mozilla. 2024. Accessed August 30, 2024. https://foundation.mozilla.org/en/privacynotincluded/.

700 Internet Safety Labs [ISL]. "Internet Safety Labs." Internetsafetylabs., 2024. Accessed August 30, 2024. https://internetsafetylabs.org.

701 DTPR [DTPR]. "Digital Trust for Places & Routines (DTPR): The Extraordinary Communities That Arise in Disaster." dtpr.io. 2024. Accessed August 30, 2024. https://dtpr.io.

RICHARD WHITT

Richard Whitt's career has spanned over three decades as a public policy attorney, technology strategist, business advisor, and entrepreneur. He spent over eleven years with Google (2007-'18) in its Washington DC and Mountain View offices, including four years as corporate director for strategic initiatives. More recently, Richard was senior vice president for government relations and public policy with Twilio Inc (2022-'24), and served as senior fellow in residence with the Mozilla Foundation (2018-'22). Richard also led technology and telecom public policy teams at MCI Communications (1994-2006), and before that worked as an associate at several large Washington DC-based technology law firms.

In 2018, under the auspices of his GLIA Foundation, Richard launched the GliaNet initiative, a proposed trust-based Web ecosystem. He currently heads the GliaNet Alliance, a coalition of technology companies building new markets anchored by Net fiduciaries and Personal AI agents. In addition, his NetsEdge LLC consultancy works with tech startups in Silicon Valley and elsewhere to develop ethical governance structures.

Richard received his juris doctor degree cum laude from Georgetown University Law Center, and his Bachelor of Science degree magna cum laude from James Madison University. He is currently a senior fellow with the Georgetown Institute for Technology Law and Policy.

Born and raised in Washington DC, Richard currently resides in Emerald Hills, California.

Thank you for reading.
I would love it if you could check out my website
for more info, and I would be even more grateful if you
could leave me a review on Amazon!

If you haven't bought the book from Amazon,
then I implore you to take a picture and upload it
with your review; that way, Amazon doesn't think you
are a bot!